The NAIL in the SKULL and Other VICTORIAN URBAN LEGENDS

The NAIL in the SKULL and Other VICTORIAN URBAN LEGENDS

›› *Simon Young* ‹‹

University Press of Mississippi / Jackson

The University Press of Mississippi is the scholarly publishing agency of the Mississippi Institutions of Higher Learning: Alcorn State University, Delta State University, Jackson State University, Mississippi State University, Mississippi University for Women, Mississippi Valley State University, University of Mississippi, and University of Southern Mississippi.

www.upress.state.ms.us

The University Press of Mississippi is a member of the Association of University Presses.

Copyright © 2022 by University Press of Mississippi
All rights reserved

First printing 2022

∞

Library of Congress Cataloging-in-Publication Data

Names: Young, Simon (Historian), author.
Title: The nail in the skull and other Victorian urban legends / Simon Young.
Description: Jackson : University Press of Mississippi, 2022. | Includes bibliographical references and index.
Identifiers: LCCN 2022003496 (print) | LCCN 2022003497 (ebook) | ISBN 9781496839473 (hardback) | ISBN 9781496839466 (trade paperback) | ISBN 9781496839428 (epub) | ISBN 9781496839459 (epub) | ISBN 9781496839435 (pdf) | ISBN 9781496839442 (pdf)
Subjects: LCSH: Urban folklore—Great Britain. | Legends—Great Britain. | Tales—Great Britain. | Popular culture—Great Britain—History—19th century.
Classification: LCC GR141 .Y68 2022 (print) | LCC GR141 (ebook) | DDC 398.20941—dc23/eng/20220207
LC record available at https://lccn.loc.gov/2022003496
LC ebook record available at https://lccn.loc.gov/2022003497

British Library Cataloging-in-Publication Data available

Contents

Abbreviations xi
Preface and Acknowledgments xiii
Introduction xix
1. The Baby Picnic 3
2. Beetle Eyes 6
3. The Bosom Serpent 8
4. Buried Alive 10
5. The Cautious Druggist 13
6. Child Pie 16
7. The Chimney Boy 19
8. Chloroformed! 23
9. Covert Catholics. 29
10. Cycling Afflictions 32
11. Death Dice 36
12. Devil Take Me! 39
13. Do You Know Her? 43
14. Downie's Slaughter. 45
15. Dressing the Workhouse Corpse 47
16. Drugged on a Train 50
17. The Eagle and the Baby 52
18. Egg Ring 56
19. Familiar Enemies 59
20. Fish Ring 61
21. The Galvanic Convict 64
22. The Ghost in Search of Help 66
23. Ghost Wager 68
24. Ghostly Donation 71
25. Hands in the Muff 72

26. Harem Prisoner 75
27. Hero Survives 79
28. Hollow Tree Death 81
29. Human Sausages 84
30. I Lost the Ring Here 88
31. I'm Jack the Ripper! 89
32. Immured Lovers 90
33. The Injured Garotter 92
34. Jolting the Coffin 94
35. The Judge and the Foreman 96
36. The Lady and the Ring 97
37. The Lawyer and the Poisoned Cakes 101
38. The Long Pack 102
39. Message in a Hat 106
40. A Million Postage Stamps 107
41. The Mistletoe Bride 111
42. A Modern Jonah! 113
43. Nail in the Coffin 116
44. The Nail in the Skull 118
45. The Omnibus Driver's Holiday 122
46. One Little Piggy 123
47. Paying for His Burial 126
48. The Pickpocket's Ring 127
49. Poison Duel 129
50. Prayers and the Thief 132
51. The Red Hand! 134
52. The Returned Watch 137
53. Selling Sovereigns 139
54. Sewer Monsters 141
55. She's My Daughter? 145
56. Shooting at a Ghost 147
57. The Shoplifter's Dilemma 148
58. The Skeletons That Eloped 152
59. The Spanish Prisoner 155
60. The Suicide Club 158
61. Swallowed Up 162
62. The Tell-Tale Eye 164
63. Tick Tock 169
64. There's Gold in Those Sewers 171
65. Tunnel Kissing 174

66. The Vanishing Lady 178
67. Watch the Clock 180
68. Wild Thing 181
69. The Wrong Bed 184
70. The Wrong Trousers 186
     Notes 189
     Bibliography 197

Once on a time, the ancient legends tell,
Truth, rising from the bottom of her well,
Looked on the world, but, hearing how it lied,
Returned to her seclusion horrified.
There she abode, so conscious of her worth,
Not even Pilate's Question called her forth,
Nor Galileo, kneeling to deny
The Laws that hold our Planet 'neath the sky.
Meantime, her kindlier sister, whom men call
Fiction, did all her work and more than all,
With so much zeal, devotion, tact, and care,
That no one noticed Truth was otherwhere.

—Rudyard Kipling

Abbreviations

ATU Uther (2004)
BC Reference from Brian Chapman
BNA: British Newspaper Archive
BS Reference from Bob Skinner
CW Reference from Chris Woodyard
DE Reference from Davide Ermacora
FG Reference from Filip Graliński
PB Reference from Peter Burger

Preface and Acknowledgments

The present volume contains seventy, largely forgotten, Victorian legends. I offer here, first of all, some words on approach so that my methods for hunting down these legends can be criticized and improved upon. When folklorists have, in the past, looked for legends in digital databases—admittedly a fairly recent activity—they have had a series of search words to hand from the story they wish to net. For instance, it would make sense with the "**Lady and the Ring**," to use "coffin," "sexton," and "ring"; a "**Modern Jonah**" would require "whale," "swallow," "alive." The success of the folklorist in this task will depend not only on the legend's frequency and the scholar's skill in using digital archives, but also, depressingly, on the rarity of certain word combinations: some stories are easier to find than others.

I experimented instead with a different method (in writing this book I have realized that this method was anticipated by Burger 2017, 202–4). I tried to find phrases that typically cropped up in newspaper reports of Victorian belief legends using the British Newspaper Archive (BNA). These phrases ranged from the very common "strange story" and "horrible story" to more recondite phrases: "stranger than fiction," "romantic story," "smoking room stories," "something out of the Arabian Nights," "not a hundred miles from," "story circulating," and so on. Using these search phrases, I went through thousands of news reports. It took me, for instance, a memorably ghastly fortnight to skim the ten thousand Victorian references to "horrible story" in the BNA. I necessarily processed reports quickly, discarding the vast majority. However, I took screen shots of any stories that I considered interesting, and it soon became possible to pick out legend types and put them into named files.[1]

Once I had a named file, I started a more targeted keyword search both in the BNA and in other electronic and physical libraries. While I began with newspaper archives, it made sense to broaden the amount of print covered as soon as the legend was identified; or, in the few cases where I was dealing with a legend that was well known to scholars, in the hunt for new instances. For

Victorian Britain this meant looking through nineteenth-century book and pamphlet archives, something that can in large measure be done digitally, as with British newspapers. However, it also meant the much more difficult task of attempting to work with chapbooks and broadsides. While ballads have been very capably catalogued (https://www.vwml.org/, accessed 29 Sept. 2020), much poetry and prose from Victorian street literature has not been, and here I fell to looking through printed collections (e.g., Hindley 1871; Meriton 2010; note that even works relating to earlier centuries, like Rollins 1927, are worth reading because of the extreme conservatism of cheap British print). Much more remains to be discovered there, but that will take a great deal of targeted work in chapbook and broadside collections.

I would only consider a story for inclusion in this collection if: either (i) I found at least three versions (with at least one published in Britain); or (ii) I found fewer references, but there was a comment that the story type was "common" in the United Kingdom. For instance, in **"Do You Know Her?"** there is only one nineteenth-century version (known to me), but there are separate comments that such stories circulated in the nineteenth century. All the stories gathered together in this book were included on the basis of one of these two criteria. In a very few cases (e.g., **"I'm Jack the Ripper!"**) I only found three sources by stepping outside the Victorian period proper.

Many interesting stories were excluded by these criteria. Indeed, I have tens of entries where I have just two instances of a given legend, or sometimes just one instance of a story that I strongly suspect was a legend. For example, I found a single Staffordshire version of "Corpse in the Car(t)" for the 1800s ("An Unlikely Story" 1866; see the introduction). Thus, I was not able to include it, despite being convinced that this was a widely circulated legend. Likewise, **"Wrong Trousers"** was, I am sure, widely told; it is too good a story not to have been. But I struggled to find more than one British example, and I am only able to include it because *FG* came to the rescue with two other instances (one from the United States and one from New Zealand set in Australia). There are many other stories that I excluded in the end for reasons of space. I am confident that with more searching and more debate, it will be possible to publish a further collection of Victorian urban legends.

In defining the legends collected here I concentrated on narrative patterns. Was there an established narrative that appeared again and again? It was sometimes tempting to pick at story complexes. For instance, there are scores of Victorian stories that involve what might be called "generosity repaid." In a society which was less meritocratic than ours and in which there was no welfare state, charity and personal patronage mattered much more. Not surprisingly, in many Victorian stories a loan or a gift is repaid many times over by the beneficiary either because he is rich (something the donor did not realize) or because he becomes rich. A man going to Australia is given a loan of £25. Several years later, after making his fortune, he gives the lender £30,000 ("Wonderful if True" 1853). A young painter gives a beggar posing for a painting a few francs; the beggar, actually Lord Rothschild, gives him 10,000 francs ("The following good story from Berlin . . ." 1881). A monograph could be written here by a historian. But from the point of view of a folklorist, this complex never resolves itself into a consistent narrative. I was much more interested in stories with strong repeating narratives. The reader must judge whether I was correct to include "**Familiar Enemies**" or "**Hero Survives**," legends that are close to legend complexes.

I likewise tried to avoid isolated motifs. For instance, there are frequent references to trapdoors and holes in the ground in Victorian urban legends. A hole in a cellar appears in Maria Monk's description of her Montreal nunnery: victims and newborn babies were thrown there (Monk 1836, 66). There were the English inns where a bed dropped its occupants down to the floor below to be killed and despoiled ("Ye Olde" 1925). There are trapdoors, too, in many Bluebeard-type murder stories—most famously Sweeney Todd's (see "**Human Sausages**"). This felt like a motif rather than a legend type, so, while acknowledging its peculiar importance in the Victorian imagination, I did not give the trapdoor an entry of its own.

Another example is the ghost's portrait: for example, E363.1(e), "Ghost of nun aids wounded French soldiers in World War II. She is identified by a picture of Joan of Arc." Despite very specific motifs like this, a generic portrait-ghost motif has never been created. On seeing a portrait, a man or woman realizes that they have seen a ghost or that they are able to identify the ghost that they have seen. This is a motif that appears in a number of legends—it is often present in the "Vanishing Hitchhiker"—but perhaps it can also be usefully classed as a legend type. There are many Victorian and Edwardian stories where the portrait is the focus—to use Gillian Bennett's phrase, "the engine" (Bennett 2005, 68, 96) of the story. Spoiled for choice, I left this story to one side. What should be clear here is that classifying story complexes, story types, and story motifs is a subjective act. It is not a question of algebraic certainty.

Once I had a belief story file, and proof that the story had circulated orally or in print, I concentrated, for the individual entries, on four points: examples of the legend from the same general period; folklore parallels; the wider historical context; and a contemporary version of the legend. I concentrated on contemporary versions because they give the concerns of Victorian society much more efficiently than any summary I could offer (a valuable point made by a peer reviewer). In choosing contemporary versions, I looked for what I felt were representative examples (that had all or most of the features of the legend). Then I typically chose more compact, less literary versions for reasons of space. An instance of "**Nail in the Skull**" that I chose runs to just over two hundred words (Timbs 1865, I, 297). Perhaps the most popular version of this story—to judge by the number of times it was reproduced—was closer to three thousand words long; one and a half times the length of my entire entry (Curling 1843).

Another issue was names for the individual story types. Folklorists of contemporary legends have experimented with various classificatory systems, none of which have become dominant (Brunvand 2012, I, 122–27). Typically, those in the field communicate with simple monikers like the "Eaten Ticket" or the "Vanishing Hitchhiker"—something possible because of the relatively small size of the back catalogue of identified contemporary legends. The ability of these folklorists to find catchy, memorable titles for the stories they describe is admirable: they create titles that often obviate the need for any longer description. Take, for instance, the inspired "Bride and Seek" (I have been unable to identify the name's origins) for the story of the newly married woman who goes missing at her bridal party during a game of hide-and-seek. She had climbed into a self-locking box, where her skeleton is found many years afterwards. I tried to find similarly memorable titles, but I fear that I was not always up to the job.[2] Note also that out of respect to previous scholars, I kept pre-existing titles for stories. Some of these, such as "**Downie's Slaughter**," work well; some rather less so, such as the "**Bosom Serpent**" or "**Long Pack**." I even reluctantly called "Bride and Seek" the "**Mistletoe Bride**," using its most common British designation.

A word now on conventions. As is typical in folklore books, I have used author-date citations. Here the number of anonymous newspaper articles—about a thousand—created a series of problems. I gave the title of the article as the author—a sensible convention followed by, among others, *Folklore*. But as titles are frequently similar—for instance, eleven cited articles begin with the words "A Horrible Story"—I have often given full titles. I have also, sometimes, included the date, such as, "'A Horrible Story,' 19 May 1867," to distinguish that title from "'A Horrible Story,' 18 Jun 1867." I, occasionally, put down, with references, how many times a story appears in the BNA in a given period to give a sense of the popularity of a narrative as it circulated, for example, "The article appeared in the BNA 60 times in August 1868." These numbers were based on an article count in the summer of 2020; as the BNA scans more newspapers, the numbers will, of course, rise.

Legend types are capitalized and have quotation marks. I have put in bold (as readers of this preface will have noticed) stories that have an entry in this volume, for ease of cross-referencing: for example, "**Tell-Tale Eye**" or "**Wild**

Thing." In referring to places in the United Kingdom, I stuck to the pre-1974 British counties, the ones referred to in contemporary reports. The town of Sale is thus in Lancashire, not Greater Manchester; Sheffield is in the West Riding not South Yorkshire. I have likewise taken Britain and Ireland as a single unit as these were, throughout Victoria's reign, part of the same country. The Republic only became a reality in 1921–22 with partition. I used the word "flap" to refer to a "state of worry, agitation, fuss, or excitement" (*OED*) in a community about a story that was believed to have taken place in the area. For instance, in 1843, it was bruited about at Colnbrook (Berkshire) that a local woman had tried to blind a child by placing beetles in its eyes ("A Monster" 1843; and crucially, "asserted by a multitude of persons" [Correspondent 1843]; see further "**Beetle Eyes**"). Unless otherwise specified, motifs are from the Stith Thompson, *Motif Index* (1955–1958).

In the production of this volume, I benefited from the help of many friends and colleagues. I would like to single out my wife, Valentina, Peter Burger (abbreviated *PB* in the text), Brian Chapman (*BC*), Davide Ermacora (*DE*), Filip Graliński (*FG*), Camille Hale, Jessica Hemming, Ron James, Bob Skinner (*BS*), Stuart Spencer, and Chris Woodyard (*CW*), the last of whom advised me constantly. I also benefited, on individual points, from the knowledge of Brent Augustus, Mike Dash, Peter Higginbotham, Sandy Hobbs, Roberto Labanti, Sofia Lincos, Kay Massingill, Emili Samper Prunera, Bob Rickard, Linda Stratmann, Bonnie Taylor-Blake, John Widdowson, and three anonymous peer reviewers. I am grateful to all. I would like, finally, to acknowledge the importance of the inspirational works of Richard Altick (1915–2008) in my own journeys into Victorian Britain.

I dedicate this book to my second daughter, Lea, whose demanding eight-year-old standards of truth tore apart many of the stories collected in this volume and their descendants. On hearing the "Vanishing Hitchhiker," Lea suggested, for instance, that either the driver had "memory problems" or that the grieving mother "made up stories." I look forward to hearing her adult views on the enjoyable travesties gathered together here.

Introduction: Victorian Urban Legends and Folklore Transmission

Introducing Victorian Urban Legends

"A VERY WEIRD STORY"

The year is 1866, and "a very weird story" is circulating "in the hill country of Staffordshire" in the English Midlands. The journalist who recorded the narrative was apologetic: "We have been unable to verify the narrative with anything like precision and content ourselves with relating it as nearly as possible as it was told to us by a clergyman during the present week" ("An Unlikely Story" 1866). The "unearthly story" had allegedly taken place on the ten-mile road between Buxton and Macclesfield.

> It was, then, one day last week, that a carrier (whose name we have been unable to ascertain), with his horse and cart was taking his accustomed journey... After he had gone some distance he was accosted by a wayfaring man, who was plodding along the road, who asked for a lift. The carrier took the man up, and proceeded onwards. After a while the carrier complained that his hands were cold, and asked his companion to drive for him for a time. The man consented and took hold of the reins. Before they had gone much farther, a stranger on horseback—the horse by the way was a white one—overtook them, and rode by the side of the cart. A conversation was commenced, which very soon took the direction of the cattle plague. Its devastating effects were discussed, and a parallel was drawn between it and other calamities, past and future. The stranger on

horseback suddenly became prophetic, saying that, next year, there would be a plague or blight among the corn, which would destroy the fruits of the earth, which would be followed, the next year, by a plague among mankind. "Christians," he said, "would lie dead in the roadsides by hundreds." "Yes," he added, lowering his voiced, and addressing the holder of the reins, "as dead as the man who is sitting by your side!" The driver turned, and, to his horror, found that he was sitting by the side of a corpse. The stranger on horseback galloped away, and the temporary driver of the cart was left to pursue his journey with his melancholy burden. ("An Unlikely Story" 1866)

Folklorists will recognize here the story type "Corpse in the Car," which should perhaps be renamed, on the basis of the above, "Corpse in the Car(t)" (Brunvand 2012, I, 148–49; Hobbs and Cornwell 1991, for more on this legend type). The earliest other reference known to me dates to 1934 and is from the Netherlands (Fr. v. R. 1934; *PB*; see also several 1938 references in Bonaparte 1941, 105, 117 and 120, for a British instance, and Bonaparte 1947, 13–40). A mysterious passenger hitches a lift in an automobile. The passenger prophesizes to the driver and after a series of revelations about the future—often the imminent death of Hitler[1]—the passenger seals the prophecy by saying that there will soon be a dead person in the vehicle. The driver picks up an accident victim who then dies on the back seat. The supernatural visitant, meanwhile, disappears, leaving only the prophecy behind.

The 1866 Staffordshire legend is an ancestor of this legend type, one which surfaced in print in the Peak District almost a century before it was recorded elsewhere. But it would be a critical error to reduce this legend to a mere twig in a folklore family tree. Here is a legend that also gives us a fascinating glimpse into the religious sentiments of Victorian Britain. Here is a popular Christianity—"drenched," recalling Matthew Arnold's words, "in the preternatural" (preface of Arnold 1883, x); a Christianity that likely embarrassed learned contemporaries. Would there even be a record—we might ask—had not a local Anglican vicar given the story and, perhaps more importantly, his authority to the journalist?

My aim in this book has been to bring together a sample—there are seventy stories included in the next pages—of Victorian urban legends like the Staffordshire cart story. Some of these legends are relatively well known, at least to folklorists—the "**Bosom Serpent**," "**Human Sausages**," and the "**Mistletoe Bride**." Indeed, ten of the seventy have already been assigned folklore motifs: the "**Fish Ring**," for instance, can be found, in the *Motif Index*, under N211.1 "Lost ring found in fish"; and under ATU 736A "The Ring of Polycrates." However, these are very much the exceptions. The rest—including Victorian classics such as

"**Chimney Boy**," "**Selling Sovereigns**," and the "**Wrong Bed**"—are unfamiliar, as they were not collected or studied in Victorian times; and they have not, for the most part, been collected or studied since.

What Is an Urban Legend?

Before we get to these legends, it is important to give some definitions. Let me start with the thorny words "urban legend" (for an overview see Brunvand 2012, I, 173–77; for more detail Smith 1999). I employ "urban legend" with a simple sense. These legends are, for me, belief narratives (as such I am close to Klintberg 1990; see also Pujol 2013, 59, "stories . . . recounted as if they were true stories"; and Hansen 2017, 6 for "credence narratives"), that is, stories in which readers or listeners are expected to believe or in which they are expected to consider belief. They are, in fact, *explorations of belief*: the reader or listener wonders about the truth of the story. I prefer this to a more typical but oversimplistic definition that a legend is "believed to be true by those who tell it and by those to whom it is told" (Georges 1971, 4; Georges, note, subsequently problematizes his own words).[2] Belief is both nuanced and changeable, and a single story can be recounted in different registers: deadpan serious, jocular, prolix, and literary . . . The *pivot*, though, in these stories remains belief, even if there is a rejection or mockery of the same.

"Urban legend" is, I admit, far from ideal as a phrase.[3] But these two words have the merit of being familiar to the public (Brunvand 2012, I, xxiii–xxv), and to academics outside of folklore studies. An alternative term among folklorists is "contemporary legend." But that term is problematic in general and becomes critically so when referring to other historical periods. Many readers would be unsettled if not confused by, say, the phrase "medieval contemporary legends." There are also unfortunate ambiguities. "Contemporary" was originally used by folklorists to refer to stories being told in the present (Smith 1989, 98; it first emerged in the early 1980s). "Contemporary" was, then, extended to mean "the here and now" in the present or past (e.g., Pettitt 1995a).[4] This change in meaning—the shift from stories *told* in *the* present to stories *set* in *a* present—came about as scholars accepted that "contemporary legends" could also be found in other historical periods. But when the term was coined in 1982 no one (at least this is my understanding) signed up to the idea that a contemporary legend could not be set some time before circa 1980: in 1940, say, or, for that matter, 1840. They meant stories *told* around 1980.

Urban legends are not *Märchen* (a wonder tale, like "Snow White") or jokes (though they often involve humor). Nor are they impossibly tall tales in the Münchausen and Sazerac tradition: for example, that nineteenth-century classic, where trapped residents escape from a fire by sliding down a jet of water from a fireman's hose ("A Tall Story" 1867). Urban legends are belief legends that touch on extreme or difficult aspects of life: crime, death, illness, sex, the supernatural, and war. They frequently involve troublesome informal social institutions (thinking of the Victorian period, duels or wagers or elopement) and anxieties over new technologies (again for the 1800s, bicycles or railways) and social changes (in Victorian Britain the enfranchisement of Catholics, say). Much as the dreamer processes his or her day at night, so society runs through its concerns in compelling and easily shared narratives.

Most of these legends were, in the late 1800s, not thought of as folklore; so they were not noticed by British folklorists. Indeed, one cogent definition of urban legends would be: "stories not collected by British and American folklorists before about 1950." Mid and late nineteenth- and early twentieth-century British folklorists were much keener on "prior folklore": fairy lore, fertility customs, traditional ghosts, pagan survivals—or what passed for pagan survivals, witchcraft, etc. (Dorson 1968, captures this enthusiasm well). They *did* collect belief legends, but only from within that narrow range: a changeling story was sought after because it involved fairies; a "weird" story about a messenger from God on a white horse was not. Certainly, no folklorist (local or national) discussed the 1866 "Corpse in the Car(t)" narrative, though it was widely circulated in the press ("An Unlikely Story" 1866). My guess is that early folklorists found the story difficult to classify. Its millenarianism was perhaps also embarrassing, a throwback to an early modern Christianity of a kind that educated Victorians liked to think outmoded; see further xi.

Twenty-first-century folklorists are, on the other hand, passionately interested in such stories: indeed, there is arguably more interest, within the discipline today, in urban legends than in "prior folklore." But these *contemporary* folklorists are, for the most part, collecting present-day legends. There is no theoretical reason why belief legends should not also be collected from among the Victorians or the Elizabethans or, data allowing, the Mycenaeans: as these same folklorists would be the first to admit. But other than two fine books on British urban legends of the world wars (Hayward 2005; 2009) there have been no retrospective attempts (known to me) by modern folklorists to reconstruct a wide range of belief legends for a given historical period (for some brave exploratory attempts in the Roman world Anderson 2006, 57; Ellis 1983 and see now Hansen 2017). There are, on the other hand, numerous examples of different national and regional studies in the present (see national entries in Brunvand 2012). So widespread have country collections of urban legends become that perhaps the most interesting data point now is the countries that have *no* publications in the field.

What Do We Mean by "Victorian"?

So much for "urban legends," but what about the word "Victorian"? This is, happily, a far easier term to pin down. By "Victorian" I refer, of course, to the reign of Victoria (1837–1901), although note that I reference, cognate stories from both before and after this period. I often, in fact, went back into the eighteenth century and forward to the Second World War (and occasionally beyond) to find parallels. The word "Victorian" is not only a temporal marker. It also has geographical implications. I limited myself (in space) to legends that were told in Victoria's territories: Great Britain, Ireland and the wider Empire. This includes stories that were set outside of Victoria's realms, but that nevertheless circulated there either orally or in writing.

Victorian belief legends can be usefully broken down into three different categories in terms of origin. There are, first, narratives from Victorian Britain and Ireland. Second, there are narratives from the British Empire and its Dominions; "**Harem Prisoner**," for instance, was a legend of the Raj (British India), which also caught on at home. Third there are narratives from elsewhere, which were enjoyed in Victorian Britain; the two most popular locations for foreign stories being perhaps the United States and Paris. These stories are the most difficult to assess. Are these stories that are temporarily borrowed from abroad (e.g., "**Death Dice**")? Do these stories subsequently take root in Britain (e.g., "**Hands in the Muff**")? Are these international stories that are told exclusively about other countries because of the embarrassment of associating them with the UK (possibly "**Message in a Hat**")? Or, in some cases, do we have stories that are projected onto exotic locations (e.g., the "**Vanishing Lady**")?

Why, in an attempt to create a list of nineteenth-century urban legends, choose Britain rather than, say, the United States or France? It would certainly be possible to write a monograph on the nineteenth-century belief legends of either of these two countries. There is no lack of stories and no lack of data. Partly my interest in Britain is a question of personal preference: I am British and many of my publications have been based in Britain or at least have begun with British sources. However, independent of this, there are two good objective reasons for choosing Britain in attempting to reconstruct nineteenth-century urban legends. Both relate to newspapers. Newspapers, as even a brief exploration of the stories gathered together here will demonstrate, are our most important sources for urban legends in the period (for nineteenth-century British newspapers, see Lee 1976; Brown 1989; Hewitt 2014; Jones 2016; Hobbs 2018).

British newspapers were, in the nineteenth century and particularly in the second half of that century, the best connected in the world. The British Empire covered a fifth of the globe, so information was flowing in from colonial possessions. Britain also had excellent contacts with continental countries and their overseas empires and British journalists had close links with American journalism (Wiener 2011). The contrast with the United States and its more limited contacts is interesting here. In my experience American journalists had direct contacts with London, Paris and later, in the 1800s, Berlin. But most other material from Europe passed through British or French hands. By using British newspapers as our starting point, we get an impressively global range of stories.

A second consideration is the ease (or lack of ease) with which we can search nineteenth-century newspaper records. Britain has only one significant database for the nineteenth century: the British Newspaper Archive (BNA), which has been created on the back of the British Library's extraordinary newspaper collections for Britain and Ireland. Its closest British rival is the scanned archive of *The Times*, though there is a wider range of datasets if one includes magazines (Mussell 2016, 23–27). The BNA is impressive, convenient and hopefully will one day be comprehensive. A British search in Victorian newspapers involves one database, whereas an equivalent search in nineteenth-century American newspapers needs multiple databases. The BNA also has good quality scanning and good quality OCR and a good search engine, meaning that it is easier to track information down within scanned pages. It does much better in this respect than, say, the rather clunky *Gallica* for France. Let's admit that the two most important questions in newspaper research are: (i) breadth of source material; and (ii) quality of search technology. By those criteria Britain wins out over other western countries, at least for the nineteenth century.

A Handlist of Victorian Urban Legends

I have not tried in the present volume to analyze Victorian urban legends (to "unpack" them; Ellis 2007, 29), something which would be premature given that many of these stories are new discoveries. My hope has been, rather, to offer an admittedly partial handlist of nineteenth-century British legends. It is, of course, impossible for folklorists in any period, including the present, to gather together all legends. Legends, after all, have different geographical spreads (e.g., the "**Ombudsman's Holiday**" is exclusive to London). Legends belong to different social classes: e.g., "**Ghost Wager**" from the urban poor (against "the nobs"). Legends also sometimes begin in specific professions: for example, the "**Ghostly Donation**," among the Anglican clergy. A totalizing catalogue is neither possible nor desirable.

The natural reflex of historically-inclined legend folklorists in the last generation has been to focus hard on one legend and then track that legend into the past and into other countries; what might be called "legend chasing."[5] There are several notable examples of this kind of study (e.g., Kosko 1966; Ermacora 2017). I have nothing but respect for this approach. In an ideal world, each and every legend would be given this treatment and I myself have attempted it with "Midwife to Murderers," a narrative that can be attested in fifteenth-century Italy and that was told well into the twentieth century in parts of the West (Young 2017). However, the publication of handlists—for example, Baughman 1966; Marzolph 2020—is a complementary approach to legend chasing: as classificatory works they orient and direct research. Yes, they are shallower, but they take us beyond individual legends and give glimpses of the ecosystem in which such legends develop.

A national survey of this kind offers many advantages for historians as well as for folklorists. It brings us insights into parts of the nation that are easily lost. For instance, in "**Dressing the Workhouse Corpse**," we eavesdrop on inmates at the workhouse, instead of on the management or taxpayers who dominate the documentary record for these institutions. In "**Sewer Monsters**" we come as close as we ever will to the intimate fears of the "toshers," sewer treasure-seekers, as they wade through the London shores. In "**Harem Prisoner**" we hear, meanwhile, a catch in the voice of the imperial class in Victorian India. Of course, a study focused on one nation will be, at times, myopic: many of the legends here were demonstrably shared among different countries. It should indeed be possible, ultimately, to write a much larger study of *Western* nineteenth-century urban legends, from Europe and what were or had been European colonies. However, this book is about one nation and its overseas possessions. I therefore start by setting out below the different forms of oral and print culture in Britain in the 1800s (the means by which folklore was transmitted).

Oral and Print Culture in Victorian Times

Victorian Oral Culture

Queen Victoria (1819–1901) died many times before her death. Indeed, on literally dozens of occasions during her reign, which began in 1837 and lasted for sixty-four years, rumors started that the queen had been murdered or had suddenly passed away; expressing anxieties or, perhaps in some cases, wishful thinking in different parts of her kingdom. For instance, in 1842 a rumor was started in Cork, by a man off the Waterford coach, that the Queen had been assassinated ("Rumour Concerning the Queen" 1842). In late March 1853 news of her death ran through Leicester in the English Midlands ("A False Rumour" 1853). In 1868 it was the turn of Bridgwater in Somerset. A school teacher had claimed that the queen was dead, and this gossip spread "and strange to say obtained credence" ("A rumour that . . ." 1868). In September 1870 "great consternation" was felt in the village of Hockliffe "in consequence of a rumour that the Queen was dead . . . A similar rumour was current at Leighton and other places" ("Exciting Rumour" 1870). In 1896 a "groundless rumour to the effect that the Queen was dead obtained considerable currency in Middlesbrough" ("Topics of To-day" 1896).

I have given here a small selection of the many Victoria death rumors—all were printed, but only once the rumor had been debunked. That such rumors sprouted up is hardly surprising. The queen stood close to the center of the imaginary life of many of her subjects, as both an authority and as a symbol (Plunkett 2005 for Victoria in the media). For present purposes, though, these accounts are interesting because they give us glimpses of an informal type of oral transmission. These rumors about Victoria's demise were circulated without any recourse to print. There is not a single reference in our sources to a handbill or to a newspaper setting off a death rumor—if there had been there would have been legal action and scandal (individuals who started rumors on this subject could expect to be prosecuted: "A rumour that . . ." 1868). The life of these reports was brief because once reliable outside information arrived, they deflated. With the 1842 Cork rumor, citizens waited anxiously for the next coach ("Rumour Concerning the Queen" 1842). With the 1896 Middlesbrough rumor it was the local postmaster who scotched the story: he will have had access to the telegraph ("Topics of To-day" 1896).

Such "flaps" show the capacity of a Victorian village or town to throw itself into brief, intense conversations without the use of print in a way that most Western communities could no longer manage, *save with the help of digital or printed media*.[6] This will come as no surprise to someone who writes on Britain in the 1800s; though oral transmission there is infrequently studied by scholars (for a rare example see Bushaway 2003).[7] But it is important to be reminded of the speed with which stories could pass around and to be able to demonstrate their, let us say, "virulence." The strength of oral transmission, likewise, becomes evident in reading the various legends gathered together in this book. Readers of this introduction will remember "the very weird story" circulating "in the hill country of Staffordshire" about a messianic prophecy and a dead body in a cart ("An Unlikely Story" 1866). There are references to similar oral "flaps" in "**Beetle Eyes**," the "**Cautious Druggist**," "**Child Pie**," and many, many others: the "'horrid narrative' is still asserted by a multitude of persons in the vicinity of the place in which it is said to have transpired" (Correspondent 1843); a rumor "is the talk of a village in the parish of Halifax, and bordering on Bradford" ("The Biter Bit" 1856); a "horrible story was circulated last week in the neighbourhood of Middlesex Hospital" ("A Horrible Story" Aug 1846) and so on. If this kind of gossip stands as unplanned oral transmission, then there was also in the 1800s planned story-telling where groups of people sat down and listened to one of their number narrate in prose or poetry. In families, these get-togethers, typically around the fire, lasted well into the nineteenth century (Vincent 1989, 24–25 suggests that they were dying out by the 1820s). But oral story-telling was by no means limited to families. There were domestic clubs and pubs where members of a circle took turns at story-telling (in dialect literature particularly, the round of tales became a frequent *Decameron*-style framing device; e.g., Axon n.d.). There were also men and women who had a reputation in the community as singers or story-tellers. In some parts of Victoria's realms, a class of oral story-tellers had survived for centuries (Delargy 1945 for Ireland; James 2019, 22–35 for Cornwall). Nor should we overlook the talented amateurs elsewhere. We have references, for instance, to "semi-professional story-tellers" in the industrializing northwest (Brierley 1892, 7). This would have included such tradition-bearers as Robert Dilrume of Saddleworth: "[Robert's] mind had treasur'd up / much antient [sic] strange record / And on a winters' [sic] night/when by a neighbours [sic] fire / He free declar'd / What he had seen and heard" (Shaw 1824, 124).

In recent years we have come increasingly to realize how important the interaction of oral and written stories proved in the ancient and the medieval world (Bisagni 2012 for a credible medieval Irish example of book learning influencing leprechaun folklore). How much more so is this true of Victorian times? Even in cases where there were long-standing story-telling traditions, such as in Gaelic-speaking Ireland, there is no question that print culture had begun, directly or indirectly, to influence both the forms of stories and their content (Khasawneh 2014). Perhaps the best studied example of this, at least for Britain, are ballads. Many nineteenth-century folklorists lovingly harvested what they believed were autochthonous treasures, which had survived in a corner of this or that parish. But it has become increasingly clear that many of these ballads had been borrowed from earlier printings: "As much as 90 per cent of the 'traditional' repertoire appeared on nineteenth-century broadsides, and in other cheap printed material" (Roud 2014, 7–8). These were not, then, strictly-speaking traditional ballads at all. They had *become* traditional ballads, a rather different thing. It is interesting in this light that some of the great nineteenth-century "singers"—the Homers of the London streets and Midland byways—were peddlers who lived by selling broadsides (Gammon 2017; Shepard 1973, 81–106; and for a fascinating local study Allan 2019). Much folklore, in Victorian times, was transmitted via the printer's press.

Other Media and Folklore

Early folklorists were not enamored of the printer's press. In the nineteenth and, indeed, for most of the twentieth centuries folklorists concentrated on the oral transmission of stories. Stories were told and passed on from person to person and from group to group, and one of the chief jobs of the folklorist was to understand how word-of-mouth circulation both preserved and altered narratives. By the 1970s a coterie of American folklorists, led by Alan Dundes, argued that folklore could also be transmitted by other means, including in print (Dundes and Pagter 1992 [1975], xvii–xviii). "For in the real world, not just a single oral medium of transmission is utilized to communicate folklore, but any available and relevant media is employed" (Smith 1992, 42); in short, if a technology can carry folklore, it does so. This idea, which was originally controversial, has slowly become mainstream. Indeed, contemporary folklorists routinely examine the way that folklore travels in writing, but also the way that folklore is transmitted by film and digitally. There has been a boom, for instance, in recent years in writings on internet folklore (for example, Kinsella 2011 and the essays in Blank 2009; Blank and McNeill 2018; Hakamies and Heimo 2019). Certainly, Victorian folklore traveled down many different routes via different technologies: some stories circulated orally, only occasionally erupting into print; some seem to have spent most or all of their lives in published works.

While writing the present book I kept a list, which soon became rather long, of the various forms of media by which the stories were passed along. There were, to start with, the different types of oral transmission: rumors, story-telling, street-criers, confessions (religious or otherwise), speeches, sermons, songs, and plays. Here we see little change compared with previous centuries. What makes the Victorian transmission of folklore unusual, compared to previous periods, is its written and particularly its printed dimension. The stories collected together in this volume were not just told orally but were also written about in (to continue the list): letters, chapbooks, broadsides, song-sheets, poetry (literary and doggerel), school primers, comics, catechisms, short stories, novels, advertisements, magazines, and, of course, newspapers. In many of these we have, as the century progresses, and particularly from the 1840s, the increasingly sophisticated use of printed images (Maidment 2016; see also Jackson 1885, 219–363); and in 1899 we have the first urban legend known to me on film (Gray 2019, 185–93; see also "**Tunnel Kissing**"). In fact, the only Victorian form of communication that I did not find carrying narratives was the telegraph; even there I suspect that a careful study would uncover folklore in late-nineteenth-century Morse (for an example of the folklore potential of the telegraph "April Fool Extraordinary" 1890, *CW*; for some other hints Cohen 1981, 191–92; Cobb 1923, vii, *BC*).

The Victorian Reading Revolution

It might be argued that with Victorian written culture there was also continuity with past centuries, much as with oral culture. The Tudors, after all, had their chapbooks and their broadsides, their novels and their letters. It is also true that literacy levels had been rising in England since at least the sixteenth century. But nothing from the previous three hundred years could compete with the reading revolution that took place in Victorian times. There were two interconnected aspects to that revolution: rapidly growing literacy levels and the greater availability of printed material. Put simply, more people could read, and it was easier to find things to read. This would all have important implications for the transmission of folklore.

When Victoria came to the throne, a little more than half of all adults were literate (Vincent 1989, 22–23; Lloyd 2007 estimates about 60% for 1840). These numbers, though, differed depending on who you were and where you lived: "Literacy," for instance, "was greater in towns and cities, and greater among men than women" (Gammon 2017, 129). By the time Victoria died, literacy levels were not far from where they stand today for adults—rural and urban, male and female (one feature of growing literacy was that female typically overtook male rates; Vincent 1989, 24–25). This was an extraordinary achievement, managed over a long generation. It was the result, in part, of legislation. "We must educate our masters," stated Robert Lowe, famously, after the passing of the Reform Act of 1867; and the political establishment took this task seriously. School became compulsory, and Parliament accepted the principle that it would fund elementary education (for an overview of the reform process see Larsen 2011, 29–50). It was perhaps primarily, the result of a change in working-class culture. Even very poor families came to expect their children to be able to read (Vincent 1989, 53–66). "Reading," we learn in an 1854 letter, "is becoming necessary to the working man" (Clay 1861, 545–47, at 547 in relation to the number of books pawned).

The second shift was the increase in the availability of the printed word. In the early parts of the century, reading material cost more than it had in the late 1700s. In the 1820s a triple-decker set of novels, say one of Scott's (then) new titles, retailed for thirty-one shillings sixpence (Altick 1998, 263), about ten percent of a laborer's annual wage. Newspapers sold for as much as seven pence (Altick 1998, 322); magazines cost anything from one shilling sixpence to six shillings (Altick 1998, 319). If you were poor in the early 1800s and had a shilling to spare for reading, then you would have been obliged to buy broadsides or chapbooks with stories, poems, or ballads. Broadsides were single sheets of paper—often large sheets—typically printed on one side. Chapbooks were pamphlets "formed from a sheet folded into four, eight, twelve, or sixteen ... usually sold uncut and unstitched" (Shepard 1973, 224–25). These were passed out very cheaply, sometimes for a penny, by traveling patterers—broadside sellers. Ephemeral works of this kind were expressively referred to as "catchpennies": they had outrageous or alluring titles that made for quick sales (and that often misled consumers).

In the 1830s, 1840s, and 1850s, a series of technological and legislative changes meant that it became cheaper to print sheets and books. Already by the 1840s it was possible to buy "penny dreadfuls" (parts of serialized sensational novels; Anglo 1977), or weekly penny magazines with a mix of fiction, anecdote, poetry and news. It was also increasingly easy to visit a public library or reading rooms. However, things had got still better by the 1890s. By then, you would, with your shilling, have been able to buy one decently stitched volume, perhaps a copy of one of Scott's aging, but still popular, classics. You could have bought, instead, four or five digests of Scott's works at a penny a piece (Altick 1998, 314). Alternatively, you would have been able to buy a newspaper a day for a week. Prices had gone down and the numbers sold gone up after the end of stamp duty in 1855: 90 million newspapers were purchased in 1854 in the United Kingdom; by the mid-1860s about 550 million were sold annually (Hobbs 2018, 5). There were also many magazines to choose from: by the end of the 1890s, there were some 304 penny magazines available in the United Kingdom; in 1860 there had been just seventeen (Phegley 2017, 279). The market for broadsides and chapbooks had collapsed as books and newspapers had grown cheaper. They were still to be found in the years before the Great War—and in some rare instances afterwards—but they had nothing like the influence that they had had earlier in the 1800s (Shepard 1973, 133–48; Atkinson and Roud 2017, 28–29).

By the late nineteenth century, then, it was not just more likely that a Briton could read; it was also more likely that he or she could afford to buy reading material. Of course, one does not need total adult literacy or anything near it for the printed word to influence folklore. We know of cases from the nineteenth century and before where books and newspapers were read aloud to groups: the printed word was transformed, in other words, into an oral act.[8] This was a way for illiterate members of a group to share in the experience of reading or for literate members who could not afford the relevant book or newspapers to make the most of a single copy. There are many images, for instance, of families gathering around as one of their number read aloud (e.g., Phegley 2017, 277, reproducing the front cover from the *Family Friend*). However, what might be called "desperate" strategies of reading aloud became less necessary in the decades leading up to the Great War. Reading aloud continued, but as a shared pleasure. It is enough to think of the Penny Readings that were so successful in late Victorian Britain (Beaven 2005, 19–27). At the same time, leisure reading was becoming a common-place pursuit and the dynamics of folklore transmission change when individuals can read a narrative for themselves in silence.

This reading revolution and its consequences for folklore are nicely summed up by Henry Houlding speaking in the 1890s about changing leisure habits in southeastern Lancashire. In the late eighteenth century, working-class families would, Houlding asserted, sit around the fire "'on winter's tedious nights, with good old folks to hear them tell the tales of ghosts and witches" (Houlding 1892, 70; recalling here *Richard II*). But by the mid-nineteenth century, when Houlding was a young man, things had changed: "We sat reading *Pickwick* and *The Old Curiosity Shop*" (Houlding 1892, 70). Individuals now had the capacity to travel independently in their imagination: "There is no frigate like a book...." However, in doing so, the older forms of group story-telling fractured. Elbourne offers this paradox about increasing literacy: "While potentially instruments for the homogenization of culture, writing and print may also provide the capacity for individual isolation within the 'global village'" (Elbourne 1980, 96) to which we might add "and in the family and the community." Folklore still traveled by oral networks, but it also switched into internal channels between author and reader. That these internal channels could cover thousands of miles or hundreds of years did not compromise the power of the messages they carried in the least.

Print Folklore in Victorian Times

Introducing Print Folklore

A "Sleeping Beauty" or "Rapunzel" is easy to find in the historical record: a narrative of this type stands out in terms of its plot, the vocabulary, and locutions employed ("once upon a time," etc.) and very often in terms of the devices and illustrations used to frame the story. This is not, however, true of belief legends that need to be identified and winkled out from magazine columns and from footnotes in books. Sometimes these legends pass themselves off as news, sometimes as experiences, and sometimes as bizarre anecdotes. They adjust to and mimic their surroundings perfectly. Indeed, the reason that they are so often circulated in print is because editors, authors, and readers are frequently unconscious of their true nature. The greatest challenge then with "print folklore" is identifying stories of this kind and the greatest shock, for anyone searching in the 1800s, particularly from the 1830s onwards, is how common they are.

The reason for this omnipresence of belief legends is relatively straightforward. As in the nineteenth century, the book, newspaper and magazine markets became less expensive, it became easier for belief legends to find their way into print. Crudely speaking, by selling a printed work for only a penny or a shilling, authors, publishers, and their agents had to sell many more to recoup their outlays. In this new economy, belief legends made for good copy. This was especially true for newspapers, by far the most widely and frequently read publications in Victorian Britain (Hobbs 2018, 42–43). Belief legends demonstrably attracted all members of Victorian society. But a highbrow publication, which retailed at a high price, such as, say, *Blackwoods* or *The Times*, would be far less likely to carry such stories than their cheaper competitors; there are cases where a story leaked into respectable publications, only to be furiously denied ("We think it our duty..." 1841; see further "**Do You Know Her?**").

Belief legends were actively used instead to sell publications to the lowbrow parts of the market or to highbrow readers who had decided to "slum it." This was the logic that had been used by chapbook and broadside writers for centuries, where a belief legend was often the basis of a sale. There are also many examples in the following pages where urban legends crop up in broadsides in the nineteenth century. For instance, "**Beetle Eyes**" was referred to in a street poem (Reynolds 1846, I, 45); "**Human Sausages**" finds expression in the much-printed cannibal song *The Workhouse Boy* (n.d.); the "**Mistletoe Bride**" owes its name to a ballad written by the late 1820s (Forman 1924, 198). This method was inherited by the newspaper and magazine sectors, where belief legends offered racy yarns that could act as fillers: one contemporary speaks, reasonably enough, of "newspaper folklore" (A Londoner 1852).

The Arrival of Fiction

An important part of the struggle to amuse new readers was the enthusiastic use of fiction by Victorian newspaper and magazine editors. Fiction had appeared in newspapers, with poetry, since the late eighteenth century. It had been used to fill gaps when news coverage ran out and as deadlines ticked closer. By the mid nineteenth century, though, fiction featured in a much more deliberate fashion, particularly in magazines. Several periodicals, including *Blackwood's* relied on serial fiction from the 1820s onward as a permanent part of their repertoire (Palmer 2016, 139). Then, from the 1840s, melodramatic fiction began to be serialized in the new penny magazines and, a little later, in newspapers. By the mid to late nineteenth century, a canny author could expect to get money for an initial serialization of a novel in a weekly or monthly publication and then be paid again for a subsequent book (Law 2000). Regional newspapers and magazines would also run short-story or poetry competitions for readers (e.g., "Notice" 1890: "The plot must be laid in Burnley or North-East Lancashire"). Some newspapers even serialized local novels with neighborhood color (e.g., for the same town, *The Love of Ennie Gold*, by Edward Slater serialized in the *Burnley Advertiser* in the summer of 1880).

Authors of novels, short stories and narrative poems naturally borrowed from belief legends. They were particularly keen to do so given the need for plot-driven rather than the character-driven short stories and more sensationalist, episodic novels in which cliff-hangers and shocks were constantly resorted to. For instance, "**Human Sausages**" became a central preoccupation of the *String of Pearls* (the sprawling epic which introduced Sweeney Todd). Likewise, the "**Pickpocket's Ring**" appears in three different nineteenth-century short stories known to me ("Adventures" 1892; McGovan 1886; "That Fatal Diamond" 1886). There are also, in the later 1800s, stories about skeletons in walls, adaptations of the "**Immured Lovers**" and the "**Skeletons That Eloped**" (e.g., "The Hidden Room" 1894; Green 1890, 57; Fields 1891). I know of no example where a legend can be demonstrated to have begun its life in a short story. There are, though, cases where published stories are asserted to have been the origins of a legend: for example, Robert Louis Stevenson's "Story of the Young Man with the Cream Tarts" is sometimes said (incorrectly) to be the inspiration for the "**Suicide Club**" (Stevenson 1915, 3–92; *pace* "Suicide Clubs" 1898).

The line between fiction and fact blurred in newspapers, and to a lesser extent in magazines. Fiction authors might adopt a more journalistic style, and journalists often hammed up their prose in tragic, sentimental or "romantic" stories. Confusion between the two was inevitable. Sometimes, doubtless, the reader was careless and misread a story as news. But sometimes mystification was encouraged by authors and editors. For instance, in 1897, Nancy Vincent McClelland, a fiction writer, published her short story "Dropped out of Existence; A Strange and True Mystery of the French Capital" in the United States, possibly the origin of the "**Vanishing Lady**." The reader would start this tight, unadorned narrative by reading a note from the editor: "The following remarkable story is true. The writer is personally acquainted with the persons who participated in the scenes which are described" ("A Mystery of Paris" 1897; Taylor-Blake and O'Toole 2010, 10). Is this fiction masquerading as news, news masquerading as fiction, or some uneasy hybrid? As we shall now see, truth was a carefully marketed commodity in the nineteenth century.

Lies in Patter

In dealing with print, folklore, and truth, it is important to begin at the bottom of the print heap with the much despised, frequently purchased (at least in the earlier parts of the century) broadsheets and chapbooks. British street literature traditionally had a very slight regard for the truth. Last speeches of those about to be executed were printed *before* hangings (Mayhew 1851, I, 234): publishers, indeed, were always anxious about pardons. Patterers, meanwhile, mimicked folklore in giving a habitation and a name to the stories they carried around with them. This is a mid-nineteenth-century street seller talking about his luck with "Love-Letters": invented letters full of *double entendre*. The principle he espouses here offers an insight into the role of street literature in spreading stories.

> We give it out that [the letters] are from a tradesman in the neighbourhood, not a hundred yards from where we are a standing. Sometimes we say it's a well-known sporting butcher; sometimes it's a highly respectable publican—just as it will suit the tastes of the neighbourhood. I got my living round Cornwall for one twelvemonth with nothing else than a love-letter. It was headed, "A curious and laughable love-letter and puzzle, sent by a sporting gentleman to Miss H-s-m, in this neighbourhood"; that suits any place that I may chance to be in; but I always patter the name of the street or village where I may be. This letter, I say, is so worded, that had it fallen into the hands of her mamma or papa, they could not have told what it meant; but the young lady, having so much wit, found out its true meaning, and sent him an answer in the same manner. You have here, we say, the number of the house, the name of the place where she lives (there is nothing of the kind, of course), and the initials of all the parties concerned. We dare not give the real names in full, we tell them; indeed, we do all we can to get up the people's curiosity. (Mayhew 1851, I, 234)

This kind of localization made for a sensible commercial strategy, but it also had important consequences for belief legends as a story took root in a given place. Indeed, there is a strong suspicion that some of the "flaps" described in this book came about because of patterers. For instance, the scandals about a given baker or butcher in, respectively, "**Child Pie**" and "**Human Sausages**" can be neatly explained by a patterer selling his wares and fixing a cannibal story on a shop. In fact, in one case, a "ballad monger," the famous James Catnach, was jailed for six months in 1818 for slandering a Drury Lane butcher with one of his publications (Hindley 1878, 84–87; Simpson 1983, 465–66). Likewise, I imagine the rush of 1860 "**Swallowed Up**" stories started with a broadsheet:

"**Swallowed Up**" had been a broadsheet staple since the late seventeenth century (Rollins, 1927, 62–67 "A most wonderful and sad judgement," 1661; Ashton 1882, 65 "God's Just Judgment on Blasphemers," 1700s; Hindley 1871 "Wonderful, Just and Terrible Judgement on a Blasphemer," 24, mid-nineteenth century?).

Lies in the Papers

The attitude of the writers and sellers of British street literature contrasted with the attitude of British journalists. By the mid nineteenth-century, British journalism had what can best be described as a culture or at least an ideal of journalistic truth: one writer played on this in an 1860 play entitled *It must be true, 'twas in the papers* ("Theatre Royal" 1862). Made up stories appeared, of course, in the British press, but these were decried by readers or by rival newspapers, and apologies appeared when editors were caught out. One example must stand for many. In 1842 the editor of the *Western Times* had to apologize for the publication of an unspecified urban legend: "We wonder how the strange story ... got into circulation—and in endeavoring to trace it are informed that it is an old story new-revived" ("The Southernhay Servants"). Victorian journalists and readers saw their newspaper culture as superior, by virtue of its honesty, to that to be found in France and the United States, the two countries with which Victorian Britain most often compared itself (Burger 2017, 310–11 records a similar journalistic ethos of truth in the Netherlands and a similar contempt for American journalism).[9]

A comparison with journalism in the United States is particularly instructive. Take, for instance, the incredible run of stories in 1835 in *The Sun* (New York) claiming that life had been discovered on the moon. Here a New York editor had opportunistically created a fictional news line believing (correctly) that his newspaper would increase its sales both during and after the moon articles (Goodman 2008). There was little in the way of moral outrage in the United States over this playful kind of news strategy. In fact, writers in the United States, including Benjamin Franklin, Poe, Twain, and, later, Ambrose Bierce, "raised the literary hoax to the status of a high art form" (Berkove 2002, 116 on the Sagebrush School; for an example of Franklin's hoaxing, Lemay 2005, 441–44; Poe 1857, III, 126 for approval of *The Sun*'s moon stunt; Boese 2002, 56–58 for Poe's hoaxes; for Twain, Caron 2008, 105–7; for Bierce, see Hall 1934, particularly iv–v). American readers seem to have been more relaxed and less, let's say, priggish, than their British counterparts. "Tall tales" or "snake stories," as they were sometimes called, were part of the fun of newspaper reading ("Snake Stories" 1885; Loomis 1946 for an overview of invented reports by Dan De Quille).

Clippings, Flaps, Experiences, and Inventions

This does not mean, of course, that nineteenth-century newspaper readers were uninterested in the kind of unlikely stories that will be encountered in this book. It means that such stories were, usually, published under special conditions rather than as everyday news. There were, in fact, four general circumstances when belief legends appeared in British magazines and newspapers: (i) clippings; (ii) flaps; (iii) individual reports; and (iv) inventions (for the ways that urban legends get into modern papers, Smith, "Read" 1992).

Clipping, to start with, was the nineteenth-century equivalent of "cut and paste" and was, in that period, used by newspaper editors around the world. An attractive newspaper story was spotted in another newspaper either by the editor, a journalist, or, in the case of large titles, paid agents. It was "clipped" (and perhaps edited down) and then inserted by the editor into his or her own newspaper, although typically with an acknowledgment pointing to the original publication or to the intermediate source. Copyright was not felt to apply to clipping; at least very few legal cases resulted. A poor editor responsible for running a newspaper single-handedly could achieve a great deal with artful clipping. Extracts might be anything from a fifty-word mini paragraph to an article of two or three thousand words; today it is possible to trace a clipping from its first appearance as it passes around the country. For instance, the report of a Scottish mermaid exploded in, of all places, an Oxford paper, 26 August 1809. By 5 September it had been excerpted in some of the London papers; then, crucially, on 8 September, it appeared in *The Times*. From there it traveled rapidly through Britain, Ireland, and abroad (Young 2018, 27–29; the Viral Text Project promises to uncover patterns in clipping circulation: https://viraltexts.org/ accessed 30 Sep 2020).

In this way, a belief legend could be printed in a small provincial paper and yet soon have tens of thousands of readers. The "Corpse in the Car(t)" legend from Staffordshire was shared by some sixty British and Irish papers in August 1866 (BNA). Victorian journalism proved, in its clipping, to be "communal rather than individual, distributed rather than centralized" (Cordell 2015, 417). Clipping was not only inexpensive, but it also effectively removed from the editor responsibility for the report. If a British editor included a passage translated from, say, an Italian paper, the editor was, by placing the Italian newspaper in the byline, deliberately putting some distance between himself and the foreign title. The reader enjoyed the narrative; the editor retained his reputation for truth, perhaps with the help of a sarcastic heading or an ironic bracketed comment: "A Very Unlikely Story," "An Unlikely Story,"

"A Strange Tale if True," "Wonderful if True," and so on. A dubious story then circulated unhindered.

The second way that belief legends got into the newspaper was through "flaps." Here there are instances when a newspaper reports a story that was doing the rounds in a local community, much as those we have described in the section above on oral transmission. The story may or may not have been true, but the editor could reasonably enough publish the story as news: after all, if the narrative was, to use Victorian words, a "bull" or a "cock," the commotion around it was still newsworthy. For instance, the "Corpse in the Car(t)" was in 1866 a local oral story in Staffordshire. In **Sewer Monsters** we learn that the story of a sewer explorer being killed by rats was talked about in London around the middle of the century: "You must ha' heard on it," one informant insisted when chatting to Henry Mayhew (Mayhew 1851, II, 154). Again, the editor typically put some skeptical distance between himself and the "facts." The Staffordshire editor, for example, noted that he had been "unable to verify the narrative with anything like precision" ("An Unlikely Story" 1866); while an 1879 urban legend in the Devizes would be, the editor insisted, "strange if true" ("A Strange Story" 31 Jan 1879). Once more, the reader got to enjoy the narrative, and the editor avoided direct responsibility.

The third category was individual accounts; that is, lived urban legends. Members of the community who were named, or whose identity was known by those who wrote, made the claim that they had had an experience that resembled a legend. Here we have not FOAF (friend of a friend), but what folklorists have referred to as "ostension" (for an introduction to ostension, see Ellis 1989 and Mitchell 2004). I would take ostension to include fantasists and tall-tale tellers, those with mental illness who "live" myths, those whose biographies really do coincide with a story type, and people who process a remarkable event in folklore terms. For instance, there were among the last group the many men and some women who said, and perhaps believed, that they had been assaulted by chloroform-wielding robbers in a way that any knowledge of that drug will show to have been quite impossible: see **Chloroformed!** and some of the cases in **Drugged on the Train.** There were the various men and women who found coins or rings in their breakfast eggs: **Egg Ring.** We also have the missionary who said that he had been swallowed by a whale and who had survived the experience: **Modern Jonah** (Campbell 1928).

The fourth category are the out-and-out inventions. In this case, typically, a correspondent or a penny-a-liner sent in a faked story. Penny-a-liners were freelance journalists who were based largely in London—only important centers had a press large enough to sustain them. They were "occasional writers" paid for news by the word, or as their name suggests, by the line. The term was almost always used in a derogatory fashion: "Many a good man and able has indeed made his first advances to journalism through humble penny-a-lining, but no man of ability remains long in the ranks" ("London Morning" 1849, 88). The penny-a-liners had a reputation for prolixity (the more words they wrote, they more they were paid); for gruesome content (they typically dealt with crime, disasters and accidents); and for making up stories. These "hacks" were, given their preferred subject matter and their lax journalist habits, particularly likely to pick up on belief legends. Either they wrote up belief legends masquerading as news (essentially a flap), or they used, in their desperation to earn money, belief legends to create news (thus, invention).

The penny-a-liner, when being "inventive," had to be very careful. If he or she referred to a court case or a murder or an event in a local workhouse, in short anything that could be checked, the story would be "called out." The editor would receive letters questioning the version of events described, and the writer might lose a source of income. There are two notable examples in the legends in this volume of a news report being publicly shredded: "**Beetle Eyes**" (Correspondent 1843) and "**Eagle and the Baby**" ("The Eagle and Child Story" 1904). It was much safer to give a story at the level of rumor or hearsay about, say, an unnamed woman seeing a ghost, or an unnamed man being robbed in an unusual way. "Safer" because it would be much more difficult to conclusively show that such stories were untrue. A fascinating example of this is the way that the newspapers filled up with hearsay when hard news was lacking in the Whitechapel murders in 1888 (Curtis 2001, 164–85).

Of course, these four categories could easily merge and become confused. For instance, a clipping may originally have been based on a flap or a personal claim. An ingenious faker might invent a local flap to get his story out. We should ask, thinking of "Corpse in the Car(t)," whether there *really* was a narrative "current in the hill country of Staffordshire" in 1866 ("An Unlikely Story" 1866). A careless journalist might record a flap as simple fact and then be blamed for dishonesty or incompetence. An unscrupulous editor could invent a story and claim that it was from a clipping from an invented newspaper or one that, at any rate, had never carried the piece.[10] At this remove, we have no way, in most cases, of establishing which of these four categories a given report belonged to. What we *can* say is that in all four cases, folklore types could easily break through onto the newspaper pages or that a new legend type could develop in print, like bacteria in a Petri dish. Flaps and clippings would be based on local traditions, which borrowed from regional folklore. Then faking journalists and story-telling members of the public might draw on (or unknowingly create) folklore.

Uneven Collection

A final complication in Victorian print folklore is the way that some narratives were neglected because they were judged to be improper. Communities find it easier to address publicly some folklore themes than others. For instance, the Victorians seem to have been more at ease with extremely violent, salacious details than modern readers. Two choice examples: "A few days ago a little boy was run over by the cars at Monson, and fearfully mutilated. His mangled remains were gathered up in a bag, and his heart, which was picked up on the track, for some time continued to pulsate in the hand which held it" ("A horrible story..." 1869); or, from 1875, "A thunder-clap ensued... heads, like black balls, were seen by those at a distance to be shot like bombshells through the air—the place was filled with dead, with fragments of clothes, with legs and arms torn from the trunk, with the viscera still palpitating of men, women and children" ("The Terrible Explosion"; for more on sensationalist Victorian violence see Boyle 1989).

Belief legends involving cannibalism or murder were not difficult to publish, in terms of content, in Victorian times. But sexual stories were far less likely to be shared then than would be the case today. This is not to say that the Victorians were horrified by sex; we have projected a far too simplistic model of Victorian prudery back into the past (Sweet 2001, xii–xv; at the same time middle class Victorians *were* often prudish compared with today's standards, Fryer 1963). Still less is it to say that Victorians were not interested in sex: the taboo nature of sex in the late 1800s made it a particularly piquant topic for Victorian story-tellers. The problem was that sex, especially outside of marriage, was judged not to be a respectable topic for conversation in middle-class society. As a result, magazines, newspapers, and novels did not feel that they could safely share sexual details, save perhaps in legal contexts (Boyle 1989, 11–20).

Sexual belief legends are hard to find in Victorian sources. They were told, but they were not recorded. "If nothing is to be found in the old archives," this does not mean that the story does not exist, but rather that it is "probably due to the fact that no notice was taken of" the story then (Bonaparte 1941, 121; Legman 1962 for difficulties in collecting sexual folklore just half a century ago). Think, for instance, of the "**Wrong Trousers**." An impoverished man returns home unexpectedly and finds his wife in bed. He removes his trousers, but she persuades her husband to go out and buy something. He agrees, slips his trousers back on, and walks down the street. When he puts his hands in his pockets, he finds, to his shock, a golden sovereign. At this point, he realizes that these are not his trousers... This story was, I suspect, told numerous times in Victorian Britain. But it would have been difficult for a Victorian newspaper to publish it. I can only cite one British example ("Curious Discovery" 1871, set in Dundee and published in a Dundee paper): long searches for other British instances have proved vain; happily, versions were recorded abroad.

Other Victorian sexual yarns include "**Hands in the Muff**," "**I'm Jack the Ripper!**," "**She's My Daughter**," the "**Shoplifter's Dilemma**," "**Tunnel Kissing**," and the "**Wrong Bed**." How do we know about these if the Victorians were so reluctant to publish sexual material? Well, they all appeared in print, but in ways that did not compromise the publisher. In "**Hands in the Muff**" and "**Shoplifter's Dilemma**," there are effective stories with coded sexual references: in fact, "**Shoplifter's Dilemma**" becomes more explicit in the twentieth century. In "**She's My Daughter**" and the more scandalous examples of "**Wrong Bed**," the story is set abroad, often in the United States. In "**I'm Jack the Ripper!**," we have to rely on post-Victorian stories for what seems to have been a Victorian story. There will, of course, have been many, many more "gentleman's jokes" ("The Box Tunnel" 1860), and they will prove difficult to find.

Another area where there were belief legends, but where contemporaries seem to have been reluctant to collect were some of the more baroque Christian narratives. Victorian Britain was, of course, a deeply Christian society. But its authors and, in the later part of the century, many of its readers, felt that "medieval" details, like a visit from the devil ("**Devil Take Me**") or a dramatic miracle story, were rather unsuited to the age of steam. Take, for instance, "**Swallowed Up**," in which a man blasphemes and is swallowed up to his chin in the earth. This story has a pedigree in Christian writing going back deep into the Middle Ages, and the evidence we have suggests that it was still circulating orally in 1860, when it surfaced briefly as a belief story in British and Irish newspapers. Stories like these were usually too unbelievable for the educated editors of newspapers to print. In fact, in 1860, the story was presented by many papers not as a morality lesson but as a joke (e.g., "Marvellous Tales" 1860).

The NAIL in the SKULL and Other VICTORIAN URBAN LEGENDS

1. THE BABY PICNIC

Summary: Jokers exchange babies at a picnic, and the families do not realize until they have made the long trip home. Earliest Attestation: 1859 (US, origins in Scotland?). Motif: Possibly related to F321.1: "Fairy steals child from cradle and leaves fairy substitute." Secondary Literature: N/A.

This story appeared in a US newspaper in 1859.

> Some time ago there was a dancing party given near Weaverville, California. Most of the ladies present had little babies, whose noisy perversity required too much attention to allow the mothers to enjoy the dance. A number of gallant young men volunteered to watch the young ones while the parents engaged in a "break-down." No sooner had the women left the babies in charge of the mischievous fellows than they stripped the infants, changed clothes, and gave to one the apparel of another. The dance over it was time to go home, and the mothers hurriedly took each a baby, in the dress of her own, and started, some to their homes, ten or fifteen miles off, and were far on their way before daylight. But the day following there was a prodigious row in the settlement. Mothers discovered that a single day had changed the sex of their babies; observation disclosed startling phenomena, and then commenced some of the tallest female pedestrianism; living miles apart it required two days to unmix the babies, and as many months to restore their naturally sweet dispositions. To this day it is unsafe for any of the baby mixers to venture within the territory. ("Scrambling" 1859, *FG*; see also "A Funny Story" 1859)

In 1875 the story was set in West Kentucky ("Op een ..." 1875, *PB* who reports that another Dutch version had servant girls jumble up the babies). A later version dates to 1878 and was set "near Waco, in Texas" ("Our Essence" 1878). Though the geographical location is different, the words used show that the 1878 story was based directly or indirectly on the 1859 story, or possibly a common ancestor. In 1881 the Weaverville story appeared again in a British magazine ("An Exchange of Babies" 1881). In 1900 the story appeared in relation to Australia:

It appears to be a social custom in the Australian bush to arrange picnics on a large scale, as being the only means of getting people together, living, as they do there, many a score of miles away from one another. Our cousins' household arrangements not being so complete as ours, on such occasions the mothers bring their babies. At one monster picnic there was a scarcity of ladies for dancing, and the mothers were all pressed into the service, leaving the babies altogether by themselves. Some few young gentlemen of a waggish turn of mind took the opportunity to change the frocks and cloaks of all the babies, without reference to sex, age or fit, and as some of the mothers went home before the others, the utmost consternation prevailed when the little ones, having been claimed by their clothes in the hurry of departure, were afterwards found to be strangers, and each distracted mother knew not with whom her child might be, or how far off. The perpetrators of the joke took care to make themselves scarce for a period, and a general interchange of babies formed the sole occupation of the ladies for days afterwards. ("A Very Nice Mixture" 1900 [New Zealand], *CW*)

The story became well enough established that by 1905 a British journalist could recall the narrative "of the Australian picnic" after a mix-up at a crèche in Newport ("The story of the confusion . . ." 1905).

The exchange-of-babies legend might come out of British fairy lore. Certainly, a similar story, first published in 1871, by Hugh Miller (1802–1856) is based on the old fear that fairies leave changelings in place of babies (still our best study of changeling beliefs is Piaschewski 1935; for Scotland, Henderson and Cowan 2001, 94–101). As a New Zealand newspaper that ran with the story explained:

[T]he form of fairy malice which was most dreaded was that of kidnapping human children, and substituting for them, fairy babies, which were called changelings, and invariably proved cross-grained, ill-tempered and voracious. A poor baby, who was attacked with any sort of wasting illness, or became unusually fretful and troublesome, was very apt to be looked upon as a changeling, and to receive anything but tenderness from the family who were forced to endure its wailing. (Cumming 1884, *CW*)

I give the story in Miller's words. It is set in Cromarty in northern Scotland:

The fairies were in ill repute at the time, and long before, for an ill practice of kidnapping children, and annoying women in the straw; and no class of people could dread them more than fishers. But they were at length cured of their terrors by being laughed at. One evening, when all the men were setting out for sea, and all the women engaged at the water's edge in handing them their tackle or launching their boats, a party of young fellows, who had watched the opportunity, stole into their cottages, and, disfurnishing the cradles of all their little tenants, transposed the children of the entire village, leaving a child in the cradle of every mother, but taking care that it should not be her own child. They then hid themselves amid the ruins of a deserted hovel to wait the result. Up came the women from the shore; and, alarmed by the crying of the children, and the strangeness of their voices, they went to their cradles, and found a changeling in each. The scene that followed baffles description. They shrieked, and screamed, and clapped their hands; and, rushing out to the lanes like so many mad creatures, were only unhinged the more to find the calamity so universal. Down came the women of the place to make inquiries and give advices, some recommending them to have recourse to the minister, some to procure baskets and suspend the changelings over the fire, some one thing, some another; but the poor mothers were regardless of them all. They tossed their arms, and shrieked, and halooed; and the children, who were well nigh as ill at ease as themselves, added by their cries to the confusion and the uproar. A thought struck one of the townswomen. "I suspect, neighbours," she said, "that the loons are at the bottom of this. Let's bring all the little ones into one place, and see whether every mother cannot find her own among them." No sooner said than done; and peace was restored in a few minutes. Mischievous as the trick was, it had this one effect, that the fairies were in less in Cromarty ever after, and were never more charged with the stealing of children. A popular belief is in no small danger when those who cherished learn to laugh at it, be the laugh raised as it may. (Miller 1871, 357–58)

The story works much better with its background in fairy and changeling belief than the picnic-party equivalents. In the case of the American and Australian mothers, we have to explain how they could have returned home with the wrong baby. Perhaps another written or oral version from Scotland inspired these stories from or about the wider English-speaking world.

2. BEETLE EYES

> Summary: Beetles are attached to a child's eyes to create a blind beggar. Earliest Attestation: 1843 (England). Motif: N/A. Secondary Literature: N/A.

Children made good beggars, and mutilated children particularly were able to collect substantial amounts in the streets of Victorian Britain (for child beggars, see Chesney 1970, 202–8; there is a long-standing historical/folklore tradition of child beggars being deliberately maimed, e.g., Henderson 2018, 213 n. 78). From this simple fact came various nineteenth-century legends about children being mutilated by ruthless parents or kidnappers. This is the necessary background for a newspaper squall in the summer of 1843. We are in Berkshire, and the original report was published in the *Reading Mercury*.

> A day or two since, a gentleman travelling along the road near Colnbrook, had his attention attracted to the screams of a child in the care of a tramping woman, who had two other children totally blind also with her. The cries of the child were so distressing that he insisted on knowing the cause, but not getting a satisfactory answer, he forcibly removed a bandage from its eyes, when, horrid to relate, he found them encased with two small perforated shells, in which were two live black beetles, for the purpose of destroying the sight. The woman was instantly seized and given into custody, and at the Magistrates meeting, at Eton, on Wednesday last, committed for trial. There is too much reason to fear that the wretch produced the blindness on the other two by similar means. ("A Monster" 1843)

We should not doubt for a moment that, if it was a question of money, cruel men and women would have blinded children. There must, surely, though have been easier ways to achieve this aim.

This story is especially interesting because, while being widely circulated, it was also instantly contested ("A paragraph…" 1843). In fact, the correspondent who had penned the report wrote, soon after publication, a letter of explanation and apology to his editor, which the editor saw fit to publish in the *Mercury*. As this letter offers a rare glimpse into the process by which "strange stories" appeared in Victorian papers, I give most of it here:

> Dear Sir, in reply to your letter … the intelligence was furnished me on most respectable authority, at the moment I was engaged in making up my weekly

correspondence to you, on the Thursday previous to the Saturday's journal in which it appeared. Not doubting its authenticity, or for one moment conceiving that the imagination alone of any evil disposed person could have furnished so horrible a narrative, I at once penned the paragraph, which appears to have caused so general a sensation, with the full conviction that it was to the very letter strictly correct. You know that I am at all times particularly cautious in these matters, but in the haste of the moment ... did not make further enquiry into it, and you may, therefore, guess my surprise on perceiving in the papers of Saturday last, a flat contradiction given to the circumstance. I have been since strictly engaged in investigating the affair, and although the "horrid narrative" is still asserted by a multitude of persons in the vicinity of the place in which it is said to have transpired, as a positive fact, I have failed in tracing its exact origin, and it does at least appear that the apprehension and committal of the woman (as represented) was altogether anticipated, as the case has certainly not undergone any investigation before the Magistrates of Eton. (Correspondent 1843)

Note that "A Monster" (1843) had been the last of several reports from the correspondent. Perhaps he just needed to fill some space.

The story, in any case, continued to be told in the press. In 1846 a letter-writer to the *Hull Advertiser* knew of how a *stolen* child had had "shells fixed over its eyes with live beetles under them to eat the poor little creature's eyes out, in order to exhibit it as an object to beg with" (A. 1846). In 1869 another letter-writer to a newspaper referred to how "a woman was convicted for applying black-beetles in walnut shells to the eyes of children in order to produce blindness" (A.V. 1869; this passage seems to have been lifted from an earlier article credited to the *Globe*, "Beggars" 1869; see also "Catharine" 1870). The *Clerkenwell News* had a similar passage in 1871: "like that horrible case a few years back—in which more than one child was intentionally blinded by the application of live beetles in walnut-shells to the globes of the eyes ..." ("The Suppression" 1871). In 1872 an author, in a book on blindness, shifted the action to London and gave the credit for the capture to the police.

> About the year 1843, a woman was taken in charge by the police for begging on London Bridge with two children, who, she stated, were both blind. On reaching the station-house it was observed that the children cried very much, and that they put their hands to the bandages that covered their eyes. On the removal of the bandages the police were filled with horror, on finding black beetles eating into the eyes of the children. (Levy 1872, 13; for London Bridge and British folklore see further **"Selling Sovereigns"**)

Did the Beetle Eyes story originate in an article in the *Reading Mercury*, or was it a much more widely known Victorian story that happened to "surface" in 1843? I have found no evidence earlier than 1843, but I suspect that it is older. In 1846 a beetle story was set in Smithfield (London) in Reynold's *Mysteries of London*. A mother describes how she will blind her children following her friend's example: "She covered the eyes over with cockle shells, the eye-lids ... being wide open; and in each shell there was a large black beetle" (Reynolds 1846, I, 45). In 1868 a routine reference is made to the trick "of confining black beetles in walnut shells and binding them over the eyes of infants" ("A Hard Road" 1868, 235: note that the author of this anonymous piece is George Augustus Sala). There was no explanation—clearly the metropolitan readers of *All the Year Round*, in which the sentence appeared, were expected to understand the motives behind this ghastly act. We also know that sometime in the second half of the nineteenth century there was a street ballad entitled "Mary Arnold, the Female Monster":

> The beetles in a walnut shell, / This mother she did place, / This dreadful deed, as you read, / All history does disgrace, / The walnut shell, and beetles / With a bandage she bound tight, / Around her infant's tender eyes, / To take away it's [sic] sight. (Ashton 1888, 375–76)[1]

The correspondent of the *Reading Mercury* who wrote up the story had likely, on this evidence, encountered an older narrative, not coined a new one.

3. THE BOSOM SERPENT

Summary: An animal enters a human body and takes up residence there causing grave health problems; the sufferer tries to remove the unwelcome guest. Earliest Attestation: Antiquity. Motif: B784 "Animal lives in a person's stomach" and associated motifs. Secondary Literature: Ermacora 2015; Ermacora et al. 2016; Bennett 2005, 3–59. Notes: the term "Bosom Serpent," while in several respects unhelpful, has been used by Bennett and Ermacora, so I employ it here.

"A man, woman, or child," writes Gillian Bennett, "is said to have a creature growing inside the body—not only reptiles ... but also amphibians. The creature has taken up residence in a vital organ, occasionally in the heart but more frequently somewhere in the gastrointestinal tract" (Bennett 2005, 4). Welcome to the "Bosom Serpent," a set of ideas that can be traced back thousands of years (Ermacora 2015; Ermacora et al. 2016). Reptiles and amphibians (and sometimes other types of creatures) dwell in the human body. Sometimes the creature is accidentally swallowed when it is young; sometimes it crawls into the human body through the mouth or another orifice while the host sleeps. Bizarre as the Bosom Serpent may seem to modern readers, these were often lived experiences. There are many accounts from nineteenth-century Britain— "I believe there are few parishes in England in which similar tales are not told" (Baring-Gould 1898, 265, *BS*)—describing sufferers liberating or failing to liberate themselves from unwelcome animal guests. This Bosom Serpent incident took place in 1844 in Cumberland:

> A married woman, residing in Distington, near Whitehaven, previous to last week, suffered severely for some months past from a pain in the stomach, and every means adopted for its removal proved of no avail. On Wednesday last, however, during a fit of coughing, she ejected from her stomach a living reptile, about 12 inches in length, resembling the water asp, and has ever since been comparatively free from the pain she had hitherto endured. It is conjectured that the reptile had been swallowed in water when very small, and that it had attained its great size in the stomach of the unfortunate woman, who had been so long tortured by her strange and unnatural lodger. ("Horrible Story" 1844)

Other accounts from the English-speaking world include the following: the black snake in a New York sailor's stomach ("A Black Snake" 1834); an advertisement, in 1854, describing how Grimshaw's Valuable Mixture drove a foot-long worm, "with a head resembling that of an Askerd or Reptile" from a woman (Barnes and Smith 2001, 137–38; Sweet 2001, 38–56 on Victorian advertising and news stories); a frog vomited by a girl from Ashford (Sussex, "A live frog . . ." 1862); grasshoppers that hatched inside a young woman from the United States ("A Very Strange Story" 1874); a snake believed to be causing chaos in the stomach of a woman in Ohio ("A Snake Yarn" 1881); a lizard alive in the stomach of a man in the same year in Detroit (a postmortem revealed a tumour; "The Detroit man . . ." 1881); a multi-colored reptile that lodged in a Cornish woman's throat ("A Strange Story" 1888); and, in 1904, a woman from Paneswick who committed suicide because she believed that she had a snake or frog in her stomach ("Snake in the Stomach" 1904). Such reports could be multiplied many times over. Victorian newspapers were surprisingly tolerant of the Bosom Serpent, declaring them "strange stories" and the like, but not usually denouncing the experiences outright. Of the stories outlined here, the writer of "A Black Snake" (1834) was the most incredulous. Medical science had already by the nineteenth

Figure 1 A French comic strip 'Une cure merveilleuse', c.1900, with a frog being pumped out of a man's stomach. In the next panel the man is shown to have recovered.

century turned almost entirely against the possibility of the Bosom Serpent, and doctors writing in such periodicals as the *Lancet* proved a good deal less tolerant than journalists (Bondeson 1997, 33–43). Revealingly, correspondents to *Notes and Queries* debated the Bosom Serpent under the heading "Newspaper Folklore" (The first letter in a series: A Londoner 1852).

4. BURIED ALIVE

> Summary: A living person in a trance is accidentally buried alive. Earliest Attestation: antiquity. Motif: S123: "Burial Alive." Secondary Literature: Bondeson 2001. Compare with: "**Jolting the Coffin**" and the "**Lady and the Ring**."

Being buried alive was, as Jan Bondeson (2001) has very capably shown, something of an obsession for Victorians. Living "corpses" appeared in factual news reports, in medical articles, in fiction, and even in art. A very small number of unlucky individuals *were* interred while still alive, but most reports came either from incorrect inferences made about noises from coffins (gasses released during decomposition) or from bodies that had later been found to have moved (again part of the process of decomposition) (Bondeson 2001, 244–45).

I have given, elsewhere in this volume, separate entries to two special urban legends about being buried alive: "**Jolting the Coffin**" and the "**Lady and the**

Ring." More typical "Buried Alive" stories break down into one of three types: survival, tardy discovery, or abandonment. The first involved, of course, "corpses" being rescued from their coffins. This is from 1856 and France:

> A young married woman of Colluire, near this city, after being ill for some time, fell, one day last week, into a complete state of insensibility, and was supposed to be dead. A medical man who was called in gave a certificate of the death, and the young woman was laid out, and in due time fastened up in a coffin. In the night some women who were sitting up to watch the deceased heard subdued groans and sighs in the coffin. They fled in dismay, and the neighbours on hearing their account of the matter proposed to have the coffin opened, but the husband of the female would not hear of such a thing, as it would be, he said, a profanation of the dead. The mother of the young woman, however, broke open the coffin with a hatchet, and it then turned out that the young woman was not dead, but had only been in a lethargy. Medical assistance was procured for her, and in a short time she recovered perfect consciousness. She is now going on well. ("A Strange Story" Nov 1856; see also, for this type, "Nearly Buried Alive" 1889)

In other cases, a coffin or grave was re-opened, but too late to save the person who had been buried alive. Note that unaccountable delays and *premortem* lacerations, found in this passage from 1893, were common in such reports.

> Information has been received at St. Petersburg of the burying alive of a peasant in the village of Maruten, in the government of Kalooga. The victim, who was shortly to be married, happened to fall asleep on a stove, the fumes from which partially asphyxiated him and rendered him unconscious. His relatives, thinking he was dead, had him buried without delay. Shortly after the funeral someone passing by the cemetery heard sounds proceeding from the newly made grave. When after considerable delay the grave was opened the victim was dead, the body presenting a horrible spectacle. The unfortunate man had torn his grave clothes and torn out one of his eyes and bitten off one of his fingers, while his face was literally in shreds. ("Buried Alive" 1893; see also, for this type, "A Major" 1892)

Sometimes the person in the coffin is found alive (just) but "expired very shortly afterwards" ("A Horrible Story" 1892).

Finally, there are stories about gravediggers or even family members ignoring clues that those who had been buried were alive. For instance, a Yorkshire sexton claimed, while drinking with friends, that he and his son had heard some noises from a pauper's coffin but had filled the grave in anyway ("A Strange Story" Oct 1877; compare with the similar "A Horrible Story" 1892). A more

Figure 2 *Illustrated Police News* (21 May 1910), 4, 'Awful Discovery: A Girl Buried Alive'.

extreme version of this came again from Russia (along with France the main source of gruesome Buried-Alive stories for the British press). The year is 1890.

> A rich popular farmer died somewhat suddenly in the village of Sooroffsky. He had been seen in the enjoyment of excellent health on Thursday, and was found dead in his bed on Friday morning. He was prayed for and duly "waked" after which he was carried to the grave, almost all the inhabitants of the village, inclusive of the priest, following him to the churchyard. Just as the body was being lowered the lid, which had been fastened rather loosely with wooden nails, began to rise up slowly and detach itself from the coffin, to the indescribable horror of the friends and mourners of the deceased. Then the dead man was seen in his white shroud stretching his arms upwards and sitting up. At this sight the gravediggers let go the chords, and along with the bystanders, fled in terror from the spot. The supposed corpse then arose, scrambled out of the grave, and, shivering from the cold (the mercury was two degrees below zero Farh.), made for the village as fast as his feebleness allowed him. But the villagers had barred and bolted themselves against the "wizard" and no one made answer to the appeals he made, with chattering teeth, to be admitted; and so, blue, breathless, trembling, he ran from hut to hut, seeking some escape from death. ("Superstition in Russia" 1890)

Several neighbors shortly afterwards tracked the revenant "wizard" down and hammered aspen stakes into his body: "There was no doubts about his death this time" ("Superstition" 1890; see also "Buried Alive: A Horrible Story" 1888, which also has aspen stakes).

5. THE CAUTIOUS DRUGGIST

Summary: A druggist suspecting bad intentions from a customer only pretends to give him or her poison. Earliest Attestation: 1847 (England). Motif: N/A. Secondary Literature: N/A.

The Victorian druggist was an important figure in the local community. Not only did he provide customers with medical advice and sometimes carry out medical procedures, but he also had the heavy responsibility of selling poisons such as arsenic, ergot, and strychnine (for background on this profession, see Jackson 1981). Until the 1868 Pharmacy Act, the sale of poison in Britain was almost entirely uncontrolled. The act formalized a poison register; required that poison be clearly labeled; and stated that poison could only be sold if the purchaser (or an intermediary) was known to the druggist (for an excellent overview of the act see Berridge 1981, 113–22). There was understandable concern that a client might buy a drug for rats and then put it, say, in his wife's tea: there were several important mid-Victorian poison cases that concentrated minds in the press and in Parliament (Flanders 2011, 183–319). It is interesting that the one Victorian urban legend we have about druggists, versions of which clump in the midnineteenth century, put him in a favorable light.

> "Fill me this bottle with laudanum," exclaimed an excited married man, rushing into a druggist's shop on the Tyne—his face bleeding from a recent encounter with his wife. "It will kill you," the druggist calmly replied. "That's what I want it for," was Romeo's rejoinder: "I'll kill myself to vex her." The druggist said it would be a pity to prevent so amiable a purpose, and filled the phial. No sooner filled than emptied. "I'm a dead man," cried Romeo, staggering into the presence of his Juliet: "I've taken laudanum." "Ha! Ha! Ha!" was the provoking response: "who cares what thou's tyen, thou ha'porth o' tripe in two bites!" The moribund little man stood aghast. He had destroyed himself to be revenged; and, instead of

running for the stomach pump, a contemptuous laugh, and a sneer at his proportions, was her receptions [sic] of his tragic announcement! He was dying to give her pain, and she was as pleased as Punch! Exasperated by his blunder, the poor sinner tottered back to the druggist's and, feeling the poison at work within him, demanded an instant emetic. "I poisoned myself," he groaned, "to vex her, and she's glad I'm going! O! Give me an Emetic, and save me!" Nothing loth, the man of medicine executed this second order. Romeo then returned to recover in the sight of his wife that she might have the mortification of beholding him restored to her arms. Now the druggist having no inclination to abet suicide, and being unwilling, by refusing to administer poison, to send our hero to a less scrupulous shop, had given him, on his first visit, a dose of tincture of rhubarb; and while the afflicted wretch was labouring under the double operation of his purge and emetic his "better half," still unmoved by his sufferings sharpened them by the scorpion exclamation: "Why, thou thin end of a penn'orth o' cheese, thou sart'ly cannot last lang for thou's swealin' [burning] away like a farden cannel leeted at byeth ends!" ("A Husband's Predicament" 1847)

Other versions of this story circulated in the next twenty years. In 1849 a tailor bought arsenic, which he swigged down with beer while he was bidding farewell to his friends; but the pharmacist had actually given him wheat flour, something that emerged when he had his stomach pumped in a nearby hospital ("Hint to Druggists" 1849). In 1864 a man wanted rat poison, but the pharmacist, realizing that his customer wished to end his life, gave him magnesia instead. The despairing man drank it in his beer and then announced to his friends that he was about to die. The landlord—who had talked to the pharmacist—pumped his stomach with a spirit siphon ("A Fellow" 1864). Stomach pumping appears in several versions as the stern lesson that the suicide must learn in returning from the brink. Suicide, it will be remembered, was a criminal act in the Victorian period (for Victorian suicide, see Anderson 1987; Gates 1988). In 1867 a man in Leeds decided to kill himself to spite his lover. The druggist gave the man carbonate of soda. The suicide took the "poison" and rolled around the floor for several hours until the druggist was asked to explain the trick ("A Discarded" 1867). The story of the druggist saving a potential suicide was also told in the early part of the twentieth century (Thompson 1923, 91–93 gives three instances: two were in his first edition in 1904, *BC*).

A different version of the story exists that involves not suicide but murder. Here the center of gravity of the narrative shifts from the druggist to the client. I know of only two versions, the first dating to 1856: the story "whether true or false" "is the talk of a village in the parish of Halifax, and bordering on Bradford."

Figure 3 An unscrupulous chemist selling a child arsenic and laudanum. Wood engraving after J. Leech. Credit: Wellcome Collection.

It appears that a certain woman, feeling her spouse an encumbrance, and, unmindful of her marriage vows and the rigour of the law, resolved on his disposal after a method, now, alas, too common. She applied to the druggist of the village for six pennyworth of arsenic. He very properly refused to sell her the article, and informed her husband of the application, at the same time inquiring of him for what purpose his wife could require such a quantity of such an article? The husband replied, jocularly, that he could not tell unless it was for the purpose of poisoning him, and telling the druggist that if she applied again he must sell some harmless article in lieu of the arsenic, and they would see what her objects were. She did apply again, and the wary apothecary delivered her some carbonate of soda, magnesia, or other comparatively innocuous drug, warning the husband of what had occurred. When he went home he found a meat pie prepared for dinner. He pretended, at first, want of appetite, and invited his wife to help herself. She refused and at last he ate a quantity of the pie. In a little time, he professed himself unwell, then feigned thirst, then alarming sickness, and finally death. The treacherous woman manifested great concern during these proceedings, but the instant death appeared to her to have occurred, she passed a rope through the chamber floor, and knit it to her supposed dead husband's neck, in order that when her neighbours were called in, he might appear to have hanged himself. She then ran upstairs to draw up and fix the rope. The instant she had disappeared the dead man revived, released himself from the rope, and passed it round the leg of the table, and the woman hung that useful domestic article, instead of the other one—her husband. The latter also ran upstairs, inquiring of the faithless woman, "what she was after, drawing the table up that way?" The affair has ended for the present in his, as the phrase is, taking the law into his own hands. He has given her, as Yorkshire folk say, "a right down good hiding." ("The Biter Bit" 1856; for home gallows compare "The Woman Who Failed" 1907, *CW*)

The story appeared again in 1861, though now it was set in north Wales. It was "much talked of in several parts of the country," though the paper could not vouch for its "strict accuracy . . . although probably there is something in it." Nor was the paper able to give names or details other than the general location of the attempt at murder: "In a place not a hundred miles from the village of Bethesda lives a married couple . . ." In the 1861 version there is no noose. The dead husband simply comes back to life, lights a pipe, and drinks some brandy while his wife summons the neighbors to see her husband's corpse ("Poisoning Extraordinary" 1861). Both the 1856 and 1861 stories are written in a comic tone, one that is strangely at odds with their content.

6. CHILD PIE

Summary: A pie is brought to a baker to be baked. It is later found to contain a baby. Earliest Attestation: 1773 (England, particularly associated with London?). Motif: N/A. Secondary Literature: N/A. Compare with: "**Human Sausages**."

In 1832 a British journalist made reference to some of the outrageous stories that sometimes did the rounds of newspapers (my italics in what follows): "To read the ordinary obituary of humanity is dull and unenticing; but an account of a man cut up into little bits and burned in detail, or *a child baked in a pie*, are treats of the highest order . . ." ("New Publications" 1832). With apologies to the disarticulated man, the child in a pie rather jumps out here. Was there a nineteenth-century tradition of baked children? Well, in 1855 a journalist had fun creating titles for newspaper paragraphs including such gems as "Accident in the City," "A Shower of Frogs," "Wife Poisoning by a Husband," and *"A Child Baked in a Pie"* ("Limited Liability" 1855). In 1860, meanwhile, there is a similar list of the kind of stories you find in newspapers: "Frightful accidents, calamitous fires, collision on the river, concussions on the railway, *a child baked in a pie*, charges of arson ..." ("Moonlight" 1860).

But what about "real" cases? In April 1773 one newspaper had complained: "The paragraph-makers last week baked a poor infant to ashes, and committed the mother to our gaol, for the amusement of the public" ("The paragraph makers ..." 1773).

I have been unable to find the invented original, but there was evidently a child pie story in the British press in April of that year. Then for 1779 there was this report:

> The following very unnatural, singular, and inhuman circumstance is nevertheless a fact: On Sunday se'nnight [a week ago Sunday], a woman brought a pie to be baked, to a baker's near Whitechapel turnpike; but not fetching the same away, it stood in the shop several days, the following week, and on being opened, was found to contain (horrid to tell) the body of a young child. It is feared, the author or authors of this infernal business will escape the vengeance of the law, especially as neither the baker or his servants, can recollect enough of the woman even to amount to a description. ("The following very unusual ..." 1779)

The story persisted into the mid-1800s. Consider this article from the summer of 1846:

> A horrible story was circulated last week in the neighbourhood of Middlesex Hospital. On Sunday a respectably-attired young man stepped into the shop of Mr. Just, baker, of No. 1, Nassau street, with a large pie to be baked; having deposited the dish on the counter, the fellow remarked that "care should be taken with that pie in baking it, as it contained a good deal of meat." He then departed. The pie was baked, but the owner omitting to send for it, some suspicion was excited, which continued to increase day after day until Thursday afternoon, when Mrs. Just suggested to her husband to keep the "dish" no longer, there being a strong and offensive effluvium arising from its contents. The crust having been raised the parties were horror-struck at finding the contents to consist of the remains of a newly-born child. Information was immediately despatched to the Marylebone Court House, and the district officer has since communicated with Mr. Wakley,

the coroner. The refined brutality of the affair renders it difficult of belief. ("A Horrible Story" Aug 1846; there are eleven occurrences in the BNA in the summer of 1846)

The story was quickly slapped down.

> A paragraph ... appeared in some of the papers of Saturday, putting forth a statement that a pie had been sent to the baker-house of Mr. Just Nassau-street, to be baked, which was afterwards found to contain the body of a new-born child. There is not one word of truth in the statement from beginning to end; and Mr. Just, who carries on a very respectable business as a baker, in Nassau-street, is determined, if possible, to find out the author of so base and wicked a fabrication invented no doubt, by some malicious villain to injure him in his business. ("A Horrible Story" Sep 1846)

It would be tempting to associate this story with the serial novel *The String of Pearls*, which introduced Sweeney Todd to the world (see further, "**Human Sausages**"). But *The String* was serialized from November 1846. If anything, perhaps the Nassau Street pie was a partial inspiration for Sweeney?

Here, meanwhile, is a story from the summer or autumn of 1860 with a "spice of humour in it." Again, it is a story of the capital. I have not been able to trace the "credulous metropolitan newspaper":

> Who has not heard of the horrifying discovery made by a certain baker in Woolwich, a few Sundays since, when opening an unclaimed pie of large proportions, he discovered beneath the tastefully disposed crust, the entire remains of a new born babe? Despite the fact that the authorities disagreed respecting the identity of the baker in whose oven the innocent was cooked, the marvellous tale gained currency, and even obtained a place in the columns of an over-credulous metropolitan newspaper. Almost every baker in the town had his turn in the responsibility, or renown, as may be, but it only required slight investigation to discover that the tale was an entire fabrication. Nevertheless, it gained ground in the public belief, and speculation was rife respecting the probable apprehension of the unlucky baker, many cute persons increasing the interest of the horrible story by guessing that the child had been placed in the pie alive, and that the ill-fated tradesman had been made the means of its death. ("Marvellous Tales" 1860)

The only related nineteenth-century report that I have been able to find is an all-too-pedestrian description of infanticide, where an eighteen-year-old woman had hidden a newborn baby, with its throat cut, in a pie dish in a box ("Committal for Child Murder" 1861, *CW*).

7. THE CHIMNEY BOY

Summary: A child from a wealthy family is kidnapped and later returns to the family while cleaning their chimney. Earliest Attestation: 1807 (England). Motif: N/A. Secondary Literature: N/A.

Victorians loved stories about lost sons and daughters being restored to their wealthy families. Such stories appeared in novels—Dickens's *Oliver* is perhaps the most famous example—but "factual" reports, most obvious farragoes, frequently appeared in the newspapers too. There was, for instance, a baby deserted at the door of an Irish workhouse who was, it transpired, the heir of an English baronet ("A Strange Story" 1883); an unnamed Russian nobleman who went to heroic efforts to track down a love child in Paris ("Curious Story" 1851); and several young women lost in the Indian Mutiny (see "**Harem Prisoner**"). One of these lost-and-found stories repeated in a formulaic fashion was that of the chimney-sweeper's boy coming down his mother's chimney. The story depended on the fact that chimney sweepers had, in the earlier 1800s, a reputation for trafficking in stolen children ("The Lost Found" 1885; Mayhew 1851, II, 393–95). Indeed, in some parts of the English countryside, naughty children were warned: "The sweeps will get you!" (Mayhew 1851, II, 394).

In "the Chimney Boy," a son from a well-to-do family is stolen and eventually ends up in the hands of a chimney sweeper. This cruel man sends the boy up chimneys.

> After serving his master for some time, one day [the child] was employed upon a large house. While cleaning out one of the flues, he dropped down into a large chamber. It was a very pleasant room. The sun shining between the curtains, gave a wonderful glory to the figures in the carpet. There was a bed on one side of the room, and a little crib upon the other. Beautiful pictures hung upon the walls. The crib looked as if no child had slept in it of late; the pillow was without a stain or wrinkle, and the linen sheet looked as if it had not been moved since it was laid upon the little bed. The little sweep glanced around the room, and feelings that he could not understand came over him. Dim recollections like a dream came into his mind. What could it mean? Tears came into his eyes. He trembled and fell to the floor. The lady of the house hearing the noise hurried to the room. Had he fallen? Was he injured? she hastily asked. He had not fallen, he assured her through his tears. He did not know what had happened to him, he said. When he looked around the room, it seemed so natural to him, as if he had some time been there and slept in the crib, that he could not help crying. Much affected, and trembling in her turn, the lady sent for her servant, and had the little

Figure 4 Chimney Sweep from Mayhew (1851, II, 173).

sweep taken to the bath, and clean clothes placed upon him. By his face, or by some well-remembered mark upon his form, the lady discovered that by this wonderful providence of God, she had found again her long-lost son. ("The Lost Found" 1867)

This is a generic Christian version of the narrative—much is made, afterwards, of God's lost children in the world. However, other versions were grounded in times, places, and families. Consider a French version from 1868: in England—the correspondent writes airily—"it would hardly be credible, but in France it is not unlikely" ("A Strange Story" 1868; a comment that suggests that the story was not extremely well known in the United Kingdom at that date).

The Countess de X____ was reading alone in her boudoir when she was surprised by the sudden apparition of a little chimney-sweep, who had slipped down into the fireplace and that stood up in the room, wonder-stricken at the elegance he saw around him. ("A Strange Story" 1868)

The little boy is identified by a tuft of hair (!) as a lost son from her first marriage, and he is adopted back into the class to which he properly belongs: "As for the boy, he has now changed his dry bread and hard blows to a comfortable home and a fond mother's tenderness, and is fast forgetting his *patois*" ("A Strange Story" 1868).

The story stretches back, in some form, into the early nineteenth century, perhaps even into the later eighteenth century. In 1807 a poem, "The Chimney Sweeper's Boy," was published, in which the stolen son of Nerina falls into the hands of the cruel sweep. One day, while working near his parents' house, the lost boy gives the traditional sweep's cry, and his voice is recognized by his mother in an adjacent house. The child is joyfully recovered (the relevant passage is quoted in "Review" 1807). In a discussion of the verses, one London author wrote:

> As to the poem itself, it suffers by having been written in the country: for had the author been informed of the fact of a discovery of a child, by the late Mrs. Montague of Portland Place, among the chimney-sweeping boys, he could not have failed of deriving much additional interest to his story from that circumstance. It is sufficiently well known, that this incident was commemorated during many years, by an annual dinner given on the first of May, to as many of the sooty tribe as chose to attend. ("Review" 1807)

This tradition of an annual dinner certainly existed, although there is confusion between two different Mrs. Montagues. There is Mrs. Montague of Portland Place (1718–1800), who gave the feast, and Lady Mary Wortley Montagu (1689–1762), whose son Edward had a habit of running away from home and school and allegedly worked for a time as a sweep.[2] The same author can be taken to imply—the poem "resembles the adventures of Mrs. Montague's child"—that the younger Montague was also found by his voice. But other traditions were current. Dickens knew the Montague/Montagu story and in 1836 wrote:

> Stories were related of a young boy who having been stolen from his parents in his infancy, and devoted to the occupation of chimney-sweeping, was sent, in the course of his professional career, to sweep the chimney of his mother's bedroom; and how, being hot and tired when he came out of the chimney, he got into the

bed he had so often slept in as an infant, and was discovered and recognised therein by his mother. (1839 [1836], 95; the mother gave food yearly to sweeps on May 1; the young Dickens himself met a sweep, 1839 [1836] 95–96: "whom we devoutly and sincerely believed to be the lost son and heir of some illustrious personage")

Consider, too, Mayhew's words in 1851:

> The lady referred to, at the time a widow, lost her son, then a boy of tender years. Inquiries were set on foot, and all London heard of the mysterious disappearance of the child, but no clue could be found to trace him out. It was supposed that he was kidnapped, and the search at length was given up in despair. A long time afterwards a sweeper was employed to cleanse the chimneys of Mrs. Montagus' house, by Portman-square, and for this purpose, as was usual at the time, he sent a climbing-boy up the chimney, who from that moment was lost to him. The child did not return the way he went up, but it is supposed that in his descent he got into a wrong flue, and found himself, on getting out of the chimney, in one of the bedrooms. Wearied with his labour, it is said that he mechanically crept between the sheets, all black and sooty as he was. In this state he was found fast asleep by the housekeeper. The delicacy of his features and the soft tones of his voice interested the woman. She acquainted the family with the strange circumstance, and, when introduced to them with a clean face, his voice and appearance reminded them of their lost child. It may have been that the hardships he endured at so early an age had impaired his memory, for he could give no account of himself; but it was evident, from his manners and from the ease which he exhibited, that he was no stranger to such places, and at length, it is said, the Hon. Mrs. Montagu recognised in him her long-lost son. The identity, it was understood, was proved beyond doubt. He was restored to his rank in society, and in order the better to commemorate this singular restoration, and the fact of his having been a climbing-boy, his mother annually provided an entertainment on the 1st of May at White Conduit House, for all the climbing-boys of London who thought proper to partake of it. (Mayhew 1851, II, 421)

In one of Mayhew's interviews with an aged sweep, the sweep states: "I don't know much about the story of Mrs. Montague; it was afore my time. I heard of it though. I heard my mother talk about it; she used to read it out of books" (Mayhew 1851, II, 417). Any expectations of this tradition being the preserve of sweep oral tradition is nicely confounded here! A similar but rather different story was known to Charles Lamb in 1824 and concerned a chimney sweep who arrived in a bedroom in Arundel Castle and climbed into bed.

Such is the account given to the visitors at the Castle ... Doubtless this young nobleman (for such my mind misgives me that he must be) was allured by some memory, not amounting to full consciousness, of his condition in infancy ... (Lamb 1836, II, 255-56)

The story of the sooty "nob" returning to his natural state must stand as important background for Charles Kingsley's *The Water Babies*, published in serial form in 1862-1863. There too a sweep, Tom, falls into an aristocratic world, and his existence is transformed.

8. CHLOROFORMED!

Summary: Chloroform is used to knock someone out so that they can be robbed—but the details of how the person was rendered unconscious are quite impossible. Earliest Attestation: 1848 (England). Motif: N/A. Secondary Literature: N/A. Compare with: "Drugged on the Train." Notes: I thank Linda Stratmann for help with this entry.

In 1846 ether and in 1847 chloroform began to be used by physicians. For the first time, it was possible to properly anaesthetize patients undergoing operations (for the chloroform revolution, see Stratmann 2003). Chloroform particularly caught the public imagination and the newspapers were filled with wonder stories about what it could do: chloroform calming a wild horse ("Extraordinary Application" 1847), curing typhus ("Chloroform in Typhus" 1848), knocking out an entire operating team when a nurse dropped a bottle ("At Taunton Hospital ..." 1847) ... It was only a matter of time before chloroform would be associated with crime. The first chloroform crime story was published in early 1848. Two apparently wealthy individuals appeared at an alehouse in the village of Mardigny (France). They were waiting for a couple of friends:

> At length, wearied with waiting, they proposed to the landlord that he should go to that place in search for the two loiterers, five francs to be his remuneration for so doing. Our host consented with joy and eagerness. He being gone, there remained of his family in the house only his wife and daughter, a little girl. Then one of the travellers produced a medallion, an effigy of the Holy Virgin, and gave

it to the mother to admire. This medallion, which had a secret receptacle for perfume skillfully disguised with chloroform [sic], exhaled an odour very pleasing to the mistress of the place, who respired it for some seconds. She then gave the effigy to her little daughter, who also breathed with eagerness the treacherous emanation. Both child and mother soon fell into an unquiet slumber, without at the same time losing the consciousness of what was passing before their eyes. The two strangers, after having placed upon the floor the two sleepers, explored the pockets of the landlady, and thence took a bunch of keys, which were applied to the drawers, in one of which they found a sum of 335 francs. This money they took away, as well as other portable articles and disappeared. ("Robbery by Chloroform" 3 Feb 1848)

The high silliness of this, particularly the misrepresentation of the power of chloroform, is striking (see further below). But journalists came to represent the drug as a serious threat to law and order in many similarly impossible stories. In the words of one overwrought Victorian editor: "A man armed with a bottle of chloroform in one pocket, and a pocket handkerchief in the other, can do as much with these simple weapons as Turpin with his small sword and blunderbuss" ("Railway Carriage Robberies" 1858). If the first stories about criminals using chloroform came in 1848, it was not until 1849–1851 that panic set in. Indeed, in 1851 there was even an attempt to introduce legislation to punish chloroformers ("Lord Campbell's 'Chloroform Clause'" 1851). "Nervous ladies and very old gentlemen have begun to protest against the march of science since they fancy it is going to the old tune of the Rogue's March" ("Chloroform as an Aid" 1851). Victorian news reports alternated between skepticism (helped along by doctors' incredulity) and solemn warnings (e.g., "Caution to Railway Travellers" 1862).

Doctors were frustrated over "the lamentable ignorance of the nature and properties of chloroform" ("Chloroform in Criminal Cases" 1865), which stories like this showed, and the first medical critique of the idea of chloroform crime came in February 1850 (Justitia 1850; quickly followed by Snow 1850; it is amusing to read these side by side with an anesthetist's very similar comments in Anderson 2007, 61). The credibility of chloroform attacks failed in terms of time and force. A doctor in mid-nineteenth-century England would chloroform a patient by holding a cloth close to the patient's mouth and nose. The patient would cooperate by breathing in the chloroform and even, then, he or she was still usually conscious for three to five minutes, and sometimes a good deal longer. The kind of scenario often rehearsed in the newspapers where a thief took a handkerchief "dexterously placing it to [his victim's] nose [and] produced instantaneous insensibility" was simply impossible ("Robbery by Chloroform" 30 Dec 1864). "How is it," asked the *British Medical Journal*, "that only people who are mysteriously robbed can be rendered instantaneously insensible by chloroform or other anæsthetic vapours?" ("Chloroform Robberies" 1871). What use is chloroform to a criminal, it was asked, even an ingenious one? "If a person is completely overpowered he may be robbed without the chloroform; if he be not [overpowered] he cannot be compelled to inhale it" ("Chloroform as an Aid" 1851; Linda Stratmann points out to me that one consequence of placing a chloroformed handkerchief on the face was blisters—doctors tried to keep the handkerchief *over* not on the face, but I know of no crime report that referred to blisters.)

Many accounts have charming descriptions of what might be called "magical chloroform": in 1848 a man fainted on a handkerchief being passed before his face several times ("Robbery by Chloroform" 21 Oct 1848; do we have here the influence of mesmerism?); a man in 1850 described the chloroform attack "like a sudden waft of wind" (Keyworth 1850); in 1864 criminals "waved a pocket handkerchief before the gentleman's face," the man collapsing ("Robbery by Chloroform in a Railway Train" 1864); in 1865 a criminal "shook a handkerchief (or something like it)" in the face of his mark, who passed out on the spot ("Chloroformed in the Street" 1865). One doctor became so frustrated by nonsensical descriptions of this kind that he saturated a handkerchief with chloroform and "shook it in the face of an aunt of mine until I was tired of shaking it any longer. I need not add that the lady was as perfectly sensible after the process as she was before" ("Chloroform in Criminal Cases" 1865). In a number of cases, chloroform was thrown in the face: something that would have stung the eyes, but otherwise had no actual effect (e.g., "Daring Robbery" 1891; an idea ridiculed in "A Chloroform Panic" 1862, *CW*).

Magical chloroform details died away as the century progressed: in later chloroform attack stories a handkerchief was forcefully applied to the mouth, though victims still lost consciousness, according to these reports, in impossibly quick times. We have some telling exceptions where chloroform may have been used in real life. Two French dentists robbed sedated patients ("Lord Campbell's 'Chloroform Clause'" 1851; "Robbery under Chloroform" 28 Nov. 1888—neither story is well sourced). In other instances, when criminals believed the hype and invested in chloroform, the drug did not work as expected. One gang experimented unsuccessfully on a kitten and a rabbit ("The Great Diamond Robbery" 1886: "its effect was tried on a kitten, but it was not successful. A similar experiment was made on a rabbit, but this also failed, and he told Jacoby that chloroform was not of any use"). In most cases where chloroform was actually employed, criminals botched things horribly (two striking examples: "Extraordinary Attempted Robbery" 1882; "Chloroform and Robbery" 1891; Stratmann 2003, 113–18, examines several cases).

Why then did people claim that they had been, to use a Victorian verb, "chloroformed" (for the verb "Robbery by Chloroform" 15 Jun 1865)? In some cases, we can demonstrate that their accounts were "ingenious inventions" to cover the loss of valuables; or for more obscure psycho-social reasons ("Contemporary Press" 1850 for the quotation; for examples of lies "The alleged robbery ..." 1858; "The Alleged 'Drugging'" 1885). Reputable men who became drunk or who found themselves in spots that they should not have been might have resorted to the chloroform excuse:

> The idea [of chloroforming] having gained general credence, it is probable, that we shall often hear of it, as prosecutors [i.e., victims] who have to account for being in disreputable places and company, instead of the usual excuse of having been dining out, will try to remember something of a handkerchief. (Snow 1850)

It is particularly striking that in several reports from the late 1840s and the 1850s a woman (often one suspects from the reports a prostitute) embraces or touches a male victim, and the man loses consciousness (when there are groups of attackers, there is often said to be a woman and several men: "Highway Robbery Under Chloroform" 1857; "Man Drugged and Robbed in a Train" 1891). John Snow, in one of our earliest medical responses to chloroform crime, implies that there were stories about prostitutes and chloroform in circulation in 1850 (Snow 1850). In the same year, a man named Fletcher was knocked out after he had refused the "solicitations" of a woman (Keyworth 1850). Take also this example, from 1851, about John Evenson, a master mariner who got chloroformed:

> As he was about to part from his friend [Mary Ann Mayne] came up and spoke to them, and having bade his friend good night [Mayne] immediately solicited [Evenson] to accompany her to her lodgings, but this he refused to do, bid her go away, and walked on. She followed him, and with a handkerchief or small shawl she had in her hand she gave him a dab on the mouth. From the moment at which the prisoner did this until about four o'clock on the following morning he was quite insensible ... ("Another Alleged Robbery" 1851)

In some cases, a similar logic of denial and invention might have applied to women who had been caught in sexual impropriety (e.g., "A Remarkable Story" 1901; some stories insinuate sexual assault).

There are other reasons, though, for claiming that you had been attacked by chloroform. In some cases, a victim who had collapsed may have assumed that they had been chloroformed, when actually their clothes had been rifled

Figure 5 *The Penny Illustrated Paper* (22 Sep 1894), 185.

once they had fallen unconscious from some unrelated medical cause. As a writer in the *Medical Gazette* put it about one chloroforming: "It is most likely, if this was anything more than the ingenious invention of the reporter, that the individual in question had a fit" (Snow 1850; see also "The Late Case" 1850, where the victim, once he got home, was "perfectly delirious for several days"). Thinking of more recent cases of incredible knockout gas stories, perhaps the police gave the idea to some victims (Anderson 2007). The description of a number of chloroform crimes sound suspiciously, it must be said, like a criminal using a choke hold and rendering his victim unconscious in that way ("Daring Street Robbery" 1851, "seized him from behind and held him with both arms around the neck"; "Robbery by Means" 1857, "threw his arm around his neck"; possibly "A Chloroform Robbery" 11 Sep 1850, a third person "put her hand across his shoulder"): the choke hold and its effects were unfamiliar in Britain until the garotting panic of 1856 and 1862 and some such attacks may have been interpreted as chloroform (see further the "**Injured Garotter**"). There might also have been questions of self-esteem: for a man, imbued with Victorian *machismo*, to admit to being subdued by violence, particularly by a single assailant, would perhaps have been more difficult than to say that he had had a mysterious cloth placed on or near his face.

There are some remarkable accounts about chloroform attacks in a room or in a house or railway compartment ("Robbery with Chloroform" 23 Dec 1879 for the compartment). The room/house/compartment is gassed, or the individuals in the room are individually drugged while they sleep. The earliest example I have found of this legend type dates to 1862 and was entitled "An Apocryphal Story." By 1876 room chloroforming was described as "an old story" ("Burglary and Chloroform"). In 1899 French criminals cunningly drilled a hole into a train carriage and inserted a tube with chloroform to gas a wealthy passenger in an adjacent carriage ("Attempted Robbery in a French Train" 1899; Anderson 2007, 53 for a modern equivalent). In practical terms, the idea of a victim being asleep, and a thief attempting to chloroform them into complete insensibility is silly. "If the person be asleep the sudden introduction of the vapour into the lungs would have the effect of awaking him" ("Burglary and Chloroform" 1876; doctors, said Snow 1850, had a great deal of experience of this because chloroform was often applied to sleeping children before an operation, and the children typically awoke). The idea of gassing the whole house with nineteenth-century technology is, of course, a complete nonstarter. There are many twentieth-century urban legends about room-gassing that presumably can be traced back to these early chloroform reports (Bartholomew and Victor 2007; for an example in literature, see Thurber 1996, 142).

9. COVERT CATHOLICS

Summary: Catholics have infiltrated the Anglican Church: Anglican vicars are, in some cases, papal sleeper agents. Earliest Attestation: 1840s. Motif: N/A. Secondary Literature: N/A.

In April 1873 J. W. Brooke, rector of Great Ponton, wrote to the *Record* (Britain's leading Anglican newspaper) with a terrifying revelation.

> A certain clergyman died in a certain diocese towards the end of the year 1871 (I do not deem it expedient to mention names at present). This clergyman had appointed as his executors a brother, who is an admiral in the British Navy, together with a friend of this brother, also an admiral, well known at the time, and of high standing. The executors were prevented from meeting together to wind up the affairs of the deceased until the middle of last year [1872], when upon examining his papers they found a parcel, as it were hermetically closed, and endorsed, "Inviolably Sacred: To be destroyed." A question arose about opening it, but they soon decided that it was their duty as executors so to do; when the parcel was found to contain two documents—one a Dispensation from the Pope, permitting the deceased to retain his position as a clergyman of the Church of England, though actually a priest of the Church of Rome; the other a list of such of the clergy in his diocese or near him, who are likewise possessed of dispensations, and upon whom he might therefore rely for friendly cooperation and sympathy. (Brooke 1873)

The editor of the *Record* noted that these statements had been in circulation for a year and that they should either be denied or explained. There was clearly a feeling that it was best to get this question out of drawing rooms and onto the printed page.

A casual twenty-first-century reader might not grasp the full significance of what Rev. Brooke was detailing. The Church of England had, from its inception in 1534, identified itself in opposition to the Roman Catholic Church. Indeed, Catholicism had been, by 1873, the national bogeyman for well over three hundred years, and anti-Catholic stories frequently circulated (most famously Monk 1836; for a remarkable late seventeenth-century example, see Fox 2000, 380–81). A revelation then that a secret network of Roman Catholic sleeper agents was operating within the Anglican Church was liable to cause concern! Yet it would come as no surprise to those who had looked with horror at philo-Catholic Anglican organizations, and this perhaps was the point: anti-Catholicism and conversions to Catholicism had both spiked in mid-nineteenth-century Britain (Peschier 2005, 10–24).

The anti-Catholic wing of the Church was quick to react. Take, for instance, Rev. G. W. Chamberlain in a public meeting at Cheltenham the very day of the publication of Brooke's letter:

> They were not English gentlemen and clergymen, but men who came with a dispensation from the Pope to remain in the church and to seek to bring its people over to Rome. He referred to a letter published in the papers that morning from the Rev. J. W. Brooke, as a startling confirmation of the suspicion that there were hundreds remaining in the Church of England dispensed by the Pope, in order to enable them to do what they otherwise could not do. ("High Mass" 1873)

At this point, the audience gave Chamberlain a resounding cheer.

But was the story true? Things subsequently got rather sticky for the Rev. Brooke, who wrote a further letter to the *Record* saying that he had been partially wrong. The executors were not two admirals but actually the Archbishop of Canterbury and the Bishop of London. Unfortunately for Brooke, both denied this, and the good reverend was obliged to back away from the story altogether. Indeed, he expressed his regret for, as one contemporary put it, "having been so deceived—in other words, so ridiculously hoaxed" (E. H. T. 1873). The same writer noted, on seeing that an Italian newspaper had picked up the narrative:

> I make bold to say that this story will come back among us some day, only strengthened and invigorated by change of air ... Accordingly, like the story of Maria Monk, the sin tables of St. Gudule, and the Monita Secreta of the Jesuits, this figment of the sealed packet will become for ever hereafter part of the stock-in-trade of your professional anti-Popery agitator (E. H. T. 1873).

The "Sealed Packet" certainly survived Brooke's climb-down. In May 1874, *The Englishman*, a patriotic review, included the story in its first number, under the headline "A Startling but True Story," and the editor added: "The following has been published before, but it cannot be sufficiently made known" (121).

Stories like this were commonplace. Indeed some "very strange stories have been often told about Jesuits labouring to advance their particular objects by assuming for years the office of minister in the Protestant Church ..." ("Some very strange stories ..." 1844; for a secret Spanish Inquisition base in London, see "Spanish Inquisition" 1837). Take this account that also originally appeared in the *Record*:

Not long since, a curate was appointed to a parish in, we think, one of the midland counties, who was obviously an able and well-read man, and made himself uncommonly agreeable to his parishioners, and all with whom he had intercourse in the neighbourhood. A gentleman, upon returning from Italy, came on a visit to a friend in the parish in question. He was promised a treat in meeting at dinner this most agreeable of curates. On them meeting, however, the curate's manner appeared wholly changed. He was apparently absent, as he was silent; and under some excuse left the dinner-table at a very early hour. Great surprise at the change was instantly expressed by the host on the curate leaving the room. His friend said, "I can explain the mystery—that gentleman was introduced to me in Italy as a Roman Catholic priest." ("Extraordinary Statement" 1843)

Rumors about secret conversions and secret Catholics were a staple of public life in Victorian Britain. In the summer of 1850, the Irish press began to publish stories that Lady Castlereagh had converted to Catholicism: "Her conversion is at present creating some sensation, as it is rumoured Lord Castlereagh is about following her pious example" ("Lady Castlereagh . . ."). In 1851 there was speculation that the Duchess of Kent (mother of the Queen) had converted ("A Very Strange Rumour"). In the 1860s it was the turn of, among others, the Countess Spencer: "The rumour that Countess Spencer has become a Roman Catholic, and that the Lord-lieutenant is about to do so, has obtained very general credence" ("Gossiping Rumours" 1869). In 1874 the gossips claimed that the Duke of Northumberland and the Marquis of Bath had gone over to Rome ("London Letter"). And the list went on. In the later nineteenth century, royalty were included in the ranks of (for most readers) dishonor: Princess Christian and Princess Beatrice were both said to have converted ("Gossip of the Week" 1888, Christian; "A Ridiculous Story" 1889, Beatrice). Then in 1889 a French newspaper, *Le Figaro*, claimed that the Queen was about "to become a Roman Catholic." Apparently, she spent "some time upon the Continent every year towards spring in order to avoid Easter devotions at home" ("Society Gossip" 1889). We might add, finally, that other countries had similar stories: in 1831 in France 400 Catholic priests planned, it was alleged, to convert to Protestantism ("A strange story . . ." 1831).

None of these stories was true, at least at the dates given. There were conversions, and these were much debated on both sides (Gorman 1910 lists all converts to Rome; his book went through ten editions between 1878 and 1910). But these stories—appearing under titles like "Gossip of the Week," "Gossiping Rumours," and "A Very Strange Rumour"—give some sense of the peculiar insecurity of Victorian Britain. Yes, this was, in economic and military terms, the most powerful nation in the world. But there was still the gnawing fear that the Pope and his minions would take over the nation; perhaps, as the stories above suggest, via Britain's aristocracy or a network of secret Catholic priests. Such attitudes have not, in the United Kingdom, been entirely consigned to the past. As recently as the early 2000s Prime Minister Tony Blair was reluctant to convert to Catholicism while in office because of the possible electoral consequences (Burton and McCabe 2009, 206–20). Kieran Flanagan has written: "When religious conversions occur inexplicably and with all manner of political unsettlements in prospect, then suspicions and anxieties are generated" (Flanagan 2009, 46–47). The opposite was evidently true in Victorian times: suspicions and anxieties created conversions, or, rather, rumors of them.

10. CYCLING AFFLICTIONS

Summary: A new form of transport, the bicycle, causes untold physical damage to practitioners. Earliest Attestation: late 1890s. Motif: N/A. Secondary Literature: very little space has been given to this subject in modern surveys of bicycle culture, for example, Herlihy 2004, 121.

By the 1890s the bicycle had become familiar on the roads of Victorian Britain in what has been called the "bicycle boom" (Herlihy 2004, 251). Men and, more controversially, women would venture out on weekend jaunts or ride to work. But, as the *Globe* put it, while discussing cyclomania in 1896: "When a new pastime takes hold of the majority of the race ... it sooner or later brings with it a new disease or two" ("The Bicycle Hand" 1894). These "Cycling Afflictions" were quickly to reach epidemic proportions, something one late Victorian rhymester had fun with:

> We've got the Bicycle Back and the Bicycle Face,
> And some all complaints to the bicycle trace;
> We have Bicycle Fingers and Bicycle Toes,
> Then the Bicycle Eye and the Bicycle Nose!
> If we cycle much more we are likely to find
> We've a Bicycle Body and a Bicycle Mind! (Ashby-Sterry 1897)

Between 1895 and 1900, a bewildering series of "Cycling Afflictions" were discussed in the newspapers, often with references to personal experiences. There was Bicycle Hand, where the hand took on the permanent form of a claw ("The Bicycle Hand" 1896). Bicycle Hand, in fact

> more usually affects women than men, probably because they are not trained to the use of hand and eye so constantly as men are. The result[s] of this disease are ruinous to beautiful hands. The roots of the fingers are spread out, and the knuckles where the fingers join the hands become portentously enlarged, while the flesh of the palm opposite the thumb gets flattened, with the result that the hand is broadened and squared. If this happened to men it would be of no consequence, but, unfortunately, as women have a nervous habit of clutching the handles with a convulsive grip, it attacks them with peculiar violence. ("The Bicycle Hand" 1896)

It will become clear, in the next pages, that "Cycling Afflictions" were particularly associated with women. This is seen most clearly with Bicycle Face.

In the summer of 1896, one man wrote to a newspaper advice column, explaining that his wife wanted to ride, "but I have heard so much about women acquiring what is called 'the bicycle face' that I am really in some doubts about the wisdom of granting my permission" (R. G. G. 1896). Bicycle Face or Bicycle Glare gave riders a "hard set agonised expression and irretrievably ruined complexion" ("Our Ladies' Column" 1897), "a fixed, wide-eyed stare, which comes from gazing straight ahead to look for the coming cow" ("The Bicycle Hand" 1896), and even "a hunted and drawn look" ("The Bicycle Face" 1897). Women and "very nervous riders" were particularly at risk ("The Bicycle Face" 1897).

There had been for some time disapproval at how women looked on bikes: "I never think a woman looks her best on a bicycle. Nine out of ten of them wear such an anxious expression, just as if they are working a treadmill" ("The Bicycle Face" 1897; Ashby-Sterry 1896). Or to quote the Duke of Cambridge: "I can't pretend my dear young lady, I don't like [cycling] as an exercise for ladies, and I wonder that you, who are so pretty, can spoil yourself with an ugly bicycle" ("I hear from Cannes" 1895). But with Bicycle Face there was the danger of a *permanent* alteration, a grown-up version of "if the wind changes your face will stick!" In 1896 one journalist reported:

> A [male] friend who was at a large dance given in London the other day, tells me that the number of girls with the bicycle face was so extraordinary, that the fact was generally noticeable. It is the constant anxiety, the everlasting looking ahead,

the strain on a nervous disposition which imparts a hard, set look to the face and gives a haggard, anxious expression to the eyes, which is quite painful to observe. (R. G. G. 1896; this is, note, the column writer's answer to R. G. G)

The solution to Bicycle Face? Chew gum (an idea from the United States, "Remedy" 1897) or just try to smile a bit more: "We think that a more pleasant expression might be cultivated even while cycling amongst cabs and drays and fast rolling carriages" ("Bicycle Face" 1896).

Then there was Bicycle Spine. The rider by bending forward and not retaining an upright posture on the bike permanently damaged his or her spine. Indeed, "deprived of its elasticity, the bones of the spine draw closer together, aggravating the normal curvature" ("The Scorcher's Spine" 1897). Dr. Bullock, who had written these words, goes onto explain how:

> The action of the complaint is the same as if a piece of whalebone were being compressed at the ends. The curve that would result in the middle of the whalebone is precisely that which the backbone of the sufferer from "bicycle spine" will assume when the complaint has become sufficiently aggravated. ("The Scorcher's Spine" 1897)

One of the consequences of this dreadful condition was "growing a hump like Punch" ("The Bicycle Hand" 1896).

Bicycle Spine was much referred to in the British press. In one newspaper article on bone libraries, in 1895, it was explained how Bicycle Spines could now be observed in public collections in America. Apparently, there were three: "Two come from Paris; and the third is that of a young American. These "bicycle spines" at present are valued at the high figure of £100 each, and the supply is not nearly equal to the demand" ("Libraries of Bones" 1895). An article in 1896, meanwhile, explained how Bicycle Spine was as yet rare in bone collections "owing to the comparative youth of the pastime; but the type is likely to become commoner, and to take a recognised place in the catalogues of osteological museums" ("A lot has been written . . ." 1896). By 1897 one journalist, with a nod to the works of Cesare Lombroso, even suggested that Bicycle Spine could become hereditary ("But really . . ." 1897).

Stories of personal experiences also circulated. Here is one from 1898:

> I have just been told of a dreadful tale which is vouched for as being true. Two girls determined to ride out to a pleasure resort over fifty miles from home. They arrived in good form, and then, after a short rest, set off back again. Long before home was reached they were worn out, but still plodded on. Friends happened

Figure 6 The backwards bike to prevent Bicycle Spine, 'Weekly London Letter' (1896).

to be waiting for them, and, seeing their condition lifted the girls off, and carried them in the house. A doctor was immediately sent for and, after examination, it was found that both their spines were seriously injured. ("One hears..." 1898)

The "ladies" need not fear, though because in 1896 a special bike was designed for the avoidance of bicycle spine. The handle bars and the steering gear were put *behind* the rider (see figure 6, "One hears..." 1898).

Other conditions included Bicycle Throat, the symptoms of which were "a mild kind of poisoning" that was "often followed by a violent headache and depression" ("Cyclist's Sore Throat" 1898). There was Bicycle Nose, which was given space in the *New York Lancet*: "It is to me quite conceivable that the quick rush through the air ... might cause considerable irritation to the nasal mucous membrane" (Stewart 1898). There was also Bicycle Eye and Bicycle Wrist ("Diseases" 1897). After 1900, as bikes became an increasingly normal part of life, only occasional reference was made to these mythical conditions. An article in 1902 on "Bicycle Troubles" made no mention of Bicycle Hand or Bicycle Face and put down other problems to "mild forms of inflammation." Bicycle Afflictions were clearly on their way out.

11. DEATH DICE

Summary: Soldiers sentenced to death are allowed to role dice to decide who dies: a miracle of some kind occurs. Earliest Attestation: thirteenth-century Spain, later associated particularly with the Germanic north. Motif: related to N1.2.1, "The miracle of broken die at gambling saves man." Secondary Literature: Krappe 1947.

In October 1881, the Manchester review *Tit-bits* (a journal which collected extraordinary stories) included this account:

As King William III of England, the Stadtholder of the Netherlands, was besieging Namur, in 1695, sundry soldiers from his army, through the want which reigned in the camp, went marauding, though such a transgression of the martial law had been forbidden on the pain of death. Most of these marauders were caught by the country people and killed; only two of them reached the camp unscathed; but they were sentenced to death. They were both brave soldiers, and the general-in-chief wanted to save one of them, and thus commuted the judgment in so far that they would have to throw at dice for their life, as was the custom in former times in such cases. On the morning appointed for the execution, both the marauders were led to a drum, in order thereupon to cast the decisive throw; while, at a few paces further, the fatal pole stood erect. Full of painful expectation, a group of officers, the regimental chaplain, and the executioner, surrounded the poor fellows. With a trembling hand, one of the condemned took up the dice: he threw—two sixes. In the next moment he saw that his fellow had also thrown—two sixes! The commanding officers were not a little struck at this strange occurrence; but their orders were precise, and so they commanded both the men to throw again. This was done; the dice were cast, and in the throw of both there turned up—two fives. The spectators now loudly called out that both should be pardoned; and the officers, to ask for new directions, momentarily put off the execution. They applied to the court martial, which they found assembled; and, after a long discussion, the disheartening reply was that the delinquents should decide their lot with new dice. Once more both of them cast, and, lo—each threw two fours "This is the finger of God," said all present. The officers again submitted the strange case to the court martial. This time, even the members of the court shuddered; and they resolved to leave the decision to the general-in-chief, who was momentarily expected. The Prince of Vaudemont came. He caused the two Englishmen to appear before him; they related to him the trying circumstances of their desertion. The Prince listened attentively, and relieved the poor culprits with the welcome "pardon," adding, "It is impossible in such an uncommon case not to obey the voice of Divine Providence." ("A Throw for Life" 1881)

A longer version had already been included in *Notes and Queries* in 1860, which in turn had been (allegedly) translated from a Dutch source, *Familie Magazijn* (Van Lennep 1860; the author was based near Utrecht; answered by Ache 1860, who was unable to establish a source). The story had "legs," and in April 1882, it reappeared in the British press, but this time the two miscreants were Prussians, soldiers of Hans Karl von Winterfeldt (1707–1757), who had killed a man while drunk. The reader was gravely informed: "This story is authentic. It is to be found in the memoirs of Prussian officer of distinction, who gives a simple, unaffected narrative of the scenes and events through which he passed, and who betrays nowhere the least disposition to exaggerate" ("A Strange Story of the Dice" 1882). The Prussian version appeared in several regional British papers between April and September 1882 (eight instances in the BNA).

In 1886 an article by one Professor W. Malmene was published describing two dice preserved at the Royal Palace in Berlin. We have here a variant connected with Frederick William of Prussia (1620–1688):

> A murder happened in Berlin in the time of the Great Elector which caused great horror, the victim was not only a young and beautiful girl, but the only daughter of the highly respected armourer Walther. Two soldiers who were paying their attentions to the maiden, were arrested and imprisoned. One of them by the name Ralph had really committed the deed in a fit of jealousy, while the other (Alfred), the more favoured of the suitors, was really innocent. Although they were put upon the rack, neither of them would admit anything, and the judges could get no clue. The witnesses who were examined testified having been in the company of both soldiers. Alfred did not deny having met Rose that evening, but declared to have parted from her very friendly. Ralph, on the contrary, could not give a very satisfactory account of his whereabouts; still he denied being the murderer, of whom no trace could be found. The Elector, in his just anger, commanded that God's judgment should decide—that they were to throw the dice to see who would die; that he who threw the smallest number should be executed as the murderer. The Elector, surrounded by his court, the judges and clergy, and also the father of the girl, old Walther were present. Ralph, the murderer, took the dice laughingly and threw to [*corr.* two] sixes, the highest number possible. Those who were present looked at each other in astonishment, because they all considered Alfred innocent, and yet after this throw there seemed to be no hope for him. Alfred knelt down, looked devoutly up to heaven, and prayed, while

everything was as still as in a church. Then he rose and called out loudly, "Help, Thou Almighty, for Thou knowest that I am innocent"; and, with joyful hope, threw down the dice, but with so much force that one of them broke in two. One side of the broken dice showed six points and the other half one point, while the other dice showed six points, therefore thirteen altogether. A general consternation followed, which was heightened when Ralph fell suddenly to the ground as if struck by lightning. After many efforts he revived, and, as soon as he had recovered consciousness, he acknowledged having done the deed. (Malmene 1886; in 1903 a series of British newspapers ran an almost identical account when the death dice were given to the Hohenzollern Museum)

The broken dice have a long genealogy in story, being recorded as far back as the thirteenth century (Krappe 1947). Other "Death Dice" stories are found on the Continent as well. In one, four deserters are made to role dice. One refuses to throw because he disapproves of gambling, and Emperor Joseph II (1741–1790) is impressed and spares all four (*Encyclopédiana* 1842, 304; thanks to Sofia Lincos for this reference).

The Dutch and Prussian antecedents of this story suggest that British journalists had periodically stumbled on Continental narratives around death sentences chosen by chance. Note that dice throwing or lot-taking was still used to decide, in the nineteenth-century, who from a group should be killed within European armies and navies: it served as a form of decimation (Abbott 2005, 100; see Dembowski 1854–1855, for a striking contemporary account). Death lottery fiction was sometimes published in the nineteenth century, particularly concerning the American Civil War (e.g., "A Lottery of Death" 1881; "The Lottery of Death" 1863; "The Lottery of Death" 1886). See also "An Englishman's Valuation" (1882), based on the work of the Scottish writer Lusinius [John Barclay], 1582–1621 (1674, 383–84). The story was later borrowed into a novel (Peake 1844, II, 252–53). However, while offering promising material, they never really coalesced into a successful legend type.

12. DEVIL TAKE ME!

Summary: Someone uses the phrase "may the devil take me," and the wish comes true; often associated with dances. Earliest Attestation: medieval. Motif: See folklore motif C12.2, "May the Devil take me if . . ." and C12.5 "Devil's name used in a curse. Appears." Secondary Literature: N/A.

Middle-class Victorians had mixed feelings about Satan. On the one hand, he was a fundamental part of the Christian universe and had biblical authority behind him; on the other, his exploits in British folklore—building dykes, being tricked by schoolteachers, scaring villagers out for a nocturnal walk—invited ridicule (Simpson and Roud 2000, 94–95). Educated Victorians preferred a more abstract, idealized devil. Satan was to them increasingly "a remote supernatural influence, not directly manifesting but rather acting as a puppet-master . . ." of those who would do evil (Bell 2012, 59, who writes this of "popular imagination"; Bartels 2017, 286 writes similarly that the devil was, in the "Victorian era," "depersonalised, tending to exercise his greatest influence as a nebulous malignant force"). One Pennine rhymester put it like this in 1899:

> Men don't believe in a devil now as their fathers used to do; / They've found the door of the widest creed to let his majesty through; / There is not a print of his cloven foot or a fiery dart from his bow, / To be found in earth or air to-day, for the world has voted it so. ("Has the Devil Gone Out of Fashion" 1899)

These same Victorians laughed at accounts in the newspapers of ignorant beliefs in other lands: the midwife's husband who, in 1851, dressed himself up as the devil to bilk a new mother out of florins in Brunn (Austria; "A Blundering" 1851); the Catholic priest who was prosecuted in 1892 in Bavaria for his part in attempts to exorcise the devil from a boy ("Witchcraft" 1892); the Italian peasants who tried to drag a hot air balloon into a church believing that the devil was hiding inside . . . ("The Devil" 1899). Even after the Great War, Poles in Kracow could gather into a mob to demand that a devilish newborn be put to death ("Devil Must Be Destroyed" 1920).[3] For British readers, this was all Romish barbarism, and most British encounters with the devil were safely closeted in folklore or fiction ("How I Spent" 1864, fiction; "The Ghost" 1893, fiction/folklore; "Rossendale Boggart Tales" 1897 folklore; for one striking nineteenth-century English encounter with the devil "Singular" 1809 and, for the hoofprints of the devil, Dash 1994).

However, about one thing all classes in the nineteenth-century English-speaking world seemed to agree. It was best not to tempt fate by wishing "the devil take me." "The direct naming of the Devil . . . has been subject to severe taboos . . . There has always been respect for diabolical power and a belief that an oath invoking the Devil could be binding if heartfelt" (Hughes 2006, 118; for a seventeenth-century example *The Mowing-Devil* 1678, 3). In the words of one early nineteenth-century poet:

> Don't use naughty words, in the next place, and ne'er in / Your language adopt a bad habit of swearing! / Never say "Devil take me" / Or, "shake me," or "bake me," / Or such like expressions. / Remember old Nick / To take folks at their words is remarkable quick. (Ingoldsby 1866 [1837], 293)

And so it proved . . . The following story was much printed in Britain in the spring of 1870. The *Boston Post* had declared "that these statements are all strictly true, and can be vouched for by the very best authority."

> Boston (Massachusetts) has a sensation story. Recently, in a town hard by, a public ball was given. The daughter of a couple who keep a boarding house set her heart on going, and in company with one of the boarders, who is designated "J." The girl's parents objected to her going to the ball, especially in company with "J.," but she said that she was determined to go, and that if she could not go with "J." she would "accept the company of the devil should he offer to attend her. On the night of the ball she slipped out of the house in proper trim except that she had to buy boots for the occasion; and having procured these she was returning to put them on, when she met "J.," as she supposed and he persuaded her to go with him to the ball at once and change boots in the ladies' dressing-room. "J." was her partner in the first dance, but disappeared until supper time, then suddenly presenting himself, with rather frivolous excuses for his absence, invited her down to the supper room. Offended by his neglect, she said she would return home at once, and he attended her thither. Very little was said by either party until they had nearly reached the house, when "J." informing his companion that he was not going in; and, presenting her with a beautiful pearl-handled penknife, and asking her when she used it to think of him, he suddenly left her. The girl, on telling her mother all that had passed, was astounded at learning that "J." had not been out of the house since early nightfall, and went to bed before the hour at which the ball began. The girl refused to believe it, but after some discussion her mother took her to "J.'s room, and there he was seen calmly and profoundly sleeping. Nothing more could be said, and the daughter retired for the night. A strange sound shortly afterwards brought the mother to the girl's chamber, and she was found

with her throat cut with the penknife given to her by her companion at the ball. She lingered until noon, and then died, declaring that, remembering what she had said in her determination to go to the dance, she used the knife because she was overwhelmed by horrible suspicions as to who it was that, personating "J.," became her partner. ("Strange Story" 1870, thirty-seven instances in the BNA)[4]

The writer of "Occasional Notes" in the *Pall Mall Gazette*, after acknowledging the Boston dance suicide, described an event "which is stated to have occurred at a country ball in England a few years ago, which we have no reason to believe is a pure fiction."

> A young lady being blamed by her mother for refusing to dance with a gentleman possessing vast wealth, but who was personally disagreeable to her, remarked that "she would as soon dance with the devil." She had hardly uttered the words when a gentleman clothed in black stood before her, and offered her his arm. With a reproachful glance at her mother which the latter never forgot she accepted the invitation of the stranger, with whom she commenced to waltz. The other couples by some strange instinct ceased dancing, and all eyes in the room were turned on the young lady and her mysterious partner as faster and faster they whirled to the sound of the music—still faster—until they almost became invisible in their unnatural activity. Then came a noise like a clap of thunder, then a sulphureous smell; the gentleman in black was missing, and the young lady lay dead on the floor. ("Occasional Notes" 1870)

All these devil dance stories recall more recent narratives about "the Devil in the Dance Hall."[5]

The idea that Christians could accidentally call the devil down upon themselves was evidently well established in the nineteenth century. One writer from Chicago shared, in July 1888 "a wild rumour" from that city about an unhappy married couple: she was Protestant, and he was Catholic.

> Lately [the wife] kicked up a row about a statue of the Virgin which in the house, and she ordered the man to throw it out, for she said she would sooner have the devil under the roof. The enraged woman was near her confinement at the time, and has since given birth to a deformed child, and as the story goes the child has hair on it like a cow, and has two horns on its head, and has a cloven foot into the bargain, so that it is a perfect picture of the devil so far as the knights of the brush and the pencil have been able to give us an idea of what that important individual is like. It seems the doctor who attended the woman wanted to kill the child, but the little thing came into the world gifted with the power of speech, and it simply

told the doctor to mind his own business else the consequences would be dreadful. (McAnally 1888; the devil child is another urban legend; see Addams 1916 for an early twentieth-century example)

The neighborhood had been "subjected to much annoyance by curious visitors coming from distant parts asking to be led into the house where the devil was born" (McAnally 1888). A similar story emerged from Minnesota in 1891 when a devil child with horns and a tail was born: "Some time in November, when a book agent appeared at the house, selling a Catholic Bible, Mrs Morris formed a violent dislike to the man and ordered him out of the house, telling him she would as soon have the devil in the house as a Bible. The agent accused her of blasphemy, and said dramatically, as she hustled him out of the door, 'I will send you a devil to plague you'" ("A Minnesota Monstrosity" 1891, *FG*). In 1896, meanwhile, there was a "Devil Scare" in New York. Children from one unnamed primary school stampeded into the street after the rumor got around that the devil was in the building. Various explanations were given for this hysteria the most credible being that a teacher had threatened that "the devil would catch the children" who disobeyed her ("The Devil Scare" 1896; for more on school scares, see Bartholomew with Rickard 2014).

There were also comic stories that depended on "Devil Take Me." I give two here involving Catholic priests. In 1874 it was reported that a Catholic preacher in Bavaria had unwisely shouted from the pulpit that Old Catholics (an independent Catholic sect) were doomed to hell "and if what I say is not true, may the devil take me on the spot" ("Ludicrous" 1874).

> Not far from the pulpit there sat an American who had a negro servant with him, to whom he beckoned to take the book up to the priest, who perhaps had never seen one of those sons of Ham in his life. The negro at once obeyed ... Although the negro went very softly, the preacher heard his footsteps and turning round, saw a black object solemnly, steadily, and surely approaching him. He looked at [the servant] with terror, and believing that he would be the next instant collared by his satanic majesty, he cried with trembling voice: "It is after all possible that there may be good people among the Old Catholics." ("Ludicrous" 1874)

On the servant not disappearing, the priest fainted away.

In a news report from 1877, an old Spaniard, on his deathbed, refused to see a priest who had been brought to the house.

> The priest withdrew, declaring that the devil would come in person to carry off so hardened a sinner as soon as he was dead. A few hours afterwards the sick man died, and while the family were watching over the body the door of the room

was opened with a great noise, and there appeared upon the scene a personage arrayed in red, brandishing a pitchfork, dragging a long tail after him, and smelling very strongly of sulphur. ("A Strange Story" 1877)

The women fled from the room, but a "man servant" with a pistol shot the devil three times. It proved to be "the parish sexton, who, by the orders of the priest had disguised himself . . . as Satan." The article finishes by stating that four priests were arrested over the matter ("A Strange Story" 1877, for possibly related British examples, see now Smith "Killing the Devil" 2019).

13. DO YOU KNOW HER?

Summary: A young woman from a wealthy background is tricked into a brothel; luckily her first client is an acquaintance who rescues her. Earliest Attestation: 1760 (England, a London story?). Motif: N/A. Secondary Literature: N/A. Compare with: "**She's My Daughter?**"

This story was told, in June 1841 by the Earl of Montcashel at the annual meeting of the London Society for the Protection of Young Females.

> A handsome, and accomplished young lady, of most respectable family connections, residing in the country, had received a pressing invitation from a lady at the west-end of the metropolis, to come to town [i.e., London] and spend a few weeks with her. The young lady accepted the invitation and came to town, where she was received with great kindness, and treated with great attention. A short time after her arrival, the lady who had given her the invitation, took her to a fashionable shop at the west end, and after looking at various articles, and making some purchases, her friend requested the young lady to remain in the shop for a few minutes while she merely went to the other side of the street, saying she would return almost immediately. The young lady of course consented, and her friend left the shop, to return, as she supposed, in a few minutes, but in this supposition she was disappointed. After some considerable time had elapsed, a female, of apparently accomplished manners, addressed her; and after stating that she had observed her anxiety at the absence of her friend, and the awkwardness of her, as a stranger, being left so, offered her a seat in her carriage, to take her to the house of her friend. The young lady expressed her gratitude for what she

considered to be extreme kindness, and accepted the offer. She was then ushered into an elegant carriage, with a coachman and footman in costly liveries, and driven away, she believed, towards the residence of her friend. Going along however, she observed she did not think that the coachman was going in the proper direction, but the lady, her conductress, assured her they were; but at length the carriage drew up, and her companion assured her that the coachman must have mistaken her directions, and had driven to her own house instead of that the young lady's friend. She then requested her to walk in for a few moments, while she gave some directions to her servants, and was shown an apartment, and as soon as she entered the door was locked, and there she was kept for some considerable time. At length, however, the door opened, and . . . a clergyman belonging to the Church of England, was admitted to her. The object for which he was introduced there could be no doubt about, but some idea might be formed of his shame and mortification on beholding, not a stranger, but a young and virtuous lady, with whose person and friends he was very intimately acquainted, and he being actually the clergyman who had prepared the lady for confirmation. The lady, it was needless to add, escaped the dreadful outrage intended to be committed on her; and though she mentioned the facts, as he had related them, to a lady, a friend of his (Lord Mountcashel's), who repeated them to him she had never disclosed the name of the clergyman. ("Striking Occurrence" 1841)

I knew of no parallel to this story, but contemporaries believed that they did. Presbyter Octogenarius wrote, in a letter to the *Standard*:

The story to which the noble lord gives the sanction of his respectable name is a fiction of, I doubt not, at least a century old. I am sure that I read it sixty years ago, though at this moment I cannot positively say where—I believe, however, in Charles Johnson's [sic] *Adventures of a Guinea*. Certainly, in some popular work of that time. (Presbyter 1841)

The editor of the *Standard* added:

We have just the impression of our venerable correspondent with reference to the Mountcashel story. We cannot say, indeed, that we read that story "sixty years since," but we are confident that we read it at the least half sixty years since: and even without this impression, we cannot but see that the story is a fiction upon the face of it. (Presbyter 1841)

The *Globe* concurred: "Clearly this is an old woman's tale; and an old woman's tale of the last century, very fit to have been worked up into the prolix pathos by the pen of Richardson" ("London" 1841). *The Times*, meanwhile, exploded in an editorial about "the extraordinary and revolting story" ("We think it our duty..." 1841).

Presbyter Octogenarius was correct. A very similar story *does* appear in Johnstone's *Adventures of a Guinea* (first published in 1760). A young lady is tricked into a house by a woman who tries to sell the girl's body to ... her own father (see also "**She's My Daughter?**"). He, of course, once the shock of recognition is past, rescues his child (Johnstone 1907, 76–80). Mountcashel, incidentally, defended himself in a letter to *The Times*, standing by the young woman's account. He admitted, though, that he too had heard of a similar story: "The occurrence is not more surprising than another that has come to my knowledge, which took place at Almack's under nearly similar circumstances. But when such adventures happen, for prudential reasons every exertion is made to hush them up" (Mountcashel 1841). The story seems to have gone underground in late Victorian England, but it appears in a 1913 blank-verse play, *Tiger*, when a father visits a brothel only to find his kidnapped daughter (Grittner 1990, 114, *BC*). Of course, women from lower-class backgrounds were sometimes "pressed" into brothels; the most famous and still mysterious case is perhaps Elizabeth Canning in 1753 (Lang 1904, 1–31, *CW*).

14. DOWNIE'S SLAUGHTER

Summary: A man is convinced that he is going to be decapitated and then dies when a wet towel is flicked across his neck. Earliest Attestation: 1824 (Scotland). Motif: N384.7 "Sham execution proves fatal"; and N384.4(c.) "Pseudo-decapitation: sharp blow on neck with wet towel" (Baughman 1966, 374). Secondary Literature: Hobbs 1973; Bennett and Smith 1993, 144–46; Burnett 1908. Compare with: "**Shooting a Ghost.**" I am grateful to Sandy Hobbs for help with this entry. The text is based, in large part, on his article "Downie's Slaughter" (1973), the first of Sandy's long career.

Downie was an unpopular college porter whose death entered Scottish and subsequently British legend. Here is a brief summary of the narrative in 1886, when the "old story of the case of a college porter" ("Can Imagination Kill?" 1886) was well enough known to be referenced.

> The students entrapped [Downie] into a room at night, a mock inquiry was held, and the punishment of death by decapitation decreed for his want of consideration to the students. It is small wonder that under the dominion of fear and belief in the earnestness of his tormentors, the sight of an axe and block, with subsequent blindfolding and necessary genuflexion, a smart wrap [sic] with a wet towel on the back of his neck should have been followed by the picking up of a corpse. ("Can Imagination Kill?" 1886)

Downie was given a fake trial and a fake execution and, to the horror of his student persecutors, died from shock. "This story has been variously regarded as true, as a folk tale, and as a hoax story invented just prior to its first appearance in print" in 1824 (Langshank [penname for Robert Mudie] 1824, 14–23; citation Hobbs 1973, 184). Hobbs makes a strong case that this was not a hoax, because the phrase "art and part as in Dauney's slaughter" was already in use in Aberdeen in 1824 (1973, 185). Unless, of course, Langshank took inspiration for his narrative from an established locution. Other versions would appear regularly through the nineteenth century and enjoyed circulation across Britain. I know of five versions of the story in the fifty years from 1824, all but (C) signaled by Hobbs (1973): (A) Langshank 1824, 14–23; (B) "The Land of Cakes" 1830, 508–9; (C) An Object (1843), a much longer version including cruentation after Downie's death; (D) [Duff] 1852—the best known version, the BNA has 37 instances of this story from 1852 to 1899, and it also traveled, with some slight variations, as "The Tragic Farce" 1862, and "Murder by Jest" 1857;[6] and (E) Maclean 1906 [1874], 185–98; for later versions, see Hobbs 1973, 184.

The story is usually set at Aberdeen University in the later eighteenth century;[7] and the name "Downie" is invariably given to the porter. One particularly interesting letter appears in 1893 when a Newcastle man, in answer to an inquiry, writes to an Aberdeen newspaper to explain what is meant by "Downie's Slaughter" after no other reader explains the term (Lawrence 1893). If this might suggest some ignorance about Downie in late nineteenth-century Aberdeen, a generation before, in 1861, "Who Murdered Downie" was used in a Scottish newspaper as a contemporary allusion with full confidence that it would be understood ("Who Murdered Downie?" 1861). I know of only one American version of the story, in early twentieth-century fraternity folklore from the University of Michigan (Hartikka 1946, 80).

The Victorians were fascinated by the idea of "suggestion": what we today would call "placebo" and "nocebo." They were perhaps helped along in this by the prestige of mesmerism and hypnotism (Hartman 2018). Some examples from the nineteenth-century press follow. In 1852 the painter, M. Karaits, was killed when he saw a funeral monument prepared by his friends as a joke, with his name upon it ("Fatal Joke" 1852). A "cripple" at Chester was healed by "faith" in

1885 ("A Modern Miracle" 1885). In 1892 a young man who had lost his reason was instructed in a dream to go to the Isle of Arran (in the Hebrides). There his reason returned ("A Strange Story of Faith Healing" 1892). A man at Cambridge with cancer was told that should he rub his face "with a dead woman's hands," he would be cured. This indeed happened ("An East Anglian Miracle" 1899). The newspapers that carried these stories saw such "miracles" as proof of the remarkable ability of the mind to affect—for good or for bad—bodily health.

There was a minor tradition of stories where condemned men were convinced that they were to die and did so, with clear relevance to Downie. In 1841, in Gibraltar, a man found himself at the gallows with a noose around his neck and a mask over his head. A last-minute confession meant that he was reprieved. But when the mask was removed, he was found to be already dead ("A Strange Story" 1841, from a French newspaper: the case never appears again in the British press and was clearly invented). In France condemned prisoners were blindfolded, put on a table, and told that they were being bled to death. Water "was allowed to trickle audibly into a vessel below." No blood was taken but the men, nevertheless, perished in six minutes ("Can Imagination Kill?" 1886).[8] A young woman believed she had eaten poison and began to die; only when her doctor took the "poison" and showed her that it was harmless did she get better ("Can Imagination Kill?" 1886). This was not just the chatter of popular legend and was often taken seriously. The last two instances appeared in an article in the *Lancet*.

15. DRESSING THE WORKHOUSE CORPSE

Summary: A workhouse inmate is imprisoned in the morgue and dresses as a corpse to frighten the management. Earliest Attestation: 1847 (England). Motif: N/A. Secondary Literature: N/A. Notes: special thanks to Peter Higginbotham for help with this entry.

Workhouses were an important institution in Victorian society (Higgs 2007; Higginbotham 2011). They were the closest nineteenth-century Britain came to a welfare system. Inmates were often treated atrociously—separated from their kin, given inadequate diets, and overworked. Indeed, this was part of the logic of the system, which strove to be unpleasant to discourage dependents.

The residents, under this difficult regime, unsurprisingly, had their own legends that they swapped among themselves (e.g., *The Workhouse Boy* n.d.; Roberts 1963, 102). But most of these stories—the stories of a largely illiterate, often despised part of society—went unrecorded. I was particularly happy, then, to find five different versions of "Dressing the Workhouse Corpse," a story of the inmates rather than the management; in fact, a story of the inmates *against* the management. The five versions are strikingly similar and yet come from different parts of the country and different dates, suggesting that this story was well known in different British workhouses in the 1800s. We have arbitrary punishment, cunning, and revenge.

The earliest version known to me dates to 1847. It is set in southeastern England.

> A pauper named "Silly Ben," the inmate of a union not far from Essex, was so refractory that the governor, in order to subdue him, ordered that he should be confined in the "dead house," where lay the body of a man lately deceased. After the lapse of two hours the porter visited the maniac, when to his horror, the poor fellow, as he imagined dropped a corpse at his feet as he opened the door. Horror-stricken, he hastened to the governor, who, upon, being informed of the circumstance, went, accompanied by several others, to the "dead house," where they beheld Silly Ben stretched upon the ground. While deploring his fate, the corpse in the coffin suddenly rose, exclaiming "Hard times, master," and then shrank back into its narrow shell. An immediate rush from the habitation of death to the governor's house was the result, when the governor and several others fainted. After a great lapse of time a crowd of officers and others repaired to the dead house . . . It was needless to say that by each endeavouring to push his neighbour forward that the awful place was searched, when the mystery was solved by its being ascertained that Silly Ben dressed the dead man in his own clothes, and having placed him against the door, put the winding-sheet and shroud upon himself, and then took the dead man's place in the coffin. Notwithstanding the fact having been proved, the governor and others, who beheld, as they imagined, the resurrection of the dead, have not even yet recovered the fearful effects of the fright. ("Extraordinary Conduct" 1847, *FG*; note that a more prolix version was published in the Essex papers)

This next version dates to 1858. The story allegedly comes from Northamptonshire, although it was published in West Riding.

A Sheffield paper tells a story of the master of the Northampton workhouse having put a refractory boy into the dead house with a corpse for punishment. The boy dressed the corpse in his own clothes, reared it against the wall, and got into the coffin. The master coming in at dusk inquired if the prisoner would have any supper, whereupon the coffined youth exclaimed, "If he won't I will." The master rushed out of the place and then died of fright ("A Sheffield" 1858; picked up by Higginbotham 2013, 48).

The next story is from Highworth (Wiltshire). This is a retrospective piece, written in 1877, remembering a story connected with a "noted character" who had just died, John Litten.

> It appears (and we believe we have most reliable information from old respected inhabitants of Highworth) that Mr. Forshaw, the then master of the Workhouse, to punish Litten for some offence against the regulations, locked him in the dead-house, where a corpse had been placed in a coffin. During the night Litten dressed the corpse in his own clothes, standing him against the wall, and, after attiring himself as the corpse, took his position in the coffin. When the master next morning tendered (as he supposed) Litten his breakfast, he received no reply. Litten thereupon rose up in the coffin and exclaimed, "If he won't have it, gov'nor, I will." This was supposed to have caused such a shock to the master's nervous system that he did not live long afterwards. ("Burial" 1858)

Another piece related to Montgomeryshire in Wales.

> An inmate of the Montgomeryshire workhouse was locked in the mortuary as punishment for misbehaviour. A corpse was lying in a coffin, but this did not disconcert the reprobate, who proceeded to avenge his treatment. Lifting the body out of the coffin, he propped it against the wall, feeling towards the door, and lay in the coffin himself. A few hours later a woman appeared with the prisoner's meal. The sight overcame her and not a word could she utter. The wag peeped over the edge of the coffin, and, addressing the corpse, exclaimed, "If you are to have no grub I can eat it for you." The woman fled. ("Mortuary Escapade" 1905, *CW*)[9]

Another version came in 1848 (the year after "Silly Ben") and is set in Weymouth (Dorset). I have deliberately placed it last because the journalist is unclear as to *why* the navvie was in the dead house—"through some cause." Having been through the other four pieces, it will be clear to the reader that the navvie had been placed there for an infraction of the rules.

> A novel occurrence happened a few days since, which, although we cannot vouch for the whole truth, we still believe to be substantially correct. A navvie having applied for temporary relief, was put into the workhouse, and through some cause placed in the dead house with a corpse. Not feeling in the least unnerved with

his quiet companion, he took it out of the coffin and exchanged dresses, placing the corpse up right in a corner of the room, and himself taking the place of the corpse. On the master entering the room in the morning, to his surprise he found, as he thought, the man was dead, and to his horror the real corpse, as he imagined, had come to life, the man having sprang up and caught him by the arm! The master has since been confined to his bed through fright. ("Weymouth" 1848)

16. DRUGGED ON A TRAIN

Summary: Travelers on trains were drugged by fellow passengers who stole their possessions or committed "outrages." Earliest Attestation: 1850s. Motif: N/A. Secondary Literature: N/A.

The train was an unusual place in Victorian Britain. Men and women who had never seen each other before, segregated only by class—there were usually first-class, second-class and third-class carriages—found themselves thrown together in facing seats (Carter 2001: 212–19). In this convivial situation, passengers would begin to talk, and sometimes they exchanged not only words but snacks, beverages, and even reading material. Beware, though, of strangers!

> An extraordinary case of robbery of the Great Northern Railway has just been brought under notice. A lady, residing in the neighbourhood of Stamford, left London by the five o'clock express on Tuesday evening. Her fellow-passengers in a second-class carriage were a well-dressed man and woman, whom she took for a newly-married couple. They were very polite in their demeanour; and on the journey the man offered the lady a copy of an illustrated newspaper, which he produced from a travelling bag. An overpowering odour proceeded from the paper on its being opened and the lady immediately became unconscious, in which state she remained until the arrival of the train at Peterborough, where she had to change carriages. Directly after the express had left the station on its northward journey, she discovered, on being applied to for her railway ticket, that she had been robbed, not only of that but of her purse and its contents ... The lady's idea is that the newspaper was saturated with chloroform, the scent of which was disguised with lavender. ("Caution to Railway Travellers" 1862)

On this occasion the drugged object was an "illustrated newspaper." But other drugged objects given by train robbers to their victims included the following: cough lozenges ("Robberies effected . . ." 1850), "refreshment" ("From Our London Correspondent" 1877), drinks ("Man Drugged" 1891), snuff ("A New Danger" 1897; "A Pinch of Snuff" 1897; "The Newest" 1898), sweets ("Drugged in the Train" 1899), cigars ("Drugged Cigar" 1907), flowers ("Drugged Cigar" 1907), chocolates ("Drugged Chocolate" 1911; "Girl and Drugged Chocolate" 1935), a carnation buttonhole ("Drugged by a Flower" 1926), and headache tablets ("Girl Complains" 1930). We should also include a number of instances where a traveler offered to clean a spot or a smudge off their victim's face with a drugged handkerchief and where the victim foolishly accepted this kindness ("Railway Robbery" 1859; "Chloroformed in a Railway Carriage" 1881). The victim in "Drugged on a Train" is unknowingly complicit in the crimes committed.

Drugged-on-a-Train stories were evidently already present in 1850 when one journalist refers to passengers being overpowered by "medicated lozenges" ("Robberies effected . . ." 1850). However, such stories only really became popular in the press at the end of the nineteenth century and in the first half of the twentieth. In the late nineteenth century, snuff was the preferred material of train criminals. "Drugged snuff," one 1898 report claimed, "is stated to have made its appearances as a medium for drugging unwary railway travellers" ("The Newest" 1898); a similar warning had appeared the year before ("A New Danger" 1897). Both offered accounts of crimes, but no names were given. By the early twentieth century, chocolate had become the weapon of choice ("Drugged Chocolate" 1911).

Attacks were typically about stealing valuables, but there were also cases where women were "outraged." Trains were, it must be remembered, a dangerous space where men and unaccompanied women met (see **"Tunnel Kissing"**). In 1897 a woman claimed that a man had drugged her drink in a pub prior to her getting on the train and that he had "indecently assaulted her" ("Drugged Drink" 1897) once in a first-class carriage.[10] In 1922 a young woman was sexually assaulted after, she claimed, she had been drugged on a train ("Alleged Outrage" 1922), and in the same year a woman told her husband, who had been out of the country for some time, that she had become pregnant after being drugged on a train. The detail came out in the ensuing divorce case ("A Cricklewood Divorce" 1922); note that in one play from 1917, "The Girl Who Didn't Care," there are introduced "such aids to abduction and seduction as drugged chocolates and a chloroform pad" ("The Elephant and Castle" 1917).

Were there really drugged passengers on trains? Some of the methods of attack—for instance the chloroformed newspaper or the chloroformed carnation buttonhole—are sheer fantasy (see further **"Chloroformed!"**). We might wish to reserve judgment about drugged snuff and chocolates. However, it is worth saying that I know of no one successfully prosecuted for a drug crime on a train; and journalists, from the late Victorian period onwards, politely signaled their doubts about stories. For example, one report about an alleged victim, James Alexander, in 1897 finished laconically: "Before leaving London" on the train, Alexander, "had brought a shilling bottle of whiskey, but the railway officials at Carlisle did not notice any bottle in the carriage" ("Drugged and Robbed" 1897). In a report from 1917 about a "curious story of theft" on Frank Bristoll in a train, a similar final sentence was tacked on: "He was a clerk with a firm of distillers ... and gave up his post because of nervous prostration and on the advice of a doctor" ("Drugged in a Train" 1913).

17. THE EAGLE AND THE BABY

Summary: An eagle swoops down and takes a baby back to its eyrie. Earliest Attestation: eighteenth century, but probably much older. Motif: remarkably this story seems never to have been given a motif. Secondary Literature: Michell and Rickard 1982, 138–43. I would like to acknowledge the help of Bob Rickard with this entry.

We are in Meigsville, Tennessee, on Christmas Eve 1868:

> A child was captured by an eagle ... He was a bright little fellow, just old enough to be learning to walk. When no one was in the house, be managed to roll out of his trandle-bed and crawl into the front yard. A great grey eagle came swooping down, and fastened its immense talons in the clothing of the little boy, then rose up with much difficulty, and sailed off across the adjacent woods, just skimming the tops of the trees. Its course lay toward the Cumberland River. A servant girl saw the eagle, and gave chase. She dashed into the tangled wood, and tried to keep a straight line, thinking the bird would do the same. The patch of wood was fully a mile and a half through, but the girl made the run to the other edge of it without feeling fatigue. Beyond the wood, and between it and the Cumberland River, lay a patch of cleared ground, partly marshy and partly cornfield, full of old stumps. When the girl left the wood, and had a clear view, she saw the eagle in the air, he seemed inclined to alight with his burden somewhere in the

neighbourhood of the river. This gave her new courage. It happened that there was a man hunting in the neighbouring marshes, and, just at the moment when the eagle reached the ground with his burden, a shot went off so dangerously near him that he mounted into the air again, but this time without the boy. The pursuing girl began a vigorous shouting as she ran, which attracted the hunter's attention, who, seeing the eagle quite near him, and a lady rushing down the slope with streaming hair and garments, and wildly shouting, concluded at once that there was something strange and, perhaps, dreadful in the immediate vicinity; he also set up a vigorous hallooing, and proceeded to reload his gun. The eagle soon became aware of the formidable opposition he would meet if he attempted to recapture his prey, hovered over the spot a moment, and then wheeled around in one grand sweep across the river, and disappeared behind the shelving rock which forms the opposite bank. When the girl came down to the hunter, she fell stiff, and was not able even to indicate what was the matter. The rough gallant then heard the scream of a child, and soon found a fine, healthy, rosy boy, with torn clothes, but otherwise uninjured, endeavouring to rise upon his little feet. The tears streamed down his innocent cheeks, and his face wore a most piteous expression. The hunter took the baby in his arms and carried it to the girl, who was now recovered. She clasped it to her bosom, covered it with kisses, and wept with joy. The parents in the meantime had missed the little one, and had become very uneasy. There was laughing and crying enough when the wanderers returned, and the wonderful voyage of the little fellow was explained. ("The American Eagle" 1869)

There are many such reports in nineteenth-century newspapers. They do not always end so well. In 1888 a baby was seized by an eagle in Wichita (Kansas): after some dangerous hand-to-hand combat with the bird, the infant's "badly lacerated" body was found ("Baby Stolen by an Eagle" 1888). In 1889 in Esterel (France) an eagle took a six-month-old baby. The father shot the eagle, and the baby dropped through the air into his arms "bright as a button" ("The Eagle and the Baby" 12 Oct 1889). In 1890 an eagle carried a baby from an unnamed village in Scotland, and the mother saved it, climbing up a rock face to the eagle's nest ("The Eagle and the Child" 1890). In 1891, in Ontario (Canada), an Indian baby was taken, and the eagle, after pecking out one of the baby's eyes, flew off with its body: the eagle was shot by the father, but the child was, by then, dead ("Baby Stolen by an Eagle" 1891). In 1889 a baby from near Nice was seized by an eagle ("Baby Carried Away by an Eagle" 1889). In 1904 another eagle took an eighteen-month baby from a crofter at Invershin (Scotland; "Carried Off by an Eagle"). The child was later recovered dead, without its eyes and "a bunch of eagle's feathers" "clutched in the baby's tiny hand."

Figure 7 'The Eagle and the Baby', *The Quiver* 1 (1865), 111.

This is just a sample of later nineteenth-century eagle-and-child stories from British newspapers. Many have, it will be understood, murky genealogies. For instance, the 1888 report from Kansas was treated with journalistic disdain: "Sceptics may, indeed, reply that the story is an 'American one,'" i.e. that it is untrue ("Baby Carried of [*sic*] by an Eagle" 1888). The 1889 report from Esterel, with the father catching his baby, was likewise greeted with raised eyebrows: "The correspondent who repeats it prudently does not ... guarantee its strict authenticity" ("The Eagle and the Baby" 12 Oct 1889). The 1890 report from Scotland was actually a rehashing of an early nineteenth-century anecdote (the original "A Glance over Selby's *Ornithology*" 1826, 661–65). The 1904 report from the same area was, meanwhile, subsequently admitted to be a hoax. "The original informant confessed that he invented the story; and it is understood that the matter is to be dealt with accordingly" ("The Eagle and Child Story" 1904). Eagle-and-child stories made for good copy, but they were not well sourced. "Since such stories filter down to us from remote or mountainous regions it is difficult to ascertain what portions of them, if any, are true" (Michell and Rickard 1982, 140).

None of this should be surprising. Eagle-human stories have long been part of the canon of world folklore: they were easily borrowed or imitated by journalists and their sources (Bottani 2002, on the possible links to what could very loosely be called "shamanism" and eagle flight, *DE*). Restricting ourselves to Britain, numerous pubs are named "the Eagle and Child," many of which are connected to the Lathom family, with its eagle-and-child crest. According to a family legend, which dates back to the fifteenth century, a Lathom had been found at an eagle's nest (Simpson 2010, 128–30; Westwood and Simpson, 400–401; note that the fifteenth-century "story" is a carved misericord and its sense is open to interpretation!) Similar narratives continued through the nineteenth century, particularly in Scotland. In 1863 Charles St. John wrote how, in the Highlands, he had heard "frequent stories of a child being carried away by an eagle, but could never trace these home to their source" (St. John 1882, 94). Most such stories went unrecorded, but we have one early example from 1703 (Martin 1703, 299) and two, at least, were written up as nineteenth-century melodrama. In the first, "Hannah Lamond and the Eagle"—widely circulated in the 1800s—the mother climbs a cliff to rescued her boy ("A Glance Over Selby's *Ornithology*" 1826, 661–65 and at 661: "'I tell the tale as 'twas told to me,' by the schoolmaster of the parish alluded to above, and if the incident never occurred, then he must have been one of the greatest and most gratuitous of liars that ever taught the young idea how to shoot.").[11] In the second, a baby is stolen by an eagle and a boy climbs to the eyrie to retrieve the child, fending off attacks ("The Eagle and the Baby" 1865). Eagle-and-child stories were collected in the twentieth century by Scottish folklorists ("A Yell man . . ." 1955);[12] and they continue to be told down to the present. Consider this account received by email in 2017:

> My 92-year-old nan often tells a story of when she was a little girl and she was in a shop with her mum in Edinburgh—she lived on the Royal Mile—when she saw a very large eagle land on a baby's pram outside the shop. She cries every time she tells this story and explains how she pulled at her mum saying "eagle, eagle," but nobody believed her until the mother of the baby went outside and started screaming that her baby was gone. They found the baby dropped from a tree and the men

who found her wouldn't let the mother near as the baby's head had smashed on the fall. My nan claims the eagle had escaped [from] a local zoo. (I wondered if it had been Edinburgh zoo but again no info found). I haven't been able to find anything further on this but her accuracy to detail and emotional state each time the story is told certainly sends shivers and prompted me to take a further look.[13]

Eagles—thinking now of ornithology rather than folklore—would have serious problems in picking up a baby, never mind a toddler. A golden eagle—remembering the Scottish examples above—weighs anything up to six kilos: the weight of a three-month old baby. There seems, though, to be a consensus that an eagle could not carry half its body weight in flight, meaning that it would be a serious struggle for it to pick up a newborn (Bodio 2012, 69; see also Michell and Rickard 1982, 138). Some of the eagle-and-child stories make polite nods in the direction of physics: "The baby [a two-year-old, 10–13 kilos?] was a heavy load for the eagle, which dropped him twice to the earth, and then swooped down for a third time for it" ("In the Talons" 1889). Of course, none of this is to say that an eagle would not *kill* a baby, left alone outside by parents: some news reports describe attacks rather than abductions, something all too credible ("A Child Attacked" 1886; "A Tall Story" 9 Feb 1885). Indeed, the eagle jumping and hopping on an infant victim might well look as if it *wanted* to fly away with its human prey.[14] Another problem, in ornithological terms, is the notion that the bird would, always assuming that it could carry a baby, take its prey to its nest and leave it there alive (often with its eaglets). For instance, in one Scottish story a rescuer arrives at the nest "where the dear little baby" lay, "wide awake, and playing with the young eagles" ("The Eagle and the Baby" 1865). An eagle, needless to say, brings meat to its young. It does not bring play companions.

18. EGG RING

Summary: A valuable object is found in an egg. Motif: N/A. Secondary Literature: N/A. Compare with: "**Fish Ring**" and "**I Lost the Ring Here.**"

The most widely publicized account of the "Egg Ring" arrived in the United Kingdom from Australia in 1879 and was published, in the first instance, in the *British Medical Journal*.

> Sir, A curious incident, which I think might interest some of my medical brethren, happened a fortnight ago; and, not having ever heard or read of a like circumstance before, I send you the particulars. On the 11th February, my wife, after mixing some corn-meal for feeding the fowl; missed her wedding ring from her finger, and, after a fruitless search, gave it up as lost. On the 8th April, while engaged eating an egg at breakfast with me, she felt the egg-spoon grate upon something hard at the bottom of the egg below the yolk. Imagine our astonishment when on further investigation, we found the lost ring firmly fixed by membranous adhesions to the bottom of the egg. I may further state that the egg was of extra large size, and was laid the day before (April 7th). Perhaps some of your readers might enlighten me as to how the ring got inside the egg, and whether it was possible for the ring to have remained inside the fowl for seven weeks. Apologising for troubling you, I remain, yours obediently, Moruya, New South Wales, April 20th, 1879. H. KIRWAN KING, M.B. (King 1879)

The information in this letter was then circulated in various forms in the British press ("Strange if True" 1879; I found eight instances of this story in the BNA for Oct. and Nov. 1879; see also, "The Adventures" 1879). Another, much more generic version of the egg-ring story appeared in 1894 with a dreadful pun:

> A lady missed her wedding-ring after feeding her fowls. Search was made high and low without success, until a day or so afterwards, when its recovery seemed hopeless, she came upon the ring in an egg she was eating, and once more became possessed of this symbol of the marriage yolk. ("Ever since . . ." 1894)

There were also reports about coins found in eggs in the later part of the nineteenth century. For instance, a sixpence in an egg in Glasgow ("A Sixpence" 1874); a shilling in an egg at Paddington Station, London ("A Shilling" 1892); a shilling in an egg in Dundee ("A Curious Egg" 1897); and a coin in yolk at Essex and Colchester Hospital ("Coin in an Egg" 1906). The trend then continued through the twentieth century with coins, rings, and diamonds turning up in breakfast eggs (Sanderson 1969; "Woman Finds" 1988; "A cracking good find" 2001). That the idea of valuables in eggs was established in the Victorian imagination is suggested by a story published in 1881. According to this delightful account, a client caused chaos in a Bristol market by finding sovereigns in eggs there. The egg seller broke all her stock looking for more coins, not realizing that her customer was Signor Bosco, a "celebrated conjuror" ("The Golden Hen" 1881).

Is it possible that at least some of these stories were true? Can objects become encased in eggs? In 2017 Gaynor from the British Hen Welfare Trust replied to an inquiry with these words:

> I can 100% tell you that it is impossible for a swallowed object to end up inside the egg. Objects that are swallowed pass through the crop/gizzard/intestine and are voided as droppings. Eggs are produced in the ovary and make their way over a 24 hour period to the vent. The only place the two systems meet is at the vent—the last inch. The egg at this stage is fully formed. What may have happened is that the hen laid a soft shell egg which got mixed up with a foreign object at the point of being voided from the body and an assumption was made that the object came from inside the egg. I love urban myths—they make my job very interesting.[15]

Compare this with a Victorian explanation for the phenomenon:

> Foreign bodies swallowed by fowls are not unfrequently found in eggs. They get enclosed in the shell of the egg, if they happen to be passing the opening of the duct which secretes the lime portion, i.e. the shell of the egg, just at the moment the soft portion of the egg is descending from the ovary. ("The Adventures" 1879)

In other terms, if someone tells you that they have found a coin or a ring in the shell of an egg it is possible that the story is true. If they tell you that the coin or ring was floating in the yolk, then the story is nonsense. In either case we have a story that will impress listeners or readers. Note that there are many analogous narratives about rings appearing in other forms of food. A woman who has lost a ring finds said ring in a carrot ("Two Gloucestershire" 1886), celery ("Lost and Found" 1879; "The Lost Ring" 1892), or a potato (Jones 1877, 438) There are also stories about rings being found in lumps of peat brought in to be burned ("Some of the Northern papers..." 1894; the ring was allegedly found by the owner on the anniversary of it having been lost).

19. FAMILIAR ENEMIES

Summary: Native armies are directed by white men, who lead them to victory. Earliest Attestation: the stories begin in the sixteenth century in the early colonial age; for example, Gonzalo Guerrero (Calder 2017), who was frequently used by the Spanish as an excuse for their military failures against the Mayans. Motif: N/A. Secondary Literature: N/A.

Mighty Victorian Britain experienced several reverses on the battlefield against pre-industrial peoples. But how was it possible that the most powerful country on the planet could be bested by such "primitive" foes? One explanation trotted out was that these enemies were salted with Europeans or natives trained by Europeans. There is a memorable story from Afghanistan that a British officer looking through his binoculars to check artillery fire was given a hand signal instructing him to adjust his aim by a sepoy who had gone over to the enemy ("A Tall Story" 1897). In other cases, "white men" were spotted among the enemy ranks: for instance, the French and Russian volunteers who supposedly fought on the Indian side in the Indian Mutiny in 1857 (Corley 1974, 188; Hibbert 1980, 233) or the Europeans glimpsed in the Mullah's army in 1903 ("The Somali War" 1903).

In more extreme cases, it transpired that victorious enemy generals were European. Thus the 1846 news spread out of Ireland that Hōne Heke (c. 1807–1850), the inspirational Maori leader, was a native of the county Tipperary:

> His real name is Hickey: he emigrated from Ireland some years ago, and was shipwrecked on the coast of New Zealand, and taken into the interior of the island by a hunting party of the natives, and was sold as a slave to one of the chiefs, who adopted him as his son, got him tattooed, and gave him his daughter in marriage. On the death of the old chief, his Irish son-in-law was chosen as his successor, on account of his skills in war. ("A Tipperary Man" 1846; the story was credited to the *Tipperary Free Press*)

Here there is both an explanation for Maori martial excellence and also perhaps some Irish story-tellers partaking vicariously in the defeat of the British in the Pacific.

Osman Digna, who fought the British in Sudan was, it transpired, French.

> Osman Digna, who, during the last ten years, has caused an immense expenditure of British blood and treasure, and who is now in command of the dervish

army, is a Frenchman, a native of Rouen. The authenticity of this strange story is vouched for by the famous African traveller, Dr Schweinfurth, by Dr Felkin, and by several other equally renowned authorities on questions relating to the Soudan. Osman Digna was born on the banks of the Seine in 1836, and was christened at the cathedral at Rouen under the name of George. When about 11 years old his father, a certain Joseph Nisbet, failed in business, and betook himself with his wife and child to Egypt, where he died a short time afterward. His widow, who found herself almost penniless, contracted a few months later a marriage with a well-known Mohammedan merchant of Alexandria Osman Digna by name. Having no children of his own he became exceedingly fond of young George Nisbet, insisted on his becoming converted to the Mohammedan faith, and entered him under the name of Osman Digna jun., at the military school at Cairo, where the lad received a careful training at the hands of distinguished French, German and British officers attached to the college as professors. ("Osman Digna" 1896)

A German paper, meanwhile, identified the missing Archduke Salvator (see **"Hero Survives"**) as Marshall Yamagata of the Japanese Imperial army, the man who, more than any other, pioneered the modernization of the Japanese military. The British press was more skeptical: "It may be added that the photographs of Marshal Yamagata reproduced in the English illustrated papers give that distinguished soldier a very Japanese cast of features" ("The Missing Austrian" 1895).

Certainly, Europeans or those of European descent sometimes did cross the battle lines. The best documented example from the British Empire is the American-born Kimble Best, who deserted from the British army and fought with the Maoris (Cowan 1911). Hiding behind most of these accounts is the conviction, though, that Europeans were not just technologically superior but that they were also racially superior to their African, Asian, and Australasian opponents. This conviction, as nineteenth-century history shows, was, from time to time, tested to destruction.

20. FISH RING

Summary: A ring is lost in the water and then is found in a fish. Earliest Attestation: antiquity. Motif: N211.1 "Lost ring found in fish"; ATU 736A: "The Ring of Polycrates." Secondary Literature: Jones 1877, 96–100; Venbrux and Meder 1995. Compare with: "**Egg Ring**" and "**I Lost the Ring Here**."

It is a very old story with antecedents in ancient Greek and Indian legend. A ring (or another valuable object, e.g., Venbrux and Meder 1995) is thrown into a body of water or lost there and then is found in the belly of a fish. The story was well known in medieval Britain, associated particularly with St. Kentigern and Glasgow (Jones 1877, 98–99). There is also a fish-ring story associated with Newcastle-upon-Tyne, where the misplaced ring of one Mr. Anderson was found in a salmon in 1559 (Brand 1789, 45; for more on this case, see Westwood and Simpson 2005, 565–66; for other traditional British examples Baughman 1966, 371 and Westwood and Simpson 2005, 813–14; for a late eighteenth- or early nineteenth-century chapbook, Meriton 2010 §574). "Ring-stories have a knack of running in one groove" ("Parallel Stories" 1873) and the story was still in that groove in the nineteenth century, as frequent press reports showed.

> A gentleman staying at Cowley Manor, the seat of W. Baring Bingham, Esq., in washing his hands after fishing, dropped a valuable gold signet ring from his finger. Immediate search in the mud was at once made, but to no effect. About six months after, an eel was sent into the kitchen for cooking, and the lost ring was found in its interior! Probably the glitter of the ring when falling in the water attracted the eye of the eel, who must have been surprised at the indigestibility of its prey. Mr. Owen of Abergavenney, the owner of the ring was so delighted at its recovery, that he sent an account to the newspapers. ("Two Gloucestershire" 1886)

And this account and others like them were published in papers and books through Victoria's reign. For instance, in 1886, the following American story crossed the Atlantic.

> Five years ago William Howe, of Moorfield, Ky., while fishing in a pond, lost a ring belonging to his sister. A short time ago he went to the pond to hunt frogs, and while cutting off the hind leg of one that he had killed, saw something shiny protruding from a bullet wound in the body of the animal, which proved to be

the long lost ring. Its identity was established by the inscription "Edna Howe." ("A new version..." 1886)

Then there is this marvelous anecdote from Ireland. The first Mrs. Massey had died in a boat accident on the Shannon. Mr. Massey had just married his second wife. His denial is, in story-telling terms, very well judged.

> Seven o'clock came, and William Massey having handed his bride elect to table, sat at the head of the hospitable board around which were assembled twenty people, and proceeded to carve the salmon which we had so recently killed. Upon placing the fish knife near the gills to take off the first cut of the head, it grated upon some unyielding substance, which prevented his making the proper incision in the fish, whereupon he took a fork and drew out from a bed, which it had formed for itself beneath the gills, a solid gold finger ring, with the word "pure" stamped upon the inside of it. It was handed about as a curiosity, and it was whispered at the table that it was one of the rings of the former Mrs. Massey; but this her husband denied aloud; and eventually his sister, the Honourable Mrs. Drew, took possession of it, and, I doubt not, has it safe at Drewsborough at this moment. (Adamson 1860, 187–89, dated to 1834)

These stories (and they could be multiplied many times over: Jones 1877, 439–41) might all be politely called "anecdotal." But sometimes journalists battered readers with circumstantial details. For instance, in 1872 an extraordinary report was published. On 28 October 1871 a ship, the *Mary Ann*, picked up a dead ox floating in the water off the Thames—as we have seen with eels and frogs, "fish" do not have to have scales in a fish-ring story. The captain and his men butchered the animal and found a golden ring inside. They were able to trace the boat that had thrown the dead ox overboard: the *Adler*. From there the ring was traced back to a wealthy German farmer who had lost his ring while making flour balls for his ox. The British captain naturally returned the ring to its rightful owner ("Remarkable Story" 1872).

Or consider this report. In early 1871 it had been noticed, in the North American newspapers, that a fisherman, John Potter, had found a signet ring with the letters "P. B." engraved in a cod he had caught off Newfoundland ("Extraordinary Story" 1871; I have been unable to find this original story, and I suspect that it does not exist). In a subsequent report we learn that Potter

> kept the prize in his possession until the 12th ult., when he was requested by a letter from the Colonial Secretary to send or bring the ring to St John's as he had received letters from a family named Burnam, in Poole, England, saying they had

reason to feel certain that the ring once belonged to Pauline Burnam, who was one of several hundred passengers of the Allan steamship Anglo Saxon, which was wrecked off Chance Cove (N. F) in 1861, the said Pauline Burnam being a relative of theirs. The fisherman, in whose possession the ring was, brought it to St John's, and presented it at the Colonial Secretary's office. He was requested to take a seat and wait a while. After about half an hour's delay he was introduced to an "elegantly dressed gentleman," a Mr. Burnam, whom the Colonial Secretary had sent for on the fisherman's arrival. Mr. Burnam at once identified the ring as the wedding ring of his mother, and which she had always worn since her marriage in Huddersfield in the year 1846. The ring was accordingly given up to Mr. Burnam, who rewarded the fisherman with bank notes amounting to £50 sterling. ("Extraordinary Story" 1871)

This delightful yarn has several suspect elements, not least the fact of Mr. Burnam's presence in St. John's.

Here is an 1887 story from Chicago, which the British editor entitled "A Little Too Fishy":

Giles Busby, a Toledo fishmonger, was cleaning a white fish last Monday, and in the large intestines of the fish he found a diamond ring. The ring had engraved upon its inner surface "JAB, Chicago, '69." Busby forwarded the ring to the Chief of Police in this city. Later on Mrs Julia Lennox, 12 Lennox-place identified and recovered the ring. She tells an interesting story of its loss. In 1869 she, Miss Bennett, became engaged to Mr. Lennox, and he gave her this diamond ring, for which he paid 450 dollars. Upon their bridal trip, in 1871, Mrs. Lennox lost the ring. While she was washing her hands in the toilet room of the Pullman car the ring slipped from her finger and dropped through the wastepipe. As the train happened to be crossing the bridge over the St. Lawrence River, near Montreal, just at that time, the bereaved bride had no hope of recovering the ring. There are no white fish in the Lawrence; the theory is that a small fish seized upon the ring, and that at some future time this small fish, while cruising about the lake, fell prey to the whitefish in which the long-lost ring was discovered. Giles Busby, the Toledo fishmonger, received from Mr. Lennox a check for 100 dollars for his honesty. ("A Little Too Fishy" 1887)

The ring had thus passed from fish to fish.

21. THE GALVANIC CONVICTS

Summary: An executed convict is revived with electric currents. Earliest Attestation: 1841. Motif: N/A. Secondary Literature: N/A.

In the late eighteenth century, doctors began to apply electric currents to the bodies of dead animals in "galvanic" experiments. By the early 1800s electricity was, in many countries including Britain, applied to human corpses, more specifically the corpses of executed criminals (the earliest case I know of from "Galvanism" 1803; see further Bennett 2018, 174–75). These experiments attracted hundreds of observers, and write-ups were printed, with the idea that perhaps life could be restored by the careful application of electricity (Ure 1819, and "Galvanic Experiments on the Human Subject" 1843). Indeed, in "the first years of the nineteenth century, galvanism was all the rage, not only in scientific books, journals, and society publications, but also in magazines and books that catered to less specialized readerships" (Schiffer 2006, 130). In 1816 a young Mary Shelley was inspired by this idea to create Dr. Frankenstein and his "creature." She reported how her husband, Percy Bysshe Shelley and Byron had conversed: "Perhaps a corpse would be reanimated; galvanism had given token of such things . . ." (Shelley 1888, x, in the preface). Then from the 1830s "Galvanised corpse" became part of the language, meaning something dead, obscenely brought to life. In 1831 a man's body jerked, "like the affected part of a galvanised corpse" ("A Condemned" 1831); by 1851, protectionism was, according to the Whigs, a "galvanised corpse" ("The Ministerial Crisis").

As the century progressed, stories began to emerge in the press of galvanic experiments where criminals had been brought back from the dead, usually briefly. The earliest of these was the revival of John White in 1841, after he had been hanged in Louisville (Kentucky). Having being left to dangle for twenty-three minutes, White was cut down and given to a group of local doctors, and the "poles of a powerful galvanic pile, which had been prepared for the occasion, were immediately applied to him" ("Execution and Resuscitation" 1841). White sat up, started breathing again, lifted his hands to his neck, but "he died in a few minutes in the most excruciating agonies" ("Execution and Resuscitation" 1841). It is difficult to know what to make of this account. Certainly, a John White was executed in Louisville in April 1841 (Hearn 2016, 185). Perhaps the best explanation is that this was a botched execution, and those carrying out the experiment revived an unconscious man. Note from the same report: "The rope not "playing" well occasioned the knot to slip up over the chin instead of being under his ear, so that his neck was not broken by the fall" ("Execution and Resuscitation" 1841).

If the White execution and its aftermath were, in part, based on fact, the same is unlikely to be true of some of the postmortem galvanic experiments described in the press in the later nineteenth century. Here we are squarely in the territory of fantasy journalism. For instance, in 1872 "a brace of Communist prisoners" in Paris were bled to death and then had a "saturated solution of chloride of calcium" injected into their veins. They were left for three months in a warm room. Then blood was pumped back into their system, and they were given the inevitable galvanic shocks. One man revived. He is "we are assured, still alive in Switzerland, under the name Fourbe" ("A very extraordinary story..." 1872; allegedly taken from Paris by a New York paper). In 1880 in Budapest, a man named Takecs, who had just been convincingly hanged and declared dead, was "brought under the influence of electro-galvanic current, and after a few hours Takacs completely recovered." "He became delirious, but was occasionally conscious, when he complained of great pain. He died next morning" ("A very strange story is related..." 1880). In 1889 details were given in a gossip column of experiments by scientists in Paris on heads taken by the guillotine. The modus operandi of this group was to inject fresh blood into the brain, and "the most horrible stories" were "afloat, and people even go so far as to affirm that the lips were made to move in reply to a question..." ("London Gossip" 1889).[16]

The best of all the stories, though, is certainly that published in 1869 (about an experiment begun in April 1868) and set at a prison in Villarica (Brazil). There one Dr. Lorenzo y Carmo's aim was to see whether he could reattach the head of a guillotined man to his body. He was given by the state two bodies to experiment on: convicts Aveiro and Carines. He managed to reattach one head and, with an electric current, was able to restart breathing. The condemned man's circulation restarted after about two hours. Three days later, electricity was removed, and breathing and circulation continued with no assistance: nourishment was given with "an oesophagian probe." At the end of seven months, the resuscitated man "was able to rise and walk, feeling only a slight stiffness in the neck and a feebleness of the limbs." The sting in the tale was that "due to the haste of the operation," the doctor had accidentally put the head on the wrong body ("A Very Strange Story" 1869. This story came from a Florentine newspaper, *L'Italie*, which was allegedly printing extracts from *Annales de la Médecine et de la Chirurgie Etrangères*. I have found no trace of this journal). British writers became lyrical at the implications of Dr. Lorenzo y Carmo's extraordinary achievement.

In families natural defects may be remedied by readjusting heads and bodies not originally proportioned for each other, and human beings dissatisfied with their sex may, under the benevolent system of Dr. Lorenzo y Carmo repair the error of their origin. It will be a question for lawyers to determine to what nationality these future beings are to belong if head and body have previously owed a separate allegiance. But if the system holds good in violent deaths, surely it may be applied to deaths ensuing, as the coroners' juries have it, from natural causes. In this case we might preserve our statesmen and celebrities for ever. Opponents of the system would, however, be found in heirs-apparent. ("A Very Strange Story" 1869)

22. THE GHOST IN SEARCH OF HELP

Summary: A messenger brings someone to a dying person's bed; the messenger, it transpires, is a ghost. Earliest Attestation: 1890. Motif: N/A. Secondary Literature: Edgerton 1968; Brunvand 2012, I, 264–65; I have taken the name "The Ghost in Search of Help" from there.

Ghost lore was an important part of Victorian supernatural culture (Davies 2007; Finucane 1996, 172–216) and survived into the nineteenth and, indeed, the twentieth century more convincingly than fairy lore and witch lore. The following ghost story did the round of the British press in early 1891.

> The lower classes at St. Petersburg are greatly excited about an alleged miraculous occurrence which is said to have taken place a few days ago. A priest went with the Holy Sacrament to a young officer, saying that he had been asked to do so by an elderly lady who had called at his house. The officer said that it was nobody that had been sent by him. "Besides," he added smiling, "I am in the enjoyment of the best of health, and by no means preparing for death." The priest looking round the room, perceived the portrait of a lady on the wall, and said it was she who had called and ordered the sacrament. "But that is the portrait of my mother, who has been dead for some time," exclaimed the officer. The priest said it was an

exact likeness of the lady who had called upon him. The officer was so impressed with the incident that he partook of the Sacrament. He died the same evening. ("A St. Petersburg Ghost Story" 1891)

In several variants of the St. Petersburg story—recorded in Russian newspapers in December 1890—the mother travels with the priest in a cab to her son's door (Edgerton 1968, 32–38, collected and translated different versions from contemporary St. Petersburg newspapers). Other versions of "The Ghost in Search of Help" appeared in the same decade. In 1890 the story was set in London in *Blackwood's Magazine*: a ghostly mother walks a priest to her son's house (Garth July 1890; our earliest account and not known to Edgerton 1968). One frustrated spiritualist reader suggests that the story was known even then: "I cannot fix time and place, but, if I have not seen it in print, I must have dreamt it. Every detail is familiar to me; but I am vexed that I cannot remember where I read it" (M. A. Oxon 1890). In 1892 there is a young girl who brings a doctor (rather than a priest) to her sick mother: the girl is, of course, a ghost (Mitchell 1892, 208; for the complicated background to this story, see Nickell 2012; on our very limited evidence doctors seem to be a later development in "The Ghost in Search of Help"). In 1894, a Father Walters is summoned by two children to their father's deathbed in Washington (DC?). The children do not come up the stairs with the priest to their father's room, and it is only when he describes the children to the father, who is indeed dying, that the mystery is resolved: "They were my children . . . My poor dead children" ("Summoned by Ghosts" 1894).

American folklorist William Edgerton reports a London version recorded in the United States in 1942 (1968, 40: "In a recent letter Professor Wax told me that she heard this version in early 1942 from an unidentified graduate student at the University of California in Berkeley who had apparently heard it only a few years before in England."). He may be referring to this story, which appeared in the press in 1939.

> Another part of London has its own legend of a phantom taxi-cab. The story goes that a South Kensington vicar was called upon by a lady in a great state of agitation, who wished him to get into the taxi which she had at the door, and go with her to see a man who was dying. Deeming it no more than his duty to answer such an appeal, the cleric went off with the lady in the taxi. He alighted when they had arrived at the house indicated, and, turning round to speak to the lady, found to his amazement that both she and the cab had vanished. The taxi does not come into the story any more, the end being the death of the man the clergyman was called to see, and the startling discovery that the lady who had brought the summons was his wife, who had been dead for 15 years. ("Ghosts on Wheels" 1937)

Edgerton (1968, 31) is determined to link the "Ghost in Search of Help" to "The Vanishing Hitchhiker." Note, though, that the early versions of the story do not usually have a vehicle.

23. GHOST WAGER

Summary: A group of aristocrats wager that one of their number will not be able to pass as a ghost without getting caught. Earliest Attestation: the 1820s (England). Motif: N/A. Secondary Literature: N/A. Notes: In preparing this entry I was able to read a prepublication version of Dash, *Calendar*. The entry would have been impossible without it

Bizarre wagers or challenges (see also "**Red Hand**" and particularly "**Selling Sovereigns**") were popular as stories in late eighteenth- and early nineteenth-century Britain (e.g., Chambers 1832, II 633–35). There was also in this period a passionate interest in ghosts. Perhaps unsurprisingly, ghosts and wagers collided in popular legend. There was "**Shooting a Ghost**," where a young man (often a soldier) bets that he will not be frightened by spirits. There is "**Nail in the Coffin**," where a party wager that one of their number dare not enter a church and hammer a nail into a coffin. Then there is the "Ghost Wager," which had as its background the surprising number of men (and very occasionally women) who pretended to be ghosts on Victorian streets and roads (Middleton 2014).

In the "Ghost Wager" a circle of "wealthy scamps of aristocracy" ("All the world" 1838; in one case the man undertaking the challenge is run around by "a livery servant in a cab," "A Ghost" 1838) bet that one of their number can (or cannot) dress himself as a supernatural being and achieve, in that costume, a specific goal. Usually the goal is to visit a certain number of places at night disguised as a phantom ("Effects of Aristocratic Example" 1837; "Mansion-House" 1838); sometimes the bet is to visit the same place a number of times (A South Londoner 1872; "A Manchester Ghost Story" 1886); on other occasions it is to frighten a number of individuals (even to cause deaths from fear, G. 1867 "The Ghost Story" 1838); to enter a certain number of houses (Patterson 1893); or, in one instance, to undress a given number of local women ("Resuscitation" 1833). The bet is carried out in the outfit of a ghost or sometimes in the figure

Figure 8 Spring-heeled Jack.

of Spring-heeled Jack, a Victorian "bogey," who was capable of outrunning and, above all, out-jumping all those who pursued him (Bell 2012; Dash forthcoming).

Such stories circulated as explanations for spates of ghost sightings in a given area or just, we might guess, from the pleasure of story-telling. Sometimes this public knowledge is given in the most general terms: "it is said," "it is stated," the "rumours that prevail," a "rumour has got into circulation here" (A South Londoner 1872; "The Ghost Story" 1838; "All the World" 1838; "Broughty Ferry" 1867). These are not all journalistic creations—though sometimes they might have been—because in some instances the allegation is made in a letter from a member of the public (e.g., "Mansion-House" 1838; A South Londoner 1872; of course, there are some cases from the nineteenth century when journalists wrote anonymous letters to newspapers). There are also references to the Ghost Wager as one of a number of competing theories. Take, for example, this report from 1887:

> Some persons described [the spook] as a man who has undertaken to visit every village in the Wirral in the character of "Springheel Jack" for a wager of £1,000; while others believe it to be a supernatural appearance, and speak of a strong smell of sulphur which accompanies his visit. ("A Ghost in Wirral" 1887)

The reports do *not* acknowledge "the unlikelihood that the local people trading in these rumors could have somehow become privy to the details of a private wager between aristocrats" (Dash forthcoming; generalized skepticism about the wager seems to have been rare, "All the world . . ." 1838) Sometimes the "ghosts" are said to get caught, but of course the case never goes to court: the rich—the lesson seems to be—can get away with things that would land someone poorer on the treadmill (A South Londoner 1872).

The first reference that we have to the "Ghost Wager" dates to 1825:

> It was rumoured that [the ghost] had been seized one night at Kensington; that he was discovered to be a Nobleman's son, whereupon the matter was "hushed up," and that he was playing these pranks for a bet, having wagered that he would "walk as a ghost" for a certain number of nights "without being taken or laid." ("The New Hammersmith Ghost" 1825)

Here is a reference from 1837:

> It is . . . currently reported that some scoundrel, disguised in a bear-skin, and wearing spring shoes, has been seen jumping to and fro before foot passengers in the neighbourhood of Lewisham, and has in one or two instances greatly alarmed females. This feat, it is said, is to decide a wager; he having undertaken to play off these freaks for a number of nights in nine different parishes without being apprehended. ("Effects of Aristocratic Example" 1837; A South Londoner 1837)

As late as 1900, meanwhile, a Yorkshire correspondent wrote of Spring-heeled Jack and his exploits of some forty years before. Needless to say, there are no records in the press, circa 1860, of the feats described here.

[Jack] laid a wager that he would appear in certain villages around Leeds near midnight, and afterwards walk around Armley Gaol wall 13 times, and although the police were trying to catch him he succeeded in escaping 11 times, but was trapped in the last lap, and sentenced to imprisonment. (Townend 1924)

24. GHOSTLY DONATION

Summary: A clergyman scares a ghost away by asking for a donation for the church. Earliest Attestation: 1886 (England). Motif: N/A. Secondary Literature: N/A.

This story appeared in the press in 1886 about a gathering at a country house:

> One of the bedrooms was known to be haunted, and was in consequence rarely used; but under the pressure of circumstances, it was in this instance appropriated to a clergyman who had joined the party somewhat unexpectedly. On the morning following the guest's arrival the host fully expected to hear some complaint, but at breakfast nothing was said, and it was taken for granted that the ghost had not appeared. Two or three days went by, and when the clerical guest announced his intended departure, the host expressed a hope that he had not been disturbed at night during his stay. "O dear no," replied the guest, "I have been most comfortable; why do you ask such a question?" "Well," returned the host, "the fact is that we were obliged to put you in the haunted room, but I did not tell you about it lest you should be nervous." "Ah! then that explains it," replied his friend; "the first night I was here I woke up and saw an old gentleman standing by my bedside, but when I asked for a subscription towards my Sunday school treat, he disappeared at once, and I have never seen him since." ("Country House Gossip" 1886)

By 1894 the story had developed into its more typical form. The man of the cloth recognizes the ghost for what it is immediately:

> The following story is being told of the Bishop of Peterborough. Happening to pay a visit to a celebrated country house the Bishop was offered the use of the haunted room. Not being afraid of ghosts he accepted this without demur. Upon

the following morning at breakfast it was noticed that the Bishop looked solemn, and he was, therefore, naturally asked if a ghost had appeared to him. "Yes," said the Bishop. "What did he say to you?" was the next question. "Oh! I spoke to it first." "Really! What did you say?" "I asked him to subscribe to my new cathedral." "And what did the ghost say?" "Nothing—it disappeared at once." ("The Bishop," 1894)

In 1909 we learn that the Bishop of Southwark told a very similar story about a clergyman who only lost the ghost when the clergyman jumped out of bed to find his pocketbook! ("The Bishop" 1908; this became part of the Bishop's speaking repertoire "Bishop's Ghost Story" 1910). By 1913 the clergyman's role was given to Archbishop Thomson (1819–1890, Archbishop of York; "The Archbishop" 1913).

These stories belong to the tradition of antisupernatural narratives in British folklore (for "folk disbelief," especially in British tradition, see Roper 2018). Most common are the numerous stories about misunderstood ghosts, typically, a dog or more commonly a donkey found in the night dragging a chain and making "unearthly noises" (e.g., "Bolton Le Sands" 1870). These stories and others like them (see **Ghost Wager**") were welcome in Victorian newspapers as they expressed the disdain for the supernatural so typical of much of the period. One suspects that the "Ghostly Donation" was also a professional story and that it was much enjoyed in Anglican circles, particularly by men who had long suffered the indignity of seeking out donations.

25. HANDS IN THE MUFF

Summary: A young woman tricks two young men into holding each other's hand. Earliest Attestation: 1851. Motif: N/A. Secondary Literature: N/A.

A story of competitive flirtation from the 1870s, published in Britain but set in North America:

Some young ladies and gentlemen who were taking advantage of the fine sleighing in Canada one fine winter were obliged to sit three on a seat. One of the seats

> held two gentlemen and a lady. The gentlemen, of course, would not allow the lady to take an exposed seat; she therefore sat in the middle. As the night was extremely cold, gentleman No. 1 passed his hand (a remarkably small one by the way) into the lady's muff. As the muff was not very capacious, the lady quietly removed one of her hands from the same. In a few moments she felt a movement on the other side, and found gentlemen No. 2. attempting to pass his hand into the muff. She then drew out her other hand and allowed him to do so. What took place in the muff afterwards she is unable to say. But each of the gentlemen privately reported to a small circle of friends how warmly the lady had returned the pressure of his hand in the muff, while the lady as privately reported to her friends the magnificent sale she had made of both gentlemen. ("The Story" 1879)

This version of the story can be traced back to an American newspaper in 1870 ("The Story" 1870, *FG*).

There is then the crueler and perhaps older variant involving mutual discovery—the two men come to realize that they are holding each other's hand. The earliest instance known to me was set, with a "coquettish little Quakeress" on a sleigh in Pennsylvania ("Story of a Muff" 1851, *FG*). In 1882, meanwhile, a young lady from Middleton (Massachusetts) "never tires of relating an amusing occurrence of the sleighing season last winter."

> She was enjoying a ride with two Hartford gentlemen and she was driving. One of the gentlemen slyly inserted a hand in her muff and lovingly pressed her disengaged hand. She blushed and withdrew it just as the gentlemen on the other side slipped his hand in the muff. She knew by the action of her adorers that the hand-pressures were frequent and loving within the silk lining of the muff, for first one face and then the other would bob forward to catch a look at the sweet face and eyes which prompted, as they supposed, the tender pressure of the hand. The by-play lasted until the young lady quietly remarked, "If you gentlemen have done with my muff, I will trouble you for it now, as my hands are quite cold." And the two gentlemen, who had been comfortably warm up to this time, suddenly felt an Arctic chill creeping up their spinal columns and the mercury of their feelings dropped to 180 degrees below zero. The two gentlemen are strangers now. ("They Are Strangers" 1882)

As this American story was circulating in Great Britain ("They Are Strangers" 1882 first appeared in the United Kingdom in Sept. 1882: in subsequent years it appears thirteen times in the BNA), an indigenous British version was launched in Liverpool: "Monday was a bitterly cutting day, but a young lady residing with her father, one of Liverpool's merchant princes, at Grassendale, managed to enjoy herself, and for some time to come she will rejoice greatly" ("Squeezing" 1884). She was out riding with two male friends (though not in a sleigh!) and the two men's hands made contact in her muff. Once they discovered the trick, "the two gentlemen suddenly felt an Arctic chill creeping up their spinal columns, and the mercury of their feelings dropped to 180 degrees below zero. They are strangers now" ("Squeezing" 1884). The Liverpool author was, to judge by these words, depending on a written version of the Middleton muff.

This story may have been particularly piquant in as much as, at least in some parts of the English-speaking world and in some classes, "muff" could be used, in the nineteenth century, to refer to the female *pudenda*. Green's *Dictionary of Slang* has a number of mainly British instances, from the seventeenth century onwards (https://greensdictofslang.com/entry/tklcnhq [accessed 13 May 2019]). The word "muff" was certainly capable of causing hilarity when mentioned in open court in a breach of promise case ("Amusing" 1878)—a man had failed to marry a woman, but she carried his gift, a muff, with her "as an emblem of his perfidy." However, that may depend on "muff" also meaning "fool."

A less successful British (?) version was published in the United Kingdom in 1881:

> Two young men met one evening, at the house of an acquaintance, some young ladies, for one of whom both gentlemen entertained tender feelings. In a spirit of frolic, one of the young ladies turned off the gas, and the young men, thinking it a favourable moment to make known the state of their feelings to the fair object of their regard, moved seats at the same instant, and placed themselves, as they supposed, by the lady's side; but she had also moved, the gentlemen were in reality seated next to each other. As the young men could not whisper without betraying their whereabouts, they both gently took, as they thought, the soft little hand of the charmer, and when, after a while, they ventured to give a little pressure, each was surprised to find it returned with an unmistakable squeeze. It may be well-imagined that the moments flew rapidly in this silent interchange of mutual affection. But one of the girls, wondering at the unusual silence of the gentlemen, stepped noiselessly out, and suddenly returned with a light, and there sat the young men most lovingly squeezing each other's hands, and supreme delight beaming in their eyes. Their consternation, and the ecstasy of the ladies, may be imagined but cannot be described. One of the young men was afterwards heard to say that he thought his friend's hand felt a little hard. ("A Little Hard" 1881)

26. HAREM PRISONER

Summary: A girl believed to have been killed during the Indian Mutiny, is found many years later to be trapped in a harem. Earliest Attestation: the stories begin almost immediately after the 1857 mutiny. Motif: N/A. Secondary Literature: N/A.

Britain may have been the most powerful nation in the world in the 1800s, but Britons had their share of humiliations in that century. Whether it was the Boers outclassing the British army, the retreat from Kabul, or the Siege of Khartoum, there were useful reminders that dominance was not omnipotence. A particularly important instance of this took place at Cawnpore (Kanpur) in northern India in the summer of 1857 during, as it is known in Britain, "the Indian Mutiny."

In that year, at Cawnpore, Nana Sahib, the local magnate, turned on his British allies, and several hundred Europeans found themselves under siege. On the verge of starvation, a free passage was negotiated between the British leader, General Wheeler, and Nana to boats on the Ganges. On 27 June the garrison and associated families went to these boats, were allowed to board the vessels but were then shot upon by Nana's troops from both sides of the river. The vast majority of the men were killed on the spot. Some 120 women and children, meanwhile, were taken to Bibighar on the edge of the city and were kept safe there with other European civilians, until 15 July, when the order was given to kill them all. Their bodies—most were murdered with blades—ended up down a well. The killing took over four hours and was evidently the stuff of nightmares (*Cawnpore* 1857; Ward 2004, 414–18; Leckey 1859, 115 for the duration of the massacre).

None survived the Bibighar massacre, or at least this is what the official accounts of the Mutiny claimed. But in the years following, rumors began to leak out that one young woman had not been killed there or had perhaps escaped before.

> We scarcely know whether our readers will be more pained or relieved to hear that Miss Emily Wheeler, the daughter of General Wheeler, of Cawnpore, is still alive. Captain Harvey, superintendent of the department for the abolition of Thuggee, has had communication with the unfortunate young lady, who, we understand is so utterly broken in spirit, that she entreats her friends not to seek to bring her back again, but to leave her to her wretched fate; yet it were better surely for the poor girl herself that her request should not be complied with. ("India" 1860)

Figure 9 'Miss Wheeler Defending Herself Against the Sepoys at Cawnpore' (Print: London Printing and Publishing Company).

The "more pained" at the head of this citation may surprise the twenty-first-century reader. But it alludes to the fear that Emily would have undergone, in the intervening years, sexual outrages at the hand of her captors; "such debasement" as one newspaper put it ("A Romance of the Rebellion" 1860). The fear of "outrages" on the part of rebels was great in the reports from the mutiny and already in August of 1857 there was the claim that one European virgin—"very young and beautiful"—had been forcibly inducted into the harem of the King of Delhi ("Outrage on British Ladies" 1857). Indeed, part of the mythology of Cawnpore is that the imprisoned British women preferred death to entry into Nana's harem (e.g., Dodd 1859, 139; "The East Indian Revolt," 1858, 49 for Nana's sexual intentions). "'Rape' became a symbol of what was understood as the Indians' transgressive assault against the British nation" (Erll 2009, 111).

The question of whether it was better or worse that Emily lived was, in any case, moot. Once Captain Harvey had made extensive investigations into her fate, he determined that she had been taken away by an Indian cavalryman, but that she had been subsequently murdered ("A Romance" 1860, excerpted from the *Friend of India*). "We have no reason," concludes a subsequent newspaper article, "to believe that any European lady ... is still experiencing the tender mercies of the heathen, which are cruel" ("A Romance" 1860). In 1865 Trevelyan, in his book on Cawnpore wrote of how Miss Wheeler had traveled for a time with the enemy and that she had not died. He explained her passivity by noting: "She was by no means of pure English blood" (Trevelyan 1866, 213): Wheeler had married a mixed-race Anglo-Indian woman. An odious form of late Victorian racism was now mixed into accounts (for late Victorian racism, see Hyam 1990, 115–36).

The whole issue is further complicated because there is confusion over which of Wheeler's daughters had (supposedly) survived: Eliza or Margaret (there was no Emily!). Margaret (aka Ulrika) had been the heroine of several fictions about British resistance against the mutineers (Leckey 1859, 154; Erll 2009, 116–17; note that "A Romance" 1860 suggests that there were also Indian legends around the girls). In our first list of the dead "the two Miss Wheelers" are included, with many other names, among those "of whose ultimate fate nothing certain is known" (Cawnpore 1857, 23).

Never mind which of the two Miss Wheelers was involved, the story refused to die. It returned almost a decade later. Here is a report from the British press in the autumn of 1869, which had appeared before in the Indian papers.

> Mr. C___, an official of high position, while on a tour through his division, had occasion to encamp near a village called S___. While there, information reached him that the missing daughter of Sir Hugh Wheeler was in the keeping of a petty Rajah in the neighbourhood, who came in under the amnesty, and thereby deprived the gallows of a legitimate victim. Mr. C___ managed to send a verbal message to Miss Wheeler to the effect that if she wished he would remove her from her present position, and restore her to her relatives and home. Miss Wheeler sent a written reply, in which she told Mr. C___ that she had been for nearly twelve years living with a native in the degrading position of an inmate in his harem, had children by him, and could not muster the moral courage to face one of her own kind, letting alone her relatives. She wished to be entirely forgotten, and to be permitted to remain unnoticed, or if thought of at all, "to be remembered as one in the grave." ("A Horrible Story from India" 1869)

Is it really imaginable that a British official would have left Miss Wheeler in place? As another newspaper put it: "The story is one not likely to obtain credence with any but the extremely ignorant" ("A Tale of the Mutiny" 1869). Letters, though, continued to appear in the Indian press, arguing for the truth of this story and others like it.

> Several communications then appeared from different persons at that time residing in India, and it was stated especially that in ___ and another locality in the ___ territory there was reason to suppose various English women were also the inmates of native harems. ("English girls in the Harem" 1892)

The story of the Englishwoman trapped in a harem rattled on down through the years. In 1880 it was no longer Miss Wheeler but "the sister of a Bedfordshire baronet" who "being then a young girl of considerable beauty, was lost during the Indian Mutiny"; believed dead she had "been found in a harem at Mecca. The lady is now in India, and questions have been sent out to secure evidence of her identity, which it is suspected there may be a desire to conceal" ("London Gossip" 1880). In 1892 a report was published in a British paper claiming that a young girl, who had been six or seven at the time of the Cawnpore massacre had been living, as late as 1869, in a harem. The correspondent had had communications with this woman, then eighteen, through a Hindu who knew a cleaner in the palace where the English girl was kept ("English girls in the Harem" 1892). In 1907 a Catholic priest was brought to the deathbed of a woman, who it was transpired was Miss Wheeler grown old and now married to her captor (Ward 2004, 504–6). In the 1930s, meanwhile, two British women claimed that they had met blue-eyed girls in the bazaar at Allahabad.

> They claimed that they were descended from an Anglo-Indian woman who had married a Muslim man during the revolt. When the women returned with some male relatives to question them further, they were unable to find the girls. (Anderson 2012, 148; evidence taken from June Wilmshurst—one of those present was June's mother; for more Anderson 2012, 138)

The number of different stories should warn us here that we are dealing with British story-telling needs, not Indian realities.[17] One woman could perhaps have been kept prisoner for some years in the Raj, but it seems unlikely that several could have been hidden away in this way. The "Harem Prisoner" was an attractive narrative for Victorians and later imperially minded Britons. It combined the mystery of the lost son or daughter (see for instance the "**Chimney Boy**"), with sensational atrocities, taboo sexual relations, and, crucially, lost innocence. The last element seems to have been the most important in the transmission of the story. A future scholar looking at "The Harem Prisoner" might ask whose innocence.

27. HERO SURVIVES

> Summary: An important individual is not really dead but in hiding. Earliest Attestation: antiquity. Motif: A 571 "Cultural hero asleep in mountain"; D1960.2, "King asleep in mountain." Secondary Literature: Henken 1996.

It is a very old idea. A national hero dies, but the people refuse to accept his or her death. The individual has really—it is whispered—been taken away. Often there is the implication that this person will return at a later date to save the nation. Medieval versions of such stories had a mystical or even supernatural edge to them. The idea, for instance, that Arthur would awake from this sleep and liberate Britain, involved things and deeds that were physically impossible (Henken 1996). By the nineteenth century, supernatural back-from-the-dead messiahs were rare, but there were many famous dead Victorians, supposedly in hiding. A notable example took place when the Mahdi finally overran British defenses at Khartoum in January 1885. General Gordon (a victim, many claimed, of the British government's incompetence) was said to have been killed. But where was his body?

> A Coptic merchant, who was one of the few men who managed to escape from Khartoum after the massacre, has arrived [in Cairo] after a long and painful journey, and has made a most astounding statement to the authorities. He asserts in the most positive manner, partly from his own observation and partly from information supplied to him on the spot by credible eye-witnesses, that shortly after the massacre which followed the entry of the rebels, and before the terrible confusion resulting therefrom had subsided, the Mahdi, hearing that Gordon had been slain, ordered his head to be brought to him. ("Is Gordon" 1885)

The head though could not be found: "The narrator, therefore, believes that there is at least a slight chance that Gordon may have made good his escape, and that he has fled to the south in the direction of Senaar" ("Is Gordon" 1885). Rumors continued. In 1888, three years later, it was reported:

> The long delay of news about Henry Stanley has produced some strange rumours. A wild story is in circulation to the effect that Stanley has this time found some one more hard to find than Livingstone—the dead General Gordon. Stanley, Emin Bey, and Gordon are said to be together. They have two steamers, and their expedition is making good progress Northwards towards Khartoum. Gordon will

not allow either of his companions to communicate, and he is "bitter of speech" against the British government. ("A Wild Rumour" 1888)

There were many others. Marshal Ney, Napoleon's favorite, had not really been killed in 1815 but had escaped to the United States: he settled in North Carolina as Peter Stuart Ney an "admirable schoolmaster and brilliant mathematician" and died there in 1843 ("A Curious Story" 1879). In 1871 it was reported that the young Lord Fitzroy Lennox had not died on board the SS *President* in 1841. Rather, "the deceased" had "obtained a situation with the London and South-Western Railway Company, and has been employed as clerk at their London Goods Terminus for the last twelve years" ("A Singular Story" 1871). In 1873 there were rumors in London clubs that Napoleon III was still alive: "The idea of such an evasion as I have related has taken root in a certain class of English society" ("Is the Emperor" 1873; Napoleon III note was a magnet for legends, e.g., "Curious Story" 1858, which alleges that the emperor was an American imposter!)

In 1891 the news emerged that Archduke Johann Salvator of Austria had not perished with his wife in a boating accident. Rather, he had escaped to Chile and had taken up a new life there ("A Strange Story" 1891). Another claim, made in 1895, was that Archduke Salvator was none other than Marshall Yamagata of the Imperial Japanese Army ("The Missing" 1895; see **Familiar Enemies**"). In 1896 there was the "ridiculous story" that the great Irish nationalist Charles Parnell (1846–1891) was still alive "and that by and by he will reappear in Irish political life": for now he was "living in a ranch in an obscure Western State" ("The *Sunday Times*..." 1896). Russian emperors were a favorite for this legend type: Tsar Alexander I (1777–1825) was widely believed not to have died ("Empty Coffin Mystery" 1933); and a similar story was told of Emperor Nicholas I (1796–1855), who, it was said, had retired to "a quiet country town in Italy" ("A Queer Story" 1865). Anastasia (1901–1918) was, by no means, the first Russian royal to survive death. The most important modern British tradition lies slightly outside our period. The death of Herbert Kitchener (1850–1916) was greeted with incredulity, and many Britons believed that he had survived the sinking of HMS *Hampshire* (Hayward 2002, 54–155; there are, note, more sources to be exploited, and Kitchener's death deserves a longer study).

28. HOLLOW TREE DEATH

Summary: A skeleton is found trapped in a tree, and objects within tell a gruesome story. Earliest Attestation: early nineteenth century (mostly found in the United States). Motif: N/A. Secondary Literature: N/A. Compare with: "**Immured Lovers.**" I thank Kay Massingill for bringing this story type to my attention.

This legend is one that was particularly popular in late nineteenth-century American newspapers (where it was set) but that was also frequently enjoyed by British readers. A tree is felled and a skeleton discovered in the hollow trunk. Objects found allow the body to be identified and the dreadful death of the trapped person to be reconstructed. In some respects, the story recalls "**Immured Lovers**," the "**Mistletoe Bride**," or the "**Skeletons That Eloped**," where the past is recreated on the discovery of a frozen death scene. Here is perhaps the most widely read version in its shortest form:

> An Ohio paper tells a very strange story of the revelations made by a stroke of lightning. The lightning, it seems, prostrated a splendid grove of oaks in the Miama Valley. Among them was one which was rent asunder from top to bottom, and, according to the narrative, the fragments in falling apart disgorged a gaunt skeleton, yellow with age, which instantly fell to pieces, and was scattered over several feet of the surrounding pasturage. With the remains were also found a few buttons of ancient pattern, and a leather pocket book, in a good state of preservation. This pocket book told the sad and tragical story of the disentombed skeleton. It contained papers which were brown and discoloured, and covered with rude pencil marks scarcely legible, but enough could be deciphered to show that they had been written by a soldier in the revolutionary army; a man in fact who had been an aid and companion of General Washington. His name was Roger Vanderburg, and he held the rank of captain. After participating in the privations of the valley forays and participating in the retreat across the Jersey, and serving a brief time at West Point, he marched with St Clair against the North-West Indians. On November 3rd, 1761 [*corr.* 1791], he was wounded and captured by the Red Skins. He subsequently escaped, however, and being hard pressed by his savage foes, took refuge in this oak tree. The hollow afforded a convenient retreat, and he allowed himself to drop into it. Then too late he found he had miscalculated the depth of the hollow, and there was no escape. The remaining hours of his life were spent writing a diary, the entries of which show a terrible record of human

suffering, and during a period of eleven days, he painfully described his sensations as he felt himself slowly starving to death. ("A Strange Story" 1873)

Other versions included a body that was found in a tree near Akron, Ohio: "With the remains were a rusty rifle, a powder flask and the remains of a buckskin hunting dress" ("A Skeleton Hunter" 1882, *BC*). There was the 1891 skeleton in an oak at Tishomingo of a man with a manacle on his leg. "The supposition is that the man had escaped from some prison and had fled with a portion of his manacles" ("A Skeleton in a Tree" 1892). In 1893 a blond-haired child with a tomahawk in her head was removed from an apple tree at Lexington ("A Skeleton in a Tree Trunk" 1893). In 1897 a body (of one David Marslin) was discovered in a tree in Burleson County, Texas. Marslin had, it was deduced, died while out hunting, and on his person he carried a "valuable deed," "so valuable that it makes Marslin's children ... very rich young people" ("Face Looked" 1897). In 1902 two petrified bodies in an oak, which had been bound together by Indians were found at Lebanon, Ohio ("Stone Bodies" 1902). In 1919 a body was found in a white oak in Minnesota. It transpired that some sixty years before, a man had tried to escape Indians and had written a description in his diary of how he had been caught in the trunk and was unable to get out ("A Gruesome Find," *CW*). In 1926 a petrified French officer D'Artagnan (the name discovered from some papers) was found in a tree at Ladysmith. He was identified as having gone missing from the 1673 expedition of Marquette and Jollette on the Mississippi. It was suggested that he had been trying to escape from some Indians when he had lowered himself into the hollow of the tree ("Weird Find"; on this fake, see Derleth 1985, 216).

"Hollow Tree Death" may have had earlier European antecedents. This story appeared in a British review in 1803:

> It is well known that during the French Revolution, the wood of Kusel, near Deux Ponts was often the scene of various actions, and that the Prussians encamped in it a considerable time; consequently the wood was so nearly ruined, that only a few oak trees were left standing, here and there. These trees were sold in the month of March last, 1803, and one lot fell to a citizen of Strasburgh [sic] for fifty florins. Soon afterwards ordering two of them to be cut down, one of them, the largest, was no sooner divided for the purpose of removal, when to the astonishment of the labourers they discovered a human skeleton, from which all the flesh having wasted away, nothing remained near the body at the bottom of the tree but some bits of blue cloth, and part of a hat. A purse half decayed was also found, containing about 100 louis d'ors in gold; and from the buttons about the blue cloth, it was concluded that the deceased had been a Prussian officer, who

not knowing the tree to be hollow or, probably sleeping near the top of the trunk of it, had slipped in, and from cold, or a variety of circumstances, being unable to extricate himself, had there perished. The fact, however, can be attested by the proprietor, the purchaser of the trees, and several other persons. ("A Shocking Discovery" 1803, translated "from the *German Politisches Journal*")

PB has kindly provided me with a similar story from the Dutch press in 1805 about a body in a tree in the forest of Cerisy near Bayeux: the skeleton belonged to a royalist rebel who had died with 800 francs on him ("Ryssel" 1805). An English novelist had a villain's body discovered in a tree (Payn 1864, II, 290–92) and complained, on learning about "A Strange Story" (1873), of "Nature's act of plagiarism" (Skinner 1903, II, 248, *PB*). The Polish press reports in 1903 that a skeleton was discovered in a rotten chestnut tree: with the body there was an iron bullet box and a coin dated to 1552 ("Szkielet..." 1903, *FG*). On the basis of this very small sample—there are more from continental Europe and Russia (e.g., "Uit Tsarentijd" 1964 *PB*)—reports from the Old World seem to lack the exciting backstory we expect from American sources.

There were also, it is worth remembering, real life cases of hollow tree deaths. In searching for these stories I came across several examples where bodies were discovered in hollow trees in the United Kingdom. In one case a man had become trapped and died (revisiting a childhood haunt "Two men..." 1928). In another there was a suicide ("Dead in a Tree Trunk" 1909). In other cases, babies' bodies had been left in tree hollows... (e.g., "A Dead Body" 1870). We also have a boy who was trapped in a tree for six days and miraculously survived ("Six Days" 1886). Stories like these should be kept in mind with Bella in the Wych Elm, the case of a woman found in a tree at Hagley (Worcestershire) in 1943, a case that has since become mixed up with witchcraft and espionage conspiracy theories (Newman 2011). They also suggest that in Britain bodies would not be long in a tree without being noticed: days, months or years rather than decades or centuries. For a really convincing hollow-tree yarn you needed the American wilderness.

29. HUMAN SAUSAGES

Summary: A man is murdered and his flesh sold as meat. Earliest Attestation: Middle Ages (I would be surprised if a thorough search of ancient sources failed to turn up an equivalent there). Motif: G10: Cannibalism. Secondary Literature: N/A. Compare with: **Child Pie**.

"[T]he sale and serving of human flesh in unsuspected forms has ever been a favourite topic with the lovers of the hideous and terrible" ("True Tales" 1868). Consider the "man representing himself to be a minister of the gospel" who, in the 1860s, stopped at an Irishman's ranch at Tobacco Plains (US). The "minister" killed the Irishman, took his place, and then employed the flesh of the poor man "in variously prepared dishes to the travellers" passing through ("Horrible Story from the Far West" 1866). Another example was reported in 1870. A tailor from Toulouse had been murdered in a tavern for his money and was then placed in a pickling tub and salted. Spaniards heading north stopped at the tavern, and they "were handed a plate of meat, the flavour of which impressed their palates as rather high" ("The Murdered Tailor" 1870). Both of these sources are "unconfirmed": no names are given, and no legal cases resulted. It is reasonable to consider them newspaper fictions. Other stories have more circumstantial details but are likewise questionable. Take here the man "named Ramas" who circa 1860 in Sardinia was said to have reduced sixteen persons to sausage meat ("Human Sausage Meat" 1894); or the "Chinamen" executed "for selling human flesh as butcher's meat" in Petrograd in 1919—a "Doubtful Story" according to the editor who gave it space in his paper ("Doubtful Story" 1919).

The illegal commercial sale of human flesh—both in legend and in fact—dates back many centuries. There is, for example, a case of a butcher being burnt alive for selling human meat at Tournus (Burgundy) in 1033 (Glaber 1989, 187–89). The butcher had resorted to human joints in a famine. However, by the nineteenth century, such stories seem to have been common-place in or about large cities and no reference to hunger was made: the key point now was that consumers could not see where their meat was coming from.

"[M]any a child has been frightened into quietude by nurses' tales about butchers and pastry-cooks selling human flesh" ("True Tales" 1868). This comment relates to nineteenth-century Paris, but similar beliefs operated in London. Thus, for several days in early the summer of 1818:

> the shop of Mr. Pizzey, a pork butcher, No. 19, Blackmoor-street, Drury-lane, was surrounded by crowds, who vented the most obnoxious epithets against him, in

Figure 10 Sweeney Todd, *The String of Pearls*, 225.

consequence of a hand-bill having been circulated, charging him with having "a number of human bodies in his shop," and adding, "two Officers searched the house, and found two dead bodies wrapped in a sack." ("For several days..." 1818)

Locals believed that Pizzey had made a pork pie of human flesh, and legal action had to be taken against the printer of the bill ("For several days..." 1818; see also Hindley 1878, 84–87 and Simpson 1983, 465–66; for more recent urban-legend commercial problems, see Smith 1984). Dickens had heard similar stories. For instance, in the *Pickwick Papers* there are sausages with trouser-buttons in them—the implication being that someone has been put through a sausage grinder (Dickens 1837, 330; see also Simpson 1983, 463–65; a similar motif in the ballad *The Workhouse Boy* n.d.). The hero of Dickens's seventh novel, *Martin Chuzzlewit*, meanwhile, wonders, on arriving in the capital, whether he will not go missing and be "made into meat pies" (Dickens 1844, 433). Dickens writes in that same book about "preparers of cannibalistic pastry" in "many standard country legends" about London (Dickens 1844, 433).

There was also a more developed story that is remembered in Britain with the name "Sweeney Todd." A barber runs a murderous trade on Fleet Street, where he drops clients through a trapdoor into his cellar; and these men are then cut up and sold as pies in the pastry shop next door. Sweeney first appeared in 1846, in a penny dreadful with the unpromising title of *The String of Pearls* (1850 for the novelized version). But the story of the two shopkeepers and the human meat trade is older and possibly originated in Paris. One version was set in that city in the time of Louis IX (1234–1270; "True Tales" 1868); another in the fourteenth century (Lurine 1844, I, 150–52); and still another in the time of Henry II (1547–1559; "A Horrible Story, If True" 1864).[18] It goes without saying that Sweeney Todd never existed, though there have been some heroic attempts to find him in the archives (for an introduction to the literature, Westwood and Simpson 2005, 465; Anglo 1977, 49–53; Flanders 2011; Smith 2002). The story, both in France and Britain, had undeniable appeal. Consider this legend masquerading as news report set in Spain from 1878, but taken from a French newspaper:

> We learn from [the *Messager du Midi*] that for upwards of a year a character residing in Aranjuez has been in the habit of selling to an unsuspecting public sausages, *pâtés*, and *boudin*, made exclusively with human flesh. So excellent were his comestibles found that he reckoned more customers than any other pork butcher in the town, and having amassed a sufficient fortune he was meditating retiring from business when hazard brought about the discovery of his malpractices. It seems that within the last year or eighteen months several persons have unaccountably disappeared from Aranjuez, and in spite of the investigations made by the police no clue has been forthcoming concerning their fate. The missing clue has at length been found; they have filled the role which by rights should have belonged to the pig, and their fellow-townsmen have unwittingly eaten them in the guise of *charcuterie*. The unscrupulous pork butcher was aided in the horrible business, says the *Messager du Midi*, by a *coiffeur*. The Spanish Figaro's shop where he shaved his customers was provided with a trap-door, by which means those among them whom he destined to death were precipitated into a cellar, where they were despatched, their bodies being handed over to the pork butcher. The disappearance of a young man called Francisco Andral, who was seen to enter the barber's shop and never came out of it alive, raised suspicion; the police followed

up the scent, and discovered the fatal trapdoor, the cellar, with its blood-stained floor, and certain other proofs, which left no doubt upon their minds as to the guilt of the accused. The two miscreants are now, it is stated, in the hands of justice, which, if the history of their atrocious crimes prove correct, will, it is to be hoped, deal with them according to their merits. ("Human Flesh Sausages" 1878)

Human sausage stories had to adapt, at the end of the century, to the industrialization of the meat trade. In 1891 news got out that a Swedish worker had killed a man in 1889 and thrown him into the works of a meat production factory in Sioux City: the human meat had then mixed with the pork being prepared there, pickled, and sold ("Man Converted" 1891). The most famous case came, naturally enough, from Chicago—the premier meat-producing city in the world in the 1800s. In 1897 Adolph Luetgert, the owner of a Chicago sausage factory, was put on trial for murdering his wife. He probably burned her body, but legend soon had it that he had sold her commercially as sausage ("Chicago Sensation" 1897; Woodyard 2013, 172–76; Bielski 2000, 17–19). Later Chicago stories tended to emphasize the accidental inclusion of human meat in sausage, most famously in Upton Sinclair's *The Jungle* in 1906 (93–94). Here we have the ancestor of the modern urban legend of the finger in the can of Diet Coke. The earliest reference I have been able to find to this story (accidental inclusion of human meat) from Britain is from 1868: "By dire mishap his apron got entangled with the chopper, and before help could be obtained, human flesh was mingled with the sausage meat" ("City Scraps" 1868; see also "A horrible story that . . ." 1888). There are some ghastly details here, but note that there is no claim that the meat was *sold*. By 1944 a British newspaper could joke about a thumb in a veal pie, apparently by then a well-known story (Drew 1944).

30. I LOST THE RING HERE

Summary: A poor boy loses a valuable ring in his care. After years away, he returns (wealthy) to the place he lost it and finds the ring immediately. Earliest Attestation: 1861, Britain (but one witness remembers the story being told in the early nineteenth century). Motif: N/A. Secondary Literature: N/A. Compare with: "**Egg Ring**," "**Fish Ring**."

There follows one of several Victorian urban legends about valuable rings:

> A servant boy was sent into the town with a valuable ring. He took it out of its box to admire it, and in passing over a plank bridge he let it fall on a muddy bank. Not being able to find it, he ran away, took to the sea, finally settled in a colony, made a large fortune, came back after many years, and bought the estate on which he had been a servant. One day, while walking over his land with a friend, he came to the plank bridge, and there he told his friend the story. "I could swear," said he, pushing his stick into the mud, "to the very spot on which the ring dropped." When the stick came back, the ring was on the end of it! (De Morgan 1861, 507)

This story had been told to the mathematician Augustus De Morgan (1806–1871) in the early nineteenth century. Indeed, De Morgan wrote of its telling:

> I heard this story when a child, and should certainly have forgotten it, but for a curious illustration which followed of the insensibility of some minds to degrees of probability. A gentleman in company said, "I knew a thing quite as extraordinary as that. A lady of my acquaintance lost her wedding-ring, and could find it nowhere. This was shortly before Twelfth-day: when the cake was cut, she found the ring in the very piece that was cut for her. She had helped her cook to make the cake, and the ring had dropped off her finger." No person in company disputed the second story being as extraordinary as the first; but, young as I was, I could not help dissenting in my own mind. (De Morgan 1861, 507)

The story was alive and well in 1893, when it was published in a Newcastle newspaper. It had been sent in by a "well-known gentleman." Note the accumulation of local details.

> Some years ago ... a youth was employed by a large firm of jewellers in Newcastle. Being highly trustworthy he was commissioned to take a very valuable diamond ring to a lady residing in the vicinity of Gosforth. Being inquisitive, he

looked at the ring near Bulman Bridge, and unfortunately it slipped out of his hands and fell into the stream below. In vain he searched for it. Afraid to face his employers, and not daring to return home, the unfortunate lad went down to the quay and shipped on board an Australian-bound vessel. A long time after, having made his "pile" in the colonies, he returned to the old town. One day whilst out walking with a friend he was seized with an irresistible desire to revisit the scene of the catastrophe. Arrived at the memorable spot, he stood gazing down into the water. "Look here," he said, at last, plunging his cane into the mud, "I feel certain it fell just there." What was his amazement on withdrawing the cane to find the long-lost ring firmly fixed on the end! ("A well-known gentleman . . ." 1893; the story quoted here is from "A remarkable story" 1893, an edited down version)

Subsequent papers copied the story but expressed skepticism ("A Remarkable Story" 1893; another five newspapers in the BNA carried the story, most from Scotland and the northeast of England). Two years later, an almost identical story appeared in British newspapers, only no town was mentioned, and the young man fled to America rather than to Australia ("The Lost Ring" 1895; the BNA has five instances of this narrative in late April 1895).

31. I'M JACK THE RIPPER!

Summary: A prostitute insistently propositions a man in the street only to find out that he is Jack the Ripper. Earliest Attestation: early twentieth century. Motif: N/A. Secondary Literature: N/A.

Perhaps the single greatest challenge with Victorian urban legends is recovering the sexual stories—the "gentleman's jokes" ("The Box Tunnel" 1860)—that circulated but that did not normally make it into the press (see also "**Tunnel Kisses**"; the "**Wrong Bed**"; and the "**Wrong Trousers**"). This is particularly true of the stories about London's prostitutes, who were counted in their tens of thousands yet about whom there are few surviving anecdotes (Mayhew et al. 2005, 10–108; Pearsall 1969, 307–87; Harrison 1979, 217–57). What British publication would have dared to carry them in the later 1800s? I include here an Edwardian narrative—that very possibly had Victorian antecedents—recorded in 1907 and set in New York. It refers to the Jack the Ripper murders, the notorious killings in Whitechapel in 1888, which were remembered for decades in the folklore of the English-speaking world (Opie and Opie 1967, 111 in England; Widdowson 1977, 148 in Newfoundland).

> It is not every man who is as ready as a nimble-witted Englishman whom a woman of forbidding appearance held up in the streets of New York one dark night. She pleaded for assistance. He was not prepared to at a moment's notice in a case of which he knew nothing. Still she pleaded, and still he tried gently to put her off. At last she threatened. "You must give me money," she said, "you shall—or I'll declare that you're Jack the Ripper." He advanced a step towards her. "Madam, I am Jack the Ripper!" he said in a thrilling whisper. She cast her shawl about her face and fled in horror. ("It is not . . ." 1907; a slightly more elaborate version in "A Startling Statement" 1907)

To be clear, a prostitute here is soliciting. Her potential client is not interested, so she threatens to inform the police that he is Jack the Ripper; a strategy that was, in fact, used ("Arrest and Release" 1889). Thus provoked, he gives his memorable Jack answer.

In 1909 an American paper set the story in London ("Outbluffing" 1909). The story was still running in the later 1930s. It was set by a British author in Berkeley Square in the capital.

> During the scare caused by Jack the Ripper, a gentleman was accosted in Berkeley Square by a lady who threatened to inform the police that he was "Jack the Ripper" if he did not furnish cash. "But I am 'Jack the Ripper,'" he answered in a flash, and she fled squealing for her life. (Leslie 1938, 336)

32. IMMURED LOVERS

> Summary: A pair of skeleton lovers are discovered walled up many years after their death. Earliest Attestation: in this form the later nineteenth century. Motif: N/A. Secondary Literature: N/A. Compare with: "Hollow Tree Death" and the "Skeletons That Eloped."

In England in 1862 an architect was tasked with creating a boudoir for an earl's new wife. The architect measures and remeasures the earl's mansion and becomes convinced that there is a hidden room.

The earl at last consented to let the walls be bored, and, when an opening had been made, not only was the room found, but a sight presented itself which almost defeats description. The apartment was fitted up in the richest and most luxurious style of 150 years ago. A quantity of lady's apparel lay about the room, jewels were scattered on the dressing table, and, but for the faded aspect which everything wore the chamber might have been tenanted half an hour previously. On approaching the bed the most curious sight of all was seen, and this it is which affords the only clue to the mystery. The couch held the skeleton of a female, and on the floor underneath the bed, half in and half out, lay another skeleton, that of a man, presenting evident traces of violence, and proving that before he expired in that position, he must have received some dreadful injury. ("Thrilling Discovery" 1862; BNA has 58 instances)

The implication was that a wife and her lover had been caught together, that the lover had been killed, and that the pair, with the wife still alive, were walled up. The story did the rounds of the British newspapers in 1862, with some disagreement about whether the room had been discovered in Cheshire or Kent ("The Late Extraordinary Story" 1862). Within a generation a distorted version of this was reported in a doctoral thesis (Hamilton 1884, 28: "a room was discovered with two skeletons; the one of a female sitting in a chair; the other of a man who had evidently been kneeling before her. There was also a weapon close beside him on the ground"). As it happens skeletons were very rarely found in secret rooms or priest holes in Britain, but in the uncommon instances when they did turn up, they tend to be carefully documented by local historians (in Fea 1901 there are only four: 99—in a wall not a room; 234 Simnel; 235—folklore?; and 261). The 1862 immured lovers appear in no serious historical study.

A similar story arrived from the United States in 1891 and was set in New Mexico. A group of surveyors found a ruined house and, likewise, realized that there was a concealed room.

They made a careful search, and found what was at one time a door, but which had evidently been walled up. They forced entrance, and on the floor of this hidden room lay two skeletons fastened together by an iron chain, the ends of which were bands of iron riveted to their wrists. The bones were those of a man and woman, and the unfortunates had evidently been left to die together a lingering death. The men wondered at the matter, but it was not until after they had left the place that the story was learned. An old Mexican, to whom they related their discovery, said that it explained the disappearance the wife of the owner of the place, who was supposed to have eloped with a young American paramour. The actions of the couple had been such as to cause talk all through the country, and it was evident that the husband had taken vengeance on the pair. ("Chained Together to Die" 1891)

Skeletons in secret rooms had long featured in European literature and traditional lore (e.g., Westwood and Simpson 2005, 591). There was also a large literature on immured nuns and occasionally of immured lovers (Thurston n.d.). But "the Immured Lovers" was a favorite of the later nineteenth century; perhaps even an anemic British imitation of "the Walled-Up Wife" (Dundes 1996). In any case, by the end of century, the lovers had leeched into fiction. Stories include "The Hidden Room" (1894) when a pair of lovers are walled up with a poisonous meal (see also Green 1890, 57; and Squires "Saved by Death" 1898).

33. THE INJURED GAROTTER

Summary: A man is garotted on the street but manages to injure his attacker: this leads to the attacker's identity being revealed. Earliest Attestation: 1862. Motif: N/A. Secondary Literature: N/A. Note: I've preferred "garotte" as opposed to "garrote" or "garrotte" as this was the usual spelling in Victorian Britain when these stories circulated.

In the classic garotte attack, a thief strangles his victim with a cord until he passes out, taking anything valuable on his person. However, the word "garotting" was also more loosely applied, in the mid and later nineteenth century, to any form of mugging. In the winter of 1856/1857 and, then again, in the winter of 1862/1863 London was swept with a garotting panic (Sindall 1987; Adeline 2019, 81 calls it a "spurious crime wave"). Reports of garotting outrages appeared in the newspapers, and fearful accounts started up in the provinces: there was even a rumor that a gang of Cockney garotters had decamped to Cambridge in 1862, leaving the town "at its wit's ends" ("The Garotters" 1862; it would be interesting to trace the panic as it spread from London out into the English counties). Members of the respectable middle classes carried weapons and wore special garotting-proof collars or employed anti-garotting strategies; for instance, carrying an open umbrella on the shoulders to prevent a garotter approaching from behind (Thomas 1862).

To read the newspapers at that time, and to believe them, you would have supposed all London was being strangled by a huge mysterious army of Anglo-Saxon Thugs, who had made a religious vow to murder first—and rob after—every well conducted citizens they could lay their hands upon. ("Letter from London" 1863; the garotting anxiety depended, in part, on stories from earlier in the nineteenth century of thuggee attacks in India, see further Dash 2005)

Yet even in the midst of the panic and particularly in December 1862 the papers acknowledged that the number of attacks had been exaggerated. In fact, many attacks had been invented outright ("False Reports" 1862). It was even whispered—say it quietly—that one newspaper "feeling the effects of full times, rather encouraged the concoction of tales of outrage, for the sake of a good sensation heading in the daily bill of contents" ("From Our London" 1862).

"[T]he most amusing stories" were told in London about the garotting attacks ("From Our London" 1862). Unfortunately, these seem not to have been picked up by the newspapers with the exception of the narrative that I call here the "Injured Garotter."

> A medical student, on his way to an hospital at the east end of London, carried in his hand an operating knife. In one of the narrow streets which he had to traverse he was seized round the throat: but he struck out vigorously, and his assailant dropped. Only waiting to take one look at him for the purpose of identification, he made his way at speed to the hospital, and related his story to his fellow students. Not twenty minutes after his arrival there, a crowd of men and women escorted to the door a respectable carpenter, poor fellow! who had just met with a sad accident at his workshop by "overreaching himself and falling on the edge of one of his tools." The patient was put to bed, and was promptly recognized as the baffled garrotter. No remarks were made on either side, but the police authorities were apprised of the circumstance, and as soon as the recovery of the wounded carpenter is complete, he will be handed over to the police. ("A Garotte Story" 1862; the BNA has eighteen occurrences for Dec 1862)

Another version was brought out earlier and was more frequently published, but was perhaps an adaptation, in pubs, clubs and drawing rooms, of "the carpenter."

> A very timid man, resident in the suburbs, always carried a loaded stick, and is constantly on the look-out. The other night, as he was walking home, near his house a man pushed rudely against him. The timid gentleman, with great presence of mind, immediately struck him a severe blow with the loaded stick, and the man ran off, leaving his hat behind him. The timid man, greatly elated, picked

up the hat, and read on the lining the name of one of his intimate friends. Dreadfully shocked, he at once hastened to his friend's house to explain matters. He was received at the door by his friend's wife, who, in a voice inarticulate with sobs said "Oh, I'm so glad to see you! Poor Edward! In bed upstairs! Covered with blood! He's been garotted!" ("Save Us" 1862; this was very popular in the press, the BNA has 59 occurrences for Dec 1862)

A variant was circulating in late 1863 in which the two friends fighting in the dark accidentally take each other's hats away while injuring each other ("Letter from London" 1863). As to injuries, much was made, in the press, of weapons used to inflict wounds so that garotters could later be recognized. For instance, *The Times* in 1856 described a weapon, for use against garotters, as being of a "very formidable nature, and likely to leave such ugly marks on the garotter as must speedily lead to his detection" (An Anti-Garotter 1856; see also "Garotte and Highway Robbers" 1863). Perhaps the stories above came out of this need to "unmask" the garotter, the terrifying other in our midst?

34. JOLTING THE COFFIN

Summary: A wife is being taken to be buried when her coffin bangs into a branch, and she awakens from a trance; on her second death, her husband warns the bearers not to hit the branch again. Earliest Attestation: eighteenth century. Motif: The closest I have found is: X1663.1(a): "Coffin falls out of hearse; dumps corpse out on ground. Wind fills its lungs with strong, healthy air, and the man revives" (Baughman 1966, 577). Secondary Literature: N/A. Notes: *CW* helped me extensively with this entry.

The story was told in Bolton-Le-Moors (Lancashire). An unpleasant wife died. Her husband paid for her funeral, but on the way to the graveyard, the coffin was jolted, and the woman was woken out of her "dream of death": she had been in a cataleptic trance. When, some years later, the wife died, the husband warned his neighbors not to jolt the coffin again.

A scolding wife so long a sleep possess'd / Her spouse presum'd her soul was now at rest; / Tom West was call'd to hang the room with black, / And all their cheer was sugar, rolls and sack. / Two mourning staffs stood sentry at the door, / And silence reign'd, who ne'er was there before; / The cloaks, and tears, and handkerchiefs prepar'd. / They march'd in pomp to Bowton Owd Churchyard; / The very dead can't pass in quiet home; / By some rude jolt the coffin lid was broke, / And madam from her dream of death awoke. / Now was all spoil'd; the undertaker's pay. / Sour faces, cakes and wine, quite thrown away. / But some years after, when the former scene / Was acted, and the coffin nail'd again, / The tender husband took especial care / To keep the passage from disturbance clear; / Charging the bearers that they tread aright, / Nor put his dead in such another fright. (H. J. O. 1891; this poem is adapted from an eighteenth-century poem: "Mulieri ne crede, ne mortuae quidem," T. G. 1735, 169)

Here is an equivalent story from late Victorian Scotland:

A Scotch Laird's wife apparently died, and was being carried, shoulder high, to her grave. On their way to the churchyard the bearers passed under a large tree, and the coffin came in contact with an overhanging bough, which pushed it off the poles, and it fell to the ground with a shock that burst it open, and revived its occupant. I am not sure whether or not the lady told her husband that she was his "dear wife," and that he was "not to be alarmed," but she went home with him, and they lived together for several years. When she died again, and the bearers were about to carry her to her grave, her disconsolate husband went up to them, and in a most impressive manner said, "Noo, for guidsake, keep clear o' yon tree this time!" (A Scotch Laird's Wife" 1881)

Other versions are set in Picardy (the woman is woken by thorns in a hedge, "Matrimony" 1818); or St. Louis (US) where an Irishman "died" (reversing the typical pattern) and on the second attempt to bury him his wife shouts out of the carriage window: "For the hope o' glory go aisy, man, or ye'll have him awake agin a'ready" ("During the Cholera . . ." 1862). The story was common enough in Victorian Britain that in 1892 a journalist talked of the version "usually current": "a hearse . . . a coffin, and a tree against which the carriage was run" ("Noteworthy" 1892). The story was told as recently as the 1980s in Appalachia (Jones and Wheeler, 1987, 76), and it can be traced back as far as the early 1700s in the United Kingdom (T. G. 1735, 169).

35. THE JUDGE AND THE FOREMAN

> Summary: A jury acquits a man who seems guilty; when the judge asks why, the foreman admits that he was the murderer. Earliest Attestation: 1763. Motif: N/A. Secondary Literature: N/A. Thanks to Roberto Labanti for help with this entry.

The following letter, by one P. E. A., appeared in *Notes and Queries* in 1862:

> A Strange Story: The following was told me the other day. Can any of your readers vouch for the correctness, and let me know when it occurred? During the assizes at Exeter (?) Judge Bolland presided at a trial for murder. The evidence left no doubt as to the guilt of the man in the dock. To the astonishment of everybody the jury acquitted him. That night the judge was dining alone; a man who wished to see him was admitted. "I am going to tell you something which I wish you not to reveal for three days." The judge agreed to this. "Well, sir," he continued, "I am the man who committed the murder. It was not the man who was tried this morning. I was foreman of the jury, and from knowing all the circumstances of the case, I pointed out to the jury various discrepancies in the evidence, and got them to bring in a verdict of not guilty. Tomorrow I leave for America, but [I] make this confession to you in case anybody else should be charged with the murder." He was not heard of again (P. E. A. 1862)

The story had been traditionally told—as one reader of *Notes and Queries* recalled (Marshall 1862; see also Matthews 1862)—of the Elizabethan judge Sir James Dyer (1510–1582; Baker 2008). In fact, a long and elaborate version of this narrative appeared in the *Gentleman's Magazine* in 1763, and the story in this form may be a good deal older (D.H. 1763; see also "In the Reign of Queen Elizabeth" 1763). In the longer version there was no "America" and the foreman explained that he had killed the man in self-defense: the judge promised not to tell the story until after the man's death. Despite its length the elaborate version was printed intermittently in the press for the next century: the BNA has examples for 1785, 1796, 1806, 1824, and 1869.

The reference in P. E. A.'s 1862 note to Judge Bolland—Baron Bolland, an early nineteenth-century judge, obit 1840 (Turner 1903, 109; judge 1829–1839, Foss 1848–1864, IX, 148)—suggests that the story had some kind of oral circulation in the midnineteenth century (Marshall 1862 points out that a short, modernized version of the Dyer story had appeared in "English and Irish Juries" 1862, 422–24). Another short version, based in part on the *Notes and Queries* exemplar, appeared in 1883 in the British press: a rather cumbersome yarn had been reduced to its pithy essence ("The following strange story" 1883). Sir James Dyce [*sic*] was now named, the meeting took place in the judge's chamber (at Exeter), and the detail about America was anachronistically retained. That version of the "Judge and the Foreman" then appeared in the American press in 1890 ("The Murderer," *CW*). The story presumably had little potential for circulation outside Common Law countries.

36. THE LADY AND THE RING

Summary: A woman falls into a trance and is buried; she awakes when a robber—often a sexton—tries to cut off her valuable ring. Earliest Attestation: early modern period, origins perhaps Germany. Motif: N/A. Secondary Literature: Bondeson 2001, 39–46; Bolte 1910, 356–65. Compare with: "**Buried Alive**" and "**Jolting the Coffin**."

It "is one of those traditions that seem to be scattered in widely separated localities, like wind-blown seed, readily finding congenial soil" (Axon 1881, 519). Yet it has never been classified with a folklore motif, or, to the best of my knowledge, been systematically investigated by folklorists (we do have the writings of historians: Bondeson 2001, 39–46; Bolte 1910, 356–65). A wife is buried with a ring, either because she is fond of it or because the ring cannot be removed from her swollen finger. A thief decides to steal the ring and, in the night, goes to her tomb. To remove the ring, he uses a knife, but in cutting at the finger, he awakens the woman: she was not actually dead! The thief flees terrified, and the woman stumbles out of her coffin and returns home. On knocking at the door, she is greeted first with horror and then with delight. She lives for many years after her "death": in some cases, "post-mortem" children are reported. One example from the many:

> There is a well known but by no means authenticated story of a thief who broke into a vault to rob a corpse of the costly jewels that had been buried with it. The pearls were taken from the neck, the diamond drops from the ears, and the rings

from the fingers—all save one that could not pass the joint. The thief drew his knife and cut off the finger. The cut awoke the lady from her trance: she started up with a scream, and so terrified the rascal that he turned to fly. ("Chit-Chat" 1861)[19]

The "Lady and the Ring" is, in narrative terms, remarkably stable. The most important changes involve the thief. His actions on discovering the woman vary. Usually (as here) he runs away (e.g., H. G. 1856, 94; H. W. R. 1891); in other cases, he stops to help the woman (e.g., Walker 1885, 139); he sometimes kills her (Bondeson 2001, 45 on Scandinavian versions where the robbers are "made of sterner stuff"); while in one particularly pleasing case he dies on the spot: "Thus death had her prey; there was but a change of victims" ("Burying Alive" 1834).

The earliest recorded version of the legend dates to 1499 and Germany, where the narrative became common (Bolte 1910, 356–57 and 363: "Ferner liegen Varianten unserer Sage vor aus Dresden, Laibach, Magdeburg, Altenburg, Hamburg, Danzig, Thorn, Glückstadt, Lübeck, Dünkirchen, Aachen, Bolkenhain, aus dem Yogelsberg, aus Nürnberg, Schweinfurt, Memmiugen, Regensburg, Freiburg . . ."; Calmet 1759, 277–78, Cologne; Hartmann 1895, 17, Salzburg). Bondeson (2001, 46) believes the story is German in origin: "It spread from fifteenth-century Germany to become well known, with different names and dates attached, in almost every European country." But the story is found all over northern Europe: it is perhaps the twin of a southern European story where carnal relations reawaken a sleeping corpse: the most famous example is the fourth story of the tenth day of the *Decameron*. The story appeared in France (Bolte 1910, 364; Hartmann 1895, 24; "Premature Internments" 1850, Poitiers; "Burying Alive" 1834, Toulouse), Scandinavia (Bondeson 2001, 45), and even crossed the Atlantic to the New World (Bondeson 2001, 45, Nova Scotia).

The "Lady and the Ring" also appeared in Britain and Ireland, and there were, in the later nineteenth century, various, rather half-hearted attempts to collate the different versions ("Parallel Stories" 1873, 572: "Of dead-alive ladies brought to consciousness by sacrilegious robbers, covetous of the rings upon their cold fingers, no less than seven stories, differing but slightly from each other, have been preserved: in one the scene is laid in Halifax; in another, in Gloucestershire; in a third, in Somersetshire; in the fourth, in Drogheda; the remaining three being appropriated by as many towns in Germany." See also Young [1875, 42–48] with special reference to the Edgcumbe family, with whom Young had contacts.)

There follows my attempt to list the British and Irish instances of the legend. There is a version from Aberdeenshire (Inverurie, "A Remarkable Incident" 4 Oct 1888); from County Armagh (Bondeson 2001, 45, on the woman's gravestone, "Marjorie McCall—lived once, buried twice"); from Bedfordshire

Figure 11 Town (1930).

(Bletsoe, Hurst 1878, 25–43 and the St. John family see further "Literary Notice"; Pickford, 1882); from Berwickshire (Chirnside, "A Remarkable Incident—Is It True" 1888; Todd 1835, 505, *CW*); from County Cork (Ballymodan; *Notes* 1874, 49); from Cornwall (Lady Edgcumbe; Bray 1853, 449–50; Frost 1882; Bondeson 2001, 41–43); from Derbyshire (Longstone family; Axon 1881, 519); from Devon (?, source a Devonshire servant; C. L. 1882: "upwards of fifty years ago by my nurse, a Devonshire woman, one of the old class of servants, unable to read or write, and who must therefore have acquired the tale orally"); from London (Cripplegate; H. G. 1856, 94–95); from Gloucestershire (Woodley Hall; Abhba 1855, a locket not a ring); from County Louth (Drogheda; Abhba 1855, a woman named Hardman); from the North Riding (Hutton Rudby; H. W. R. 1891); from Somerset (Watchet; Tripp 1882; S. A. S. 1855); from the West Riding (Halifax; Walker 1885, 137–42; Martin 1855); and at an unspecified location a story about the Countess of Bridgewater (Drysdale 1887, 413); and another about a Miss Killigrew (discussed over dinner in 1803; Frances 1864, 1–2 at 2: "A maid who belonged to Mrs. Killigrew, after her death lived with Mrs. Walters, grandmother to the Grimstones: from her they had this story"). There will, of course, be many more.

The story is frequently claimed to be "true." This is perhaps particularly the case with the British versions, which tend to be set in the relatively recent past. The story is almost always pushed back two or three generations; its connection with the present, kept by that most fallible thing, "living memory." The only "contemporary" case of the "Lady and the Ring" known to me in English is an

1880 short story based on the legend ("Mrs. Fitzpatrick's Diamond Ring" 1880 set in Warwickshire; see also, for a story with some common points, "Bernard Wren's Yarns" 1888, Cork, *CW*).

The curious visit the gravestone of the woman who survived (H.G. 1856, 94; Calmet 1759, 278; "A Remarkable Incident" 4 Oct 1888; the marked grave is particularly common in the German versions, Bolte 1910, 357–59). Story-tellers recall their connection, through a relative or an elder neighbor or a servant of the family, with the protagonists of the story (Walker 1885, 140; "A Remarkable Incident" 4 Oct 1888; H.W.R. 1891; Frances 1864, 1–2). Then there are the shrill assertions of authenticity: "The foregoing narrative ... is founded on an actual occurrence ..." ("Mrs. Fitzpatrick's Diamond Ring" 1880, 528); "It is impossible to disbelieve a story, so circumstantially told ..." (Walker 1885, 140). Perhaps what we see here are genuine examples of "**Buried Alive**," having the "Lady and the Ring" foisted on them. A living woman is accidentally put into a coffin, and the community is so shocked by her coming back to life that the "Lady and the Ring" narrative is attached to give a little more romance to the remarkable event.

When people knew one version and then encountered others, there were sometimes problems in terms of belief. "The existence of a score of parallel legends is ... 'unfortunate for the story'" (Axon 1881, 519; the quotation within the quote is from Reisbeck). One Scottish correspondent, for instance, was shocked to hear that a second "Lady and the Ring" existed and confessed: "I was telling the story to a friend the other day as an undoubted fact" and went on to hope that her friend did not discover the alternative version and think her a liar ("A Remarkable Incident" 4 Oct 1888). Julian Charles Young, on being confronted with several versions, wrote: "It is possible that there may be foundation for" all the stories. Or, he considered, only one might be true "and that through lapse of time, error of memory, and diversity of narration, the story may have been applied to the wrong persons" (Young 1875, 48 and, on the same page, "Of one fact I have long been convinced, viz., that there is no task more difficult than that of substantiating a sensational story which has obtained general circulation, even though told by the most veracious lips.") Others, meanwhile, were entirely unworried by the existence of a story of "nearly similar character" and took both or a series as being true ("Premature Internments" 1850; see Axon's comments 1881, 518).

37. THE LAWYER AND THE POISONED CAKES

Summary: A lawyer proves his client is innocent by eating her poisoned cakes and then discreetly taking an antidote. Earliest Attestation: based on a real event in 1842. Motif: N/A. Secondary Literature: N/A.

In 1875 (and again in 1886) several British newspapers offered this gem.

> The following extraordinary story is told of a Chicago counsel: Mr. Van Arman was engaged to defend a woman who had caused the death of her husband by administering a poisoned cake. He swallowed a piece of the cake as a proof of the innocence of his client. Immediately afterwards a telegram was brought to him announcing the sudden illness of his wife. He obtained permission to leave the court for five minutes to answer the message. On his return he finished his speech for the defence, and obtained a verdict of acquittal. It transpired afterwards that the dispatch received was a false one, and that his temporary absence was employed swallowing an antidote and getting rid of the effect of his dangerous meal. The truth was known too late for the Court of Assizes to reconsider its judgment. The counsel, whose zeal outran his discretion, has gained great éclat by his desperate act. ("A Wonderful Story" 1875, in 1875 24, and in 1886 two newspapers in the BNA gave this account)

In 1891 the story reappeared in Britain in a slightly different form. Van Arman was now an unnamed "quick-witted and daring Western lawyer," and instead of a telegram, the lawyer made "a bee-line for an adjoining room, where he had an emetic in readiness and an antidote" ("A quick witted . . ." 1891; three records in the BNA). By 1893, in a New Zealand paper, the hero was "a famous criminal lawyer in Southern Michigan . . . M'Sweeney" who used a stomach pump ("A well-known Kansas citizen . . ." 1893, *CW*).

This is, pleasingly, an urban legend based squarely on a real event. Van Arman gave the "real facts of the story for the first time," in 1877.

> It was in 1842. I was then twenty-two years old, and had been admitted to the bar two years, and was in partnership with Attorney Brown, at Marshall, Michigan. A woman had been indicted at Hillsdale for poisoning her husband. He lived more than a year after the poisoning, and, of course, she could not be indicted for murder; yet giving poison was a penitentiary offence—amounting to a life

sentence—and I was engaged to defend her. The woman's husband was a witness against her.... It was proven on the trial that the husband had eaten a cake in which arsenic had been put, and the chemist testified that one grain was a fatal dose. Well, I took the chemist, judge and jury to a bakery, and had the baker mix a cake in their presence, and put in two grains of arsenic, and bake the cake while they looked on. When done it was brought to the court by the judge. I began by saying that the celebrated chemist had sworn that one grain of arsenic would produce death. In this cake were two grains, a fact which judge, jury and chemist acknowledged. I thereupon ate the cake, after which I began my address to the jury and spoke for three hours, at the end of which time I drew their attention to the fact that I was not dead yet and demanded the acquittal of my client, which the jury did without leaving their seats. ("Taking Arsenic" 1877, 144)

And how did he do it? "Oh ... at that time I was used to eating from six to seven grains of arsenic without feeling the worse for it" ("Taking Arsenic" 1877, 144).

38. THE LONG PACK

Summary: A thief is brought into a house in a "long pack": a bullet into the pack finishes the plans of a local band to raid the house during the night. Earliest Attestation: eighteenth century (associated particularly with the Borders). Motif: N/A. Secondary Literature: N/A. Notes: I thank *PB* for introducing me to this story.

There are, as we shall see, a number of versions of the "Long Pack" recorded in nineteenth-century Britain and the United States. Here is one set in Ohio in 1869:

A travelling pedlar going his rounds near Cincinnati last month, presented himself about nightfall at a farmhouse, and asked shelter for the night. The farmer was absent, and the servant refused to admit the stranger, who then asked if he might leave his pack, and call for it on the morrow, alleging that he was wearied out, and could not carry the load any further. This request was granted, and a great pack, which contained his wares was deposited in an outhouse for the night. Fortunately, however, the farm girls, instigated by curiosity, like true daughters of Eve, resolved to see what the pack contained, and greatly to their consternation found that it was a living man. They had the wit to retreat without betraying their discovery, and alarmed the men. The latter, armed with six-shooters, soon riddled the pack and its contents with a general discharge of bullets. A frightful cry proceeded from the pack and a man armed with a bowie knife cut his way out of it, and rolled out covered with blood into the midst of his assailants. Another shot or two finished him, and upon examining his person he was recognised as a miscreant murderer who had long been the terror of the country, and had committed innumerable murders and outrages for some time past. ("A Sensation Story" 1869)

This Ohio story has two of the three elements usually found in the Long Pack. There is (i) the pedlar who leaves the pack; (ii) the discovery and the shot into the pack—writers almost always make a good deal of the blood seeping out. In most versions, the "murderer" is the "inside man" who will open up the house to a larger band of crooks: he often has a whistle (as well as various weapons) with him ("Old Stories" 1863, 266; Bailey 1874, 264). The story typically ends with (iii) the occupants of the house scaring the band away.

The earliest version of the "Long Pack" known to me is a short story written by James Hogg (1770–1835) and published as a chapbook in 1817. The story is set sometime after 1723 in Northumberland, and the narrator claims that he learned the narrative from the man who had, as a young servant, taken the shot: "I have often stood at his knee, and listened with wonder and amazement to his stories of battles and sieges, but none of them ever please me better than that of the long pack" (Hogg 1817, 24; note that Hogg later reprinted the fiction in his *Winter Evening Tales*, 1820, I, 134–44). The story was known as—and Hogg adopts the term—the "Long Pack" or the "Lang Pack," and we have respected his choice here. Hogg probably had the story ultimately from Bellingham (Northumberland)—about sixty miles away from his home at Ettrick. The "Long Pack" had, according to Richardson, writing in 1846, "an almost unexampled popularity in the north of England" (Richardson, 1841–1846, III, 11; I'd take this to be "the north-east" of England; I have never come across this story or anything like it in the northwest). An 1864 guide book notes that two Bellingham houses "dispute" the legend; that is, the legend was set in both (*A Handbook* 1864, 259).[20] In 1934 John Rentilson visited Bellingham and wrote up the story for the *Jedburgh Gazette*: Jedburgh is some thirty miles to the north of Bellingham, just across the border, in Scotland. His account is interesting because he notes that when young, "at the jail gates," he and his friends had listened to "stories about ghosts, witches and warlocks."

Figure 12 Frontispiece from [Hogg], *The Long Pack* (1840).

"The Lang Pack" was one our favourite yarns, and as it was told we used to huddle closer together, expecting some spectre to spring up at any moment. (Rentilson 1934)

I have not been able to establish Rentilson's age, but to judge by some incidental comments, he and his friends perhaps listened to the Long Pack in the late 1800s (Rentilson 1934, many of his "old cronies" had died by the time of publication).

Several subsequent versions of the story show their debt to these early sources from the Scottish-English border. Indeed, these debts can often be tracked to textual details. For example, Hogg's three servant heroes were Alice, Edward, and Richard: in an 1890 American version of the story they are Alice, Edward, and Pedro ("The Peddler's Ruse" 1900). In a particularly enjoyable mangling of tradition, a Dutch writer sets the story in a village named Long Park: here Long Pack had been mistranscribed *and* misunderstood ("Onder de inbrekers" 1885, *PB*)!

The story itself appears in the press in the last third of the nineteenth century, though the Ohio news report above is, to the best of my knowledge, unique. Usually, it appears in short stories or folklore reflections. In 1863 the Long Pack appeared in *Chambers's Journal*: "Whereas the hundred-and-one big books read but lately have passed away and left no impress, here come these old stories back as I heard them in days gone by, when I was young…" ("Old Stories" 1863). The story is set at an undisclosed location in Britain. In 1874 Henry D. B. Bailey claimed that the narrative was told about a house in New York (Bailey 1874, 259–65). In 1877 it appeared in a collection of burglar stories by one Frederick Arnold: this time the pedlar called on a Yorkshire farmhouse (Arnold 1877, 313–27). In 1892 a nurse tells of her experience with the pedlar to her young charges (Hardy 1892). In 1899 Herbert Russell used the "Long Pack" for his serialized story "An Idol of Clay" set near Guildford (Russell 1899). In 1900 the story was set in Illinois ("The Peddler's Ruse" 1900).

The narrative does not appear in Baughman (1966). Indeed, it has not been given a motif number, and in English folklore collections I only know a short entry in *Lore of the Land* (Westwood and Simpson 2005, 557–58). But the "Long Pack" was, on the evidence given above, well known in parts of the Borders and perhaps further afield. It was so well known, in fact, that some authors toyed with the story and their readers' expectations. In an 1892 version a pedlar leaves a heavy pack in a man's house. It transpires that the pack is full of stolen treasure; the pedlar was attempting to frame the man ("A Roadside Romance" 1891). In 1894 a British newspaper published an American story set at a tavern called the "Long Pack" in California. An embittered innkeeper agrees to look after a pedlar's pack. The pack moves and the innkeeper prepares to shoot it, but on opening the pack he discovers his granddaughter, the child of an estranged daughter ("The Innkeeper's Ghost" 1894). There are related stories: for instance, a sea captain takes on board a merchant and his wax figures—actually pirates ready to take possession of the ship ("The following strange story…" 1829, *CW*; I am reminded of the thieves brought in oil jars into Ali Baba's house.)

39. MESSAGE IN A HAT

Summary: A woman meets her future husband by placing a secret message in something she has made and that will be sold on. Earliest Attestation: 1871 (US) although one of the versions from that year is a play on the story—"an old trick"—that suggests that it dates back still further. Motif: N/A. Secondary Literature: N/A. Notes: *CW* provided the US originals of these stories.

In 1871 the following story appeared about a young woman in Norwalk (Massachusetts) who was employed

> as a hat trimmer in a manufactory of that city. One day being more than usually disgusted with her tedious and prosaic occupation, on the impulse of the moment she wrote her name and address upon the lining of a hat which she had finished, and patiently awaited the result. The hat with hundreds of others, was sent off to the "trade," and finally purchased by a young New Yorker, who chanced to discover the name upon the lining. Being of a romantic turn of mind, he wrote to the young lady, an intimacy followed, and the result was the marriage of the two last week. ("The South Norwalk Sentinel..." 1871)

This was apparently a common story on the East Coast in the later nineteenth century. In 1886 a hat trimmer pasted her address into a hat in Danbury (Connecticut) and ended up marrying a New Orleans merchant ("Romantic, if True" 1886).

Then there is a story that subverts the original:

> This is an old trick, played by several of our girls, one of whom in particular had an eventful experience. She stitched her name inside the lining of a hat beside the statement: "I am thine; wilt thou be mine?" and sent it adrift. After various vicissitudes, it was purchased by a gentleman, and took a position on his head. One day the lining became loose, and in endeavoring to fasten it his eyes rested on the sentiment and name. When Martha returned to her home that day, she was taken to a retired part of the cottage and warmed up with a strap. The gentleman who got that hat was her father. ("The Danbury News..." 1871)

This unromantic story (but one that depends on an even greater coincidence) is a reminder why there are unlikely to have been many messages in hats with addresses: managers and family would have violently disapproved of this kind of behavior on the part of young women.

CW has brought to my attention other stories of this type including a school teacher from Maine who wrote her name on an egg and got married to the purchaser ("An Egg" 1890; "What an Egg" 1891). There is also a saccharine narrative about a girl who knit gloves and who left a message in a pair asking for a wax doll for Christmas; the present, of course, arrived ("Cora" 1880). A later short story, dating from the First World War, has a young girl make fudge for American soldiers. She includes her name and address with inevitable consequences (Douglas 1914; this perhaps came from a British source; or possibly it is set in the American Civil War, there is a reference to "three years").

The Norwalk story circulated in Britain ("A Romantic Story" 1871; "Romantic if True" 1886), but I have, to date, found no story set in the United Kingdom. The story very likely originated in pre-Fordist America where girls working on manufacturing lines got bored—note the reference to the heroine's "tedious and prosaic occupation"—and, consequently, dreamed ("The South Norwalk Sentinel..." 1871).

40. A MILLION POSTAGE STAMPS

Summary: Members of the public are persuaded to collect hundreds of thousands of used stamps for various causes. Earliest Attestation: 1849. Motif: N/A. Secondary Literature: N/A.

In 1840 Britain released the first postage stamp, an innovation that spread quickly around the globe. An urban legend about postage stamps seems to have been told within a very few years of the stamp's arrival. In 1849 there was a bride whose "DRACO of a papa will not let her marry until she has collected a million postage stamps" ("Fashionable Hobbies" 1849). Apparently, in that year, you could "hardly step into a drawing-room without being stopped for old postage-stamps" ("Fashionable Hobbies" 1849). By 1857 the backstory had developed.

> I heard at the time that some person had found out a way to clear the red from the old stamps,[21] and to put some fresh adhesive gum on their backs, and sell them as new, by which of course a very large profit was made. Being unable to get enough in any ordinary way, he hit on the plan of circulating a story that a young man of inferior fortune had fallen in love with a lady whose father would not consent to the match unless she collected a million of old postage heads. Many

sympathisers were found to save all they could, and to forward them: but the ruse was suspected and the obliterating stamp changed, and the robbery on the revenue was put a stop to. (A. A. 1857; this *might* be our earliest evidence for a British chain letter: much depends on how "circulating a story" is construed)

The story of the million postage stamps returned in the 1850s, in an entirely different guise—philanthropy. The first clue we have that something charitable was afoot comes in the review *Notes and Queries*, in July of 1857: a reader wrote in to ask whether it was true that Christ Church Hospital would give free treatment in exchange for a million stamps ("Antiquary cannot..." 1857). Then two months later the same review published the following query:

> A number of persons are collecting old postage stamps, under the idea that they will be able, by presenting them, to gain admission for a child to some benevolent institution. None seem to know what institution; can any of your correspondents inform me? (A. B. M. 1857)

The answers sent in to the review show that committees had been founded, that vicars had been preaching to congregations and that the well-intentioned had gone door to door, all to encourage the collection of used stamps (M. C. 1857). The problem with the million-stamp story is that no one could explain "what marketable or persuasive value a million [stamps] could have" (Harlow 1940, 88; a point also made forcefully by Laughton 1898; one theory was that they were for papering rooms, "Fashionable Hobbies" 1849). Nevertheless, the names of various charitable institutions and wealthy individuals were bandied around. So enthusiastic did the public become that one of these, Miss Burdett Coutts, made an unprecedented statement via the newspapers that she was *not* asking for stamps to be collected on her behalf ("Miss Burdett Coutts and the Million" 1858; see also "Queer Hoaxes" 1858, 454: *Notes and Queries* offered an apology for using her name in connection with stamp collection, "Miss Burdett Coutts does..." 1859).

Notes and Queries opined: "It is to be hoped that the paragraph on the collection of postage stamps in the Report of the Postmaster-General which has just been published will put a stop to the folly" ("Miss Burdett Coutts does..." 1859). Yet, of course, the "folly" continued. In 1860 a group of friends in Yorkshire started collecting a million stamps because they had been told that the British state would pay thirty pounds and papier maché factories forty for that number (Veritas 1860: for its use in the early 1860s see Laughton 1898, 425). Then the stamp-collecting folly traveled abroad: an Englishman was said to be prepared to give a fortune to a German orphan if only the Englishman was

Figure 13 Portrait of Edna Brown, (source 'Millions of Letters' 1895).

given a million stamps; in Belgium the stamps were to fund missionaries to the Congo (Germany, "Queer Hoaxes" 1858, 455, see also "An Old Hoax" 1890; Belgium, Laughton 1898; an exported British urban legend?)

By the 1890s the million-stamp story was an established part of the canon of Victorian legends. One Irish journalist referred to it as an "old hoax" in 1890. However, it was about to get a fresh burst of life thanks to the "chain" or "snowball" letters, which took off in that decade. In September 1894, a young American woman, Edna Brown, resident in Kaneville, Illinois (population one hundred), sent out a letter about a neighbor. This is one of the many copies of that letter printed in the American and British press.

> A medical institution has offered to treat a young lady of Kaneville who has been a cripple since she was six years of age, if she could collect one million canceled postage stamps, so we have started this chain of letters, in which we ask your aid. Make three copies of this letter as I have done, only change the date and put the next highest number on the top, numbering the three the same, and sign your name. Return this letter, with ten or, more canceled stamps, to Edna R. Brown, Kaneville, Kane county, Illinois. Also the names and addresses of the three to whom you have written. They, in turn, are asked to do the same. Any one receiving No. 60 will please return the letter without making copies, as that ends the chain. Any one not wishing to write three letters is asked to return this letter to

Miss Brown, that we may know that the chain is broken. Although this may seem a small matter, yet any one breaking the chain will involve serious loss to the enterprise. Yours sincerely. ("The Innocent Letter" 1895)[22]

Replies flooded in from "Russia, Germany, Denmark, Holland, Italy, Spain, India, China, Japan, South and Central America, and especially England and Scotland" ("The American Chain Letter" 1895). So serious did the situation become in the English middle classes that one furious father wrote to a newspaper about how his daughters had received two letters from Miss Brown in a day:

> I think it is high time to caution a confiding public against the latest example of the hydra-headed begging letter which is going the round of English country houses and imposing on the good nature of our philanthropic but generally unmathematical daughters. (Pater Filiarum 1895)

By 1895, 6000 letters a day were being delivered to the hamlet of Kaneville, and by the fall of that year 2,000,000 letters and some 30,000,000 stamps had been received ("The American Chain Letter" 1895; "Millions of Letters" 1895, *CW*). A similar chain letter, sent to fund a hospital in New South Wales, was started in 1896 by one Audrey Griffin. The bulk of letters in Sydney proved so great that by 1902 it had led to a change in Australian postal policy ("Snowball" 1906).

Did either of these schemes make any money for the causes they were supporting? One American report claims that Edna Brown in Kaneville had saved 200 dollars from her scheme, for her lame friend—not much, although she did allegedly marry her friend's brother, so there was a consolation ("The American Chain Letter" 1895; other sources talked of much more money "A Clever Swindle" 1895.) If we can believe the figure of thirty million stamps—and I would recommend *extreme* skepticism—then the real amount of money might have been higher. Rare stamps could be sold on to collectors (Harlow 1940, 88–97; see particularly his point on 89: "by 1873 the older and rarer stamps were becoming sufficiently valuable to make the stunt [of gathering a million stamps] more plausible"). But, surely, even four hundred or six hundred dollars was not enough to justify opening two million envelopes?

This has always been the problem with the million-stamps story. The original narrative of the confidence trickster claiming he needed a million stamps to satisfy a weird father-in-law (or a bride her father) just about worked. But why did Christ's Church Hospital or, for that matter, anyone else want what amounted to hundreds of thousands of "bits of dirty paper" (Laughton 1898)? We must hope that, as the sacks full of letters were brought to their doors, Edna Brown and Audrey Griffin came up with a satisfactory answer to that question.

41. THE MISTLETOE BRIDE

Summary: A bride, during a wedding game of hide and seek, closes herself in a self-locking chest. She is not found. The chest is only opened a generation later, when her skeleton is discovered. Earliest Attestation: 1809. Motif: related but distant types include K1555.0.1; "Dying woman lures paramour into chest; Asks husband to bury chest with her"; S12:1: "Murder by slamming down chest-lid: Done while victim is looking into the chest." Secondary Literature: Westwood and Simpson 2005, 302–3; Bishop and Roud 2012, 308–10, 489–90.

It is the most claustrophobic of all British legends:

> that of a bride who, in a game of hide and seek concealed herself in a chest and was never found. Many years afterwards the chest was opened and disclosed the remains of the bride herself, her wedding dress and her wreath. (Lambert 1922)

The story is associated with several British manor houses: six is the number normally given. "That such an accident should happen twice," commented one author, "is exceedingly unlikely. But six times! No! Utterly incredible!" (Jaggard 1944). Its name—the "Mistletoe Bride"—comes from a famous song "The Mistletoe Bough," which was a favorite of carol singers in the nineteenth and early twentieth century: "in the southern shires" (Forman 1924, 273); "it is familiar to every town and village at Christmas, when it inevitably takes it places in the repertoire of 'the waits' among the more ancient hymns and carols" (Forman 1924, 273). The song itself, by Thomas Bayly, can be traced back no further than 1828 (Bishop and Roud 2012, 308–10, 489–90 date it to the early 1830s, according to Forman 1924, 198. It appeared in a song set: "The copy of this publication in the British Museum is dated from Bath, June 1, 1828.").

> "I'm weary of dancing now," [the bride of Lord Lovell] cried, / "Here, tarry a moment, I'll hide, I'll hide; / And Lovell, be sure thou'rt the first to trace / The clue to my secret hiding place." / Away she ran and her friends began / Each tower to search, each nook to scan; / And young Lovell cried, "Oh, where doest thou hide? / I am lonely without thee, my own dear bride." / … They sought her that night and they sought her next day, / They sought her in vain till a week passed away; / In the highest, the lowest, the loneliest spot, / Young Lovell sought wildly but found her not. / Then years flew by, and their grief at last / Was told as a sorrowful tale of the past; / And when Lovell appeared the children cried: / "See the old

Figure 14 The chest and its victim's portrait hanging above, Rogers, *Italy*, 96. 'Alone [the portrait] hangs/ Over a mouldering heir-loom, its companion,/ An oaken-chest, half-eaten by the worm,/ But richly carved by Antony of Trent/ With scripture-stories from the Life of Christ.'

man weeps for his fairy bride. . . . / At length an old chest that had long lain hid / Was found in the castle; they raised the lid, / And a skeleton form lay mouldering there, / In the bridal wreath of that lady fair." (Bishop and Roud 2012, 309)

There are, though, earlier references in prose. In 1823 Samuel Rogers had put the story to verse and set it in Italy—Rogers's poem may have been the inspiration for Bayly (Bishop and Roud 2012, 489). In Rogers's 1830 edition he admitted: "This story is, I believe, founded on fact; although the time and place are uncertain. Many old houses in England lay claim to it" (259). Rogers is clear, too, that the story is *not* based on an Italian source: "Except in this instance and another ... I have everywhere followed history or tradition; and I would here disburden my conscience in pointing out these exceptions ..." (1830, 259). The narrative also appeared in the theater. In 1829 a British author, while commenting on a play entitled *The Spring Lock*, recalled a legend that he and his audience were evidently familiar with:

> that awful story of a young girl having concealed herself in a chest, or cabinet, which fastened by a secret spring; the chest, and the room in which it was lodged, being known only to herself. One hundred years afterwards the deserted chamber being discovered, and the chest broken open, a skeleton appeared: a melancholy commentary upon the legend of the lost girl, suggesting also a train of reflections from which the heart recoils, as when in a dream we are forcibly detained upon a crumbling precipice. ("Theatrical Examiner" 1829)

Note that a play *The Mistletoe Bough*, "taken from an old ballad," appeared in 1834 ("Greenwich Fair" 1834).

The earliest version of the Mistletoe Bride known to me dates to 1809 and is set, by a British journalist, in Germany ("A Melancholy Occurrence" 1809; David Emery tracked down this reference, www.liveabout.com/bride-and-seek-the-missing-bride-3299076 [accessed 1 Oct 2020]).

42. A MODERN JONAH!

Summary: A man is swallowed by a whale and survives. Earliest Attestation: antiquity. Motif: See folklore types: X1723.1.2 Lie: man swallowed by fish and later rescued alive; AT 1889G—man swallowed by fish. Baughman 1966, 579–80 gives a series of humorous American versions of X1723.1.2. Objects found in the fish's belly include an old lady rocking on her rocking chair and a New York brass band. Secondary Literature: Davis 1991; Ziolkowsk 2007, 65–92. Notes: I thank *DE* for help with this story.

Jonah, it is well known, was hurled into the sea and swallowed by a great fish, surviving in the animal's belly for three days. This attractive story had little science to recommend it. Of the great sea "fish," only the sperm whale has a gullet large enough to swallow a human being whole; and the person would not survive the experience (Davis 1947, for 1893 or 1894). But the story did have Biblical authority and it is hardly surprising that not only were there literary and folklore Jonahs (Ziolkowsk 2007, 65–92), but there were also yarns about men who had "really" been eaten by a sea creature and who had survived to tell of their experiences. The most famous of these was James Bartley, whose ordeal was much covered by the British press in 1891 and early 1892. The story seems to have originated in the United States (the earliest version I know appeared in the *St. Louis Globe-Democrat* "A Modern Jonah" 28 June, with this byline, "special correspondence of the Globe-Democrat," *CW* and *FG*).

In Britain a tiny notice, "James Bartley" appeared in the *Hull Daily Mail*, 13 July 1891. Sixteen newspapers in the BNA then ran with an initial long story between July and September. The earliest I have found is "Man in a Whale's Stomach," 15 July 1891. A second run of the same article (nine in the BNA) came out in January and February of 1892. A shorter article appeared in April 1892 in some papers, for example, "A Splendid Yarn" 1892: this is the version quoted below. Davis (1991, 236) is incorrect in saying that the first article came out in August 1891 in Yarmouth. His point (233) that news about the Gorleston Whale (washed up in East Anglia) was the inspiration for Bartley is not credible given the American origins of the story.

Here is a contemporary but abbreviated version of Bartley's ordeal:

> The story of James Bartley, the lucky harpooner of the good ship Star of the East, who is said to have been brought safely to light after passing twenty-four hours in the belly of a whale, is indeed a splendid yarn. While coasting off the Falkland Islands the boats were put off in pursuit of a whale, one was upset by the wounded animal; the men were thrown into the water, and before the crew of the other boat could pick them up one man was drowned, and James Bartley had disappeared. His comrades concluded that he had gone to the bottom, and set to work to cut out the blubber from the dead whale. Fortunately for their missing companion they did not confine their attention to blubber alone. The stomach of the whale was hoisted on to the deck, cut open, and inside was found the missing sailor "doubled up and unconscious." When revived he remained, as the story goes, for a fortnight in the captain's cabin a raving lunatic, but when recovered he soon was in splendid spirits again, and now apparently, "fully enjoys all the blessings of life that comes into his way." What experts say to this legend of the deep may be gathered from the opinion of whaling captains—they never knew a parallel case before. What tyros in the whale fishing business will most probably think is that it was passing strange for whalers who had given up their mate for lost to bother themselves about the worthless belly of a whale ("A Splendid Yarn" 1892)

Bartley's experiences—one paper quoted Oscar Wilde: "The story might not be true but it is perfect" ("Swallowed by a Whale" 1892)—was endlessly recycled over the next decades with new details accruing or "established" facts being improved upon (Davis 1991 for a wonderful overview; for the larger fascination with whaling in ballads Lloyd 2019). Similar stories continued to surface. Here is a delightful story from *The Times*' letter page of an adventure that possibly dates back to late Victorian or Edwardian Britain. One S.E. Campbell recalled meeting, some years before, a "missionary to the Southern Whaling Fleet" in his father's house, from whom he had heard this first-hand account.

> Whales, as is generally known, have such small throats that they could not possibly swallow a man, but there is one kind which has large throats [sperm whale, see above]. My father's friend [the missionary] has been so often overboard that he could hold his breath longer than most men. One day while they were fishing, he fell overboard into the shoal, and was swallowed by a whale. Luckily he was seen to fall, and the whale was harpooned. It is a fact that when a whale is harpooned it at once evacuates the contents of its stomach, and the missionary came to the surface and was saved. (Campbell 1928)

This account *conceivably* represents a man being taken into the whale's mouth, which, in some cases, would be ample enough to contain a man. As John Bland-Sutton put it in 1925, "The open mouth of a big whale may measure 20 ft. in length, 15 ft. in height, and 9 ft. in width. Such a chamber would easily accommodate twenty Jonahs standing upright" ("Psychology" 1925). Whales did also sometimes maul both whalers and their boats (e.g., "A Modern Jonah" 20 Feb. 1892). Bland-Sutton himself includes an account from 1771 (I have been unable to check the original) of one Marshall Jenkins, whose boat had been destroyed and who had "been taken into the mouth" of a whale "which had then sunk with him. On returning to the surface, the whale had ejected him onto the wreckage of the broken boat, much bruised but not seriously injured" (Bland-Sutton 1925, 104: "*Boston Post Boy*, October 14th, 1771"). We perhaps have here a whale declining or being unable to swallow a sailor and spitting him out.

There are other stories of men being immediately cast out of a marine monster's mouth—something more credible than a prolonged stay in a whale or shark's stomach. This one dates to 1892. Notice the suspicious lack of details. Coming several months after Bartley, it might owe its existence to that widely circulated report.

> A British war-vessel was sailing in the Mediterranean, when a man fell overboard. A huge shark instantly arose, and the unlucky seaman disappeared within

its mouth. The captain fired a gun at it from the deck, and as the shot struck upon its back it cast the man out again, and he was rescued by his companions. They forthwith harpooned the fish, dried him, and presented [the shark] to his intended victim. ("A Modern Jonah," 12 Aug 1892; compare to the story in Davis 1991, 229)

43. NAIL IN THE COFFIN

Summary: "Person goes to cemetery on a dare: he is to plant a stake in a grave or stick a knife or fork or sword or nail into a grave (or coffin). The knife is driven through the person's loose cuff, or the nail is driven through part of the sleeve, or the stake is driven through the person's long coat tail." Earliest Attestation: eighteenth century in Britain. N384.2(a), quoted in summary. Secondary Literature: N/A.

Towards the end of a long life, Lord Brougham (1778–1868) remembered this story told by his father, Henry Brougham (1742–1810):

[Henry Brougham] had dined one day in Dean's Yard, Westminster, with a party of young men, one of whom was his intimate friend, Mr Calmel. There was some talk about the death of a Mrs Nightingale, who had recently died under some melancholy circumstances, and had been that day buried in the Abbey. Some one of the party offered to bet that no one of those present would go down into the grave and drive a nail into the coffin. Calmel accepted the wager, only stipulating that he might have a lanthorn. He was accordingly let into the cathedral by a door out of the cloisters, and then left to himself. The dinner-party, after waiting an hour or more for Calmel, began to think something must have happened to him, and that he ought to be looked after; so my father and two or three more got a light and went to the grave, at the bottom of which lay the apparently dead body of Mr Calmel. He was quickly transported to the prebend's dining-room, and recovered out of his fainting-fit. As soon as he could find his tongue, he said, "Well, I have won my wager, and you'll find the nail in the coffin; but, by Jove! the lady rose up, laid hold of me, and pulled me down before I could scramble out of the grave." Calmel stuck to his story in spite of all the scoffing of his friends; and the ghost of Mrs Nightingale would have been all over the town, but for my father's obstinate incredulity. Nothing would satisfy him but an ocular inspection of the grave and coffin; and so, getting a light, he and some of the party returned to the grave. There, sure enough, was the nail, well driven into the coffin; but hard fixed by it was a bit of Mr Calmel's coat-tail! (Brougham 1871, I, 205–6)

A correspondent to *Notes and Queries* was having nothing of this.

A similar story has been frequently told with a change in the locality and in the *dramatis personae*. As applied to the present case, one might remark on the inherent improbability of the whole narrative—the open grave or vault in the Abbey; the idea of a person left to himself to ramble about the building at midnight without any attendant; the church left open for the roysterers to go in and out as they pleased. But the simplest answer to the whole is the fact that Mrs. Nightingale died on August 17, 1734, and that Lord Brougham's father was born in June, 1742—eight years after the transaction in which he is alleged to have performed so prominent a part. (Picton 1871, 277)

The correspondent suggests that the father had told his son this story and that his son, Lord Brougham, had, through confused memories, made his father into one of those who had been present (Picton 1871, 278). I have been unable to confirm the correspondent's claim that this story had been set elsewhere.

The earliest reference I have found to the "Nail in the Coffin" comes from 1832: "A well-known story is related of a member of a party of revellers, who engaged, in a fit of bravado, to enter the vault of a church at midnight, and in proof of his having done so, to stick a fork in a coffin which had been recently deposited there" (Chambers 1832, II, 634). The fork carrier "fell into a swoon" when he found that he could not escape. "An incident of this nature," the author continues, "is credibly recorded to have taken place in London in the last century, the scene being one of the vaults beneath Westminster Abbey" (Chambers 1832, II, 634). The story was often given in the later nineteenth- and early twentieth-century press: sometimes Westminster Abbey is named, and sometimes no location is given ("A Ghost" 1871; "More Curious Wagers" 1892; "Surprising Wagers" 1912; "Strange Wagers" 1924; "One Guinea" 1933). Baughman found some dozen examples in the United States (1966, 373).

44. THE NAIL IN THE SKULL

Summary: A nail is discovered in a skull, and this leads an investigator to a murderer. Earliest Attestation: eighteenth-century Britain. Motif: S115.2.1: "Murder by driving nail through head" (nothing in Baughman 1966). Secondary Literature: Ermacora (forthcoming). Notes: I owe *BS* for drawing my attention to this legend type and *DE* for sharing his forthcoming monograph with me.

The Victorians knew that hammering nails into heads could prove fatal. Experiments were carried out in the 1800s to establish skull damage should nails be driven in (Erichsen, "Driving" 71). There are well-attested cases, then and now, of the mentally ill battering nails into their skulls (e.g., "Driving Nails" 1890). There were also acts of infanticide: it is apparently easy to push a sharp object into the brain before the baby's skull has properly fused, usually with fatal consequences (e.g., "Infanticide" 1853; "On Saturday . . ." 1886; see also Ermacora, forthcoming). Then there were stories—and here the folklore begins—of adults being murdered by a spouse with a hammer and nails: something rather more difficult to achieve. The story of a nail in the head was fairly common in the nineteenth century and had folklore and even biblical antecedents. Examples pepper European history, the most famous involving Boniface VIII (possible killer) and Celestine V (victim) (Ermacora forthcoming). See Judges 5:24–26 for the story of Jael and Sisera. Jael hammers a tent peg through the sleeping Sisera's skull. The earliest British reference to a nail in the skull appears to be an allusive sentence in Chaucer ("Prologue to the Wife of Bath's Tale," line 775: "And somme [wives] han dryve nayles in hir brayn / Whil that they slepte, and thus they han hem slayn," *DE*).

"Nail in the Skull" broke down, in Britain, into two closely related narratives, both of which involved a hero "detective," a grave digger, a man's skull (often an innkeeper), a nail, and a faithless wife. All the versions I have found are English; the story first arrived in America (while being set in England) in 1830 ("Murder Will Out" 1830). Here are the two oldest versions of the narrative, the first with and the second without a toad, which marks the difference between the two variants.

> Dr Airy, Provost of Queen's College, Oxon (1599–1616), passing with his servant accidentally through St Sepulchre's Churchyard, in London, where the sexton was making a grave, observing a skull to move, showed it to his servant, and then to the sexton, who, taking it up, found a great toad in it, but withal

observed a ten-penny nail stuck in the temple bone; whereupon the Doctor presently imagined the party to have been murdered and asked the sexton if he remembered whose skull it was. He answered it was the skull of a man who died suddenly, and had been buried twenty-two years before. The Doctor told him that certainly the man was murdered, and that it was fitting to be inquired after, and so departed. The sexton thinking much upon it remembered some particular stories talked of at the death of the party, as that his wife, then alive, and married to another person, had been seen to go into his chamber with a nail and hammer, &c; whereupon he went to a justice of the peace, and told him all the story. The wife was sent for, and witnesses were found who testified that and some other particulars; she confessed, and was hanged. (Timbs 1865, I, 297 "written about the beginning of the last century, in the Rawlinson MSS"; Forker 1986, 18 "may be … apocryphal")

When Doctor Donne, afterwards Dean of St. Paul's, London, took Possession of the first Living he ever had, being a speculative Man, he took a Walk into the Church-yard, where the Sexton was digging a Grave, and throwing up a Skull, the Doctor took it up, to contemplate thereon; and found a small Sprig, or headless Nail sticking in the Temple, which he drew out secretly, and wrapt it up in the Corner of his Handkerchief; he then demanded of the Gravedigger, whether he knew whose Skull that was? He said he did, very well, declaring it was a Man's who kept a Brandy shop, an honest drunken Fellow, who one Night taking two Quarts of that comfortable Creature, was found dead in his Bed the next Morning: Had he a Wife, said the Doctor? Yes, Sir: Is she living? Yes: What Character does she bear? A very good one; only indeed the Neighbours reflected on her, because she married the Day after her husband was buried, though to be sure, she had no great Reason to grieve after him. This was enough for the Doctor, who under Pretence of visiting all his Parishioners, called on her; he asked her several Questions, and amongst others, what Sickness her first Husband died of? She giving him the same Account he had before received, he suddenly opened the Handkerchief, and cried, in an authoritative Voice, Woman, do you know this Nail? She was struck with Horror at the unexpected Demand and instantly owned the Fact. (Pilkington 1754, I, 150–52; Pilkington has Jonathan Swift, 1667–1745, tell the story to his workmen)

Note that both versions here include the nail being hammered into the temple, hinting at a horrible intimacy in death: the husband's head was—to judge by other similar stories—placed on his wife's lap while she took the nail and knocked it in (Ermacora forthcoming). The connection with the brandy shop is also part of a wider theme: in several versions, the dead man was an innkeeper or was

Figure 15 Trusler (1811, 37).

staying at an inn (Curling 1843, innkeeper; Tregortha 1808, 445–49, innkeeper; Trusler 1811, 37–40, guest in inn; "Murder Will Out" 1830, guest in inn). The association with alcohol, of course, makes it easier to explain the man's passivity.

These are not the only accounts where the legend is attached to famous Englishmen. Another version allegedly took place in the eighteenth century in Chelmsford and had author Joseph Strutt (1749–1802) as the detective: a wife and her second husband were found to be guilty of the murder of her first husband (an innkeeper; Tregortha 1808, 445–49; this is the earliest example I can find of the Strutt version). Another much printed account has a returning soldier solve the mystery in Abbots Lillington, a Cumberland village (an innkeeper's wife was the murderer; Curling 1843). The story was published as an elaborate literary work (Curling 1843; "The Murder" 1865; "Murder Will Out" 1830). It was also written up as a poem: "Murder Will Out: A Tale Founded on Fact" (Trusler 1811, 37–40), and we know that it appeared in a collection of Catholic catechism stories (Spirago and Baker 1904, 392–93) and, in 1876, in a Protestant sermon:

> But there were other ways in which sin finds men out. It sometimes discovers men by certain circumstances—by their being brought into contact with certain individuals. This was illustrated by the case of a blacksmith who had been murdered by his wife driving a nail into his skull after giving him a sleeping draught. The nail was found in the skull many years afterwards by a stranger and on it being produced before the guilty woman she made a full confession of her guilt and was executed. ("Mr. Hallowes's Sunday Afternoon Theatre Service" 1876)[23]

There were other stories based around nails in the skull, although there is no question that the toad and toadless variants given above are the most common in Britain. A version that appeared in 1865, set in the 1700s, had a group in Ireland encounter a moving skull in a stream on the edge of cemetery; it transpired an eel was inside! A nail was in the skull and a woman present, Esther Mahoney, admitted to having hammered a nail into a friend's fiancé's head, while he was drunk, twenty years before ("The Murder" 1865). In 1877 a story appeared claiming that an Englishman murdered his wife with a nail in the skull, became an actor, and many years later, playing Hamlet was confronted by her skull with the nail still in it. He confessed on stage! ("An English Green-Room" 1877, *CW*). The story about the actor (involving Hamlet?) seems also to have been known in France:

> About thirty years ago a story was written by a Frenchman on this same ghastly subject, laying the scene in private life in France, and making the perpetrator of the deed a woman. It had a great success, and to this day is occasionally revived, and goes the rounds of the newspapers... ("An English Green-Room" 1877)

We even have "real life" cases. In 1830 a soldier (based in Ireland) confessed to killing a woman with a nail in London some years before. This confession came to be associated with the discovery of a skull with a nail in the left eye socket. The magistrates established that the soldier could not possibly have been guilty and that, as such, he was a fantasist; he certainly proved to be an unstable individual ("Extraordinary Circumstance" 1830; "The Alledged [sic] Murder" 1830). The nail was probably accidentally associated with the skull, but the soldier's desire to confess and, above all, the association of the nail and skull among locals hint at knowledge of the story (or one similar). We have one precious example where we see the oral circulation of Nail in the Skull—toad and all—as a real incident: "Mr Stewart tells me a passage that Mr James Ramsay, when chaplain to their regiment, told him and several of the officers when in Yorkshire. Mr Ramsay had this account from the first hands" ("Curious Discovery" 1833, credited to "Wodrow MS"). Then in 1857 British newspapers ran a report about a boy who had hanged himself in a barn in Nassau (New York State). A medium was subsequently told by the boy's spirit that this was not true and that his mother had "driven a nail in his skull and hung him up afterwards." Following much local controversy, the body was dug up, and the skull was "found perfect in every part" ("The Superstitions" 1857).

45. THE OMNIBUS DRIVER'S HOLIDAY

Summary: An omnibus driver has a day off after years of work and spends it on the omnibus. Earliest Attestation: well known by 1886. Motif: N/A. Secondary Literature: N/A.

Today the phrase "Busman's Holiday" is well established in British English. In the words of the longer *Oxford English Dictionary*, it is "leisure time spent in occupations of the same nature as those in which one engages for a living" ("Bus (n)"). A chef, for instance, goes abroad only to end up cooking for friends and family in the kitchen of his French *gîte*.

The phrase was based on a late Victorian story to which we have several references, but of which few details survive, about an omnibus driver given a rare day off. The omnibus was, of course, a covered horse-drawn cab, particularly common in the capital and the ancestor of London's modern bus fleet. There were, circa 1850, about 3,000 of these omnibuses, and the average vehicle carried some fifteen persons: the maximum was twenty-two (thirteen inside and nine outside). Each omnibus had a driver and a conductor (who collected fares). Mayhew suggests that there were some 7,000 drivers and conductors living in London (Mayhew 1851, III, 338).

As to the story, in 1886 we read of "the old story of the omnibus driver" ("Mr. Arthur Cecil..." 1886); in 1893, "the good old story about the omnibus driver" ("Bank Holiday"); in 1898 "the traditional conduct of the omnibus driver out for a holiday" ("Mr. J. L. Toole..."); and in 1903 the "very old story of the omnibus driver..." ("Town Topics"). But what was this story? The fullest version that

I have found dates to 1891 and a report on the Kaiser's visit to London in that year. Much is made by the journalist of the fact that the German king spent his time in London much as he would have in Berlin: reviewing troops, going to the opera, and so on. "He reminds one," the journalist goes on to say, "of the omnibus driver who, having a day's holiday after twenty years' continuous service, spent it on the box-seat of his own bus, sitting by the driver who had taken his place" ("It is true that . . ." 1891). Other reports echo this version ("Bank Holiday" 1893; "Mr. J. L. Toole . . ." 1898; "Mr. Gladstone" 1888). In one later report, the omnibus driver is out riding a friend's cab ("Town Topics" 1903).

How old is this "old story"? Mayhew, who loves such details, does not tell it or even allude to it in 1851 in his work on omnibuses. He does, though, give some sense of how incredibly hard the omnibus drivers worked, with the example of one man who had not had a day off in six years and who had driven some 170,568 miles in that time (Mayhew 1851, III, 338)—the equivalent of riding seven times around the equator. A London newspaper story from 1866 details a day out with omnibus drivers who celebrated their holiday with a picnic and a series of holiday games ("A 'Day Out'" 1866). The author does not mention a busman's holiday, nor did the editor use it for the title, although the phrase would have been a gift to either. I would assume then that the story was not widely known in London in that year. An old story, but probably not much older than the 1870s or 1880s.

46. ONE LITTLE PIGGY

Summary: Three children are left alone and one slaughters another in imitation of his father killing pigs. Earliest Attestation: well known by 1867. Motif: N334.1: "Children play hog-killing: one killed"; AaTh 2401 "how children played at slaughtering together"; the story often travels under the German name "Wie Kinder Schlachtens miteinander gespielt haben." Secondary Literature: Richter (1986).

Pigs usually appear in news reports in nineteenth-century Britain for winning prizes at country fairs or for mauling young children (e.g., "At Llanydyssil Village . . ." 1890). However, in 1867 the following report came from Saskatchewan, Canada.

> A French Canadian had killed several pigs, and his little children had looked on in approving wonder on the process. Soon after the parents went to church, and on their return was [sic] met at the door by their oldest child, Gustave, an eight-year-old boy, who exclaimed in childish glee, "I have killed little piggy; come and see." He was covered with blood. What they saw may be inferred from the confession of the boy as to what had taken place. When the parents had gone to church, Gustave proposed to his little brother that they should play killing pig. In this request, it is supposed that the unfortunate little fellow acquiesced. The youngest was to be the pig, the eldest the butcher. Gustave eagerly assisted his brother to undress for the tragedy, and, taking a small rope, tied him down securely to a rough lounge that stood in the room; he then procured the butcher-knife that his father had used in slaughtering the pigs the day before and plunged it into the throat of his passive and helpless brother. The wound was a mortal one, and it is supposed that death must have immediately resulted. After the child had bled his little life away, the unnatural brother, with the most incredible heartlessness, took the cord which confined the body to the lounge, and tying one end around the feet of the corpse, threw the other over the beam, and lending his weight, and strength, hoisted the body to the position in which it was found; then not satisfied with the programme thus carried out, the little butcher must needs disembowel his dead brother almost in the exact manner in which his father had the pigs the day before. ("A Horrible Story" 18 June 1867; 82 occurrences in the BNA)

A much longer version appeared in North American papers, based on a letter from an eye-witness who had, he claimed, accompanied the parents back from church and with them discovered the "pig" ("A Horrible Story" 19 May 1867, *CW*). Anyone reading the article quoted above and particularly the letter might be seduced into belief. But this is an old European story, which dates back at least to the sixteenth century (Richter 1986, 2–3) and which had been picked up in the first edition (it was subsequently eliminated) of the Brothers Grimm's *Kinder- und Hausmärchen* (Grimm 1812–1815, I, 101–3). Even in early versions it was told with strong circumstantial details: "Zum Stil der Novitätenerzählung gehört dabei die feste, Wahreit heischende Ortszuweisung" (Richter 1986, 4).

The story evidently took root in North America. In 1885 this account was connected to Tallaged [*corr.* Tallageda], Alabama.

> J. H. McGowan killed and dressed a pig for barbecue last Friday. His three children, aged eleven, nine and four, saw the process of butchering. Next day McGowan left home, and the children agreed to repeat the process of the day before. Having no pig, the two eldest proceeded to butcher the youngest. They

cut its throat and hung it up by the heels, and were proceeding to disembowel it when their mother discovered them. ("A Horrible Story and Its Moral" 1885)

In 1892 an American health magazine included this story:

> The papers recently recorded the murder of a little girl by her brother, who cut her throat with a butcher knife the next day after having seen his father slaughtering pigs. When inquired of respecting the whereabouts of his missing sister, he led the way to the spot in the garden where she was lying in a pool of blood, and coolly remarked to his horrified parents, "I've been killing pigs." ("An Infant" 1892)

The author also recalls a butcher's son "in an Eastern city," killing several of his playmates in an unused cellar ("An Infant" 1892).

"One Little Piggy" catches two nineteenth-century concerns. The first is worry about the slaughter of animals in close proximity to families and impressionable children:

> When there is to be found in every town in this vast country from one to several hundred slaughter-pens devoted to the destruction of the lives of helpless animals ... it is not to be wondered at that such horrible incidents are occasionally recorded, and indeed the marvel is, that similar occurrences are not more frequent. ("An Infant" 1892)

The second is the danger of parents leaving children alone. Consider this related legend from the Continent:

> A German, named Actenburg, a strolling musician of the village of Thiscrup, in Jutland, left home on the 18th ult., with his wife and daughter to play a wedding party at the neighbouring town of Holt, leaving behind three boys, aged respectively, thirteen, eleven and nine. The children who had great repugnance to go to school, deliberated amongst themselves as to the best means of freeing themselves from that disagreeable duty, and at last they resolved to cut out their tongues! The boy of eleven took a large table knife and placing himself before a looking-glass, resolutely made a profound incision in his tongue. Not being able to terminate the mutilation, he begged his elder brother to do it for him, and the latter, taking hold of the tongue with a piece of line between his fingers, pulled it forward and cut off a piece an inch long. Blood flowed in abundance, and the children becoming terrified, uttered piercing cries. The neighbours rushed in, and seeing what had taken place procured medical assistance; but though everything

was done for the child that art could suggest, his life is considered in danger. ("Very Strange Story" 1857)

There are also stories, reminiscent of the modern urban legend the "Baby Roast," about unsuitable babysitters (Brunvand 2012, I, 26–27). Consider this 1890 report "vouched for by a gentleman of unimpeachable veracity" ("Devoured" 1890). The murderers were two deaf-mutes:

> A horrible case of cannibalism is reported from County Quebec. The infant son of a farmer named Cote was eaten alive while the parents of the little child were absent berry picking. ("A Horrible Story from Ottawa" 1890)

47. PAYING FOR HIS BURIAL

Summary: A philanthropist gives a poor woman money, after being shown her husband in a coffin; on forgetting something the philanthropist returns to the house and finds the "corpse" sitting up and counting the money. Earliest Attestation: 1855 (US). Motif: N/A. Secondary Literature: N/A.

The earliest "Paying for His Burial" story known to me dates to 1855:

> A female called a few days since on a lady of some influence in Brooklyn, and told a sad and plaintive story of suffering and privation, and, moreover, that her husband had just died, and that she lacked the means of a decent burial. Her tale of woe so wrought upon the lady that she proceeded to visit her immediately, to satisfy herself there was no imposture. On entering the apartment she beheld the coffin, and was satisfied all was right, and not wishing to harrow the feelings of the bereaved woman, she left a considerable sum of money and immediately departed. After passing two or three blocks from the dwelling, thinking all the way of the strange complexions to which we are liable, she missed her pocket handkerchief and returned to see if she had not dropped it in the house. The stairs were ascended hastily and the room entered without much ceremony, when what did she behold, the woman's husband sitting up in the coffin counting over the money! ("The Dead Alive" 1855)

This story was circulated in Britain in 1855: five examples in the BNA; then it was reprinted as "A Sad Sell" (1856) and "Truth Stranger" (1860). Other versions subsequently appeared, associated with other American cities. In 1857 the story was set in Philadelphia. A woman had been "frequently called upon by a child to relieve the wants of her father, represented as dangerously ill, and at length as dying." She goes to the child's house, leaves "additional aid," but has to return, having forgotten her purse, and finds "the dead man sitting up in his coffin eagerly counting its contents" (Everett 1879, III, 577–78).[24] In an 1870 version set in Boston a man goes to a woman's house, sees the coffin and dead husband and returns because he has forgotten his gloves. He "left the house a sadder and a wiser man" ("According to . . . ," 22 examples in the BNA). By 1892 a New Zealand newspaper story had set the story in Australia ("A Ghastly Fraud," *CW*).

48. THE PICKPOCKET'S RING

Summary: A pickpocket accidentally leaves a valuable ring in his victim's pocket. Earliest Attestation: 1869. Motif: N/A. Secondary Literature: N/A.

It is one of the commonest Victorian and Edwardian crime stories. I offer a series of short examples.

A pickpocket in New Orleans recently stole a portemonnaie containing a few dollars from a lady's pocket, and by accident dropped in its place a valuable diamond ring. ("A pickpocket . . . 1869)

A woman in Cape Town had her purse abstracted from her pocket whilst riding in a tramcar. In her pocket, however, she subsequently found a ring, which must have slipped from the pickpocket's finger, and which she afterwards sold for £30. ("A woman . . ." 1902)

In stealing a lady's purse in Melbourne, Victoria, a pickpocket let a diamond ring, worth £50, fall into her pocket from his finger, and was unable to recover it. ("In stealing . . ." 1904)

The narrative may have its origin in the trick whereby organized pickpockets left their loot in the pockets of accomplices, to cut the risk of being arrested with stolen property on their person. Newspaper stories show that occasionally pickpockets deposited stolen watches and wallets in the *wrong* pockets ("From Our London Correspondent" 1895).

Often the "Pickpocket's Ring" is longer, and the presence of the diamond ring on the pickpocket's finger puts travelers on buses and trams off their guard. This, apparently, is a respectable individual. The loss of the ring, then is doubly apt: a punishment for thieving but also for dastardly social misrepresentation.

> An extraordinary incident happened one day last week to a young lady—a day governess in English provincial town. The lady was in a tramway car when a stylish gentleman came and was careful to show prominently a valuable diamond ring he wore on one his fingers, aping at the same time the manners of aristocrat. It was not long before he got out, and the young lady on getting to her stage on her way home stepped out as well, but to find on putting her hand in her pocket that her purse was gone. She, however, found a strange article in her pocket, which, to her astonishment, turned out to be the identical ring which her fellow-traveller had been so ostentatiously displaying. Examination proved that the ring was no flash article, a jeweller appraising it of the value of at least £30. Fortunately for the lady, there was only two shillings in the purse she lost. The ring had evidently slipped off the pickpocket's finger when was in the act of abstracting the purse. ("An Extraordinary Incident" 1888)

The "Pickpocket's Ring" was popular. It was found on the Continent (e.g., "De Vergissing Van Een Dief" 1906, *PB*) and (as the examples given above show) in the wider English-speaking world. It also seems to have circulated orally, at least in Britain. A journalist gave, for instance, a highly circumstantial version from the capital that had been passed on by word of mouth. In that case the thief, "who was fashionably dressed" followed the woman (he had realized that he had lost his ring) and she only escaped by getting into a hansom cab. She found the ring in a pocket later, at home ("From Our London Correspondent" 1895). The story also appeared in fiction. I know, in fact, of three short stories that used the narrative: in one, a thief goes to the police to get his ring back (McGovan 1886: fiction masquerading as memoir); in another, a thief, many years after losing his ring, retrieves it ("Adventures" 1892, the best of the three); and in the third, a British pickpocket in Paris ends up in prison as the ring he reported losing turns up in a victim's pocket ("That Fatal Diamond" 1886). There are also then other unlikely-sounding stories—cousins of the pickpocket's ring—where, in a robbery the traffic between thief and victim goes both ways.

A very pretty and true story comes from Naples:

> The other evening a gentleman was assaulted by three thieves, one of whom, after relieving him of all his money and valuables, demanded his overcoat. "But," objected the man, "I shall die of cold," whereupon the thief forced his victim to put on his old ragged coat, and all three thieves disappeared in a twinkling, laughing heartily. The gentleman, making a virtue of necessity, plunged his hands into the threadbare pockets to keep warm, and, to his stupefaction, found there everything of which he had been despoiled. ("A Curious" 1899)

49. POISON DUEL

Summary: Two men duel using poison as a weapon. Earliest Attestation: medieval (origins in the Arab world?). Motif: H223: "Ordeal by Poison." Secondary Literature: N/A.

Duels were matters of honor and offended honor. Two gentlemen (with their "seconds," who acted as referees) met to fight using weapons chosen by the man who had been challenged. Usually, a duel was fought until honor was satisfied, meaning until one of the two was injured. However, deaths sometimes resulted and duels, which were illegal, did occasionally end with combatants and seconds fleeing the country (two general guides, neither of which mentions the poison duel are: Hopton, 2007; Kiernan 1988). With their unpredictable drama such combats were a favorite of eighteenth- and nineteenth-century literature: what reader will ever forget, say, the duel between Pierre and Dolokhov in *War and Peace* or between Albert and the Count in *The Count of Monte Cristo*? They were also a gift to journalists. There were so many variables involved: not just the cause of the duel and participants, but also the form that the duel would take. What weapons would contestants use? Beyond the obvious—swords, pistols—there were also other ways of wounding your opponent: including cannons, golf balls, whips, and, of course, poison ("A Singular Duel between Two French Coachmen" 1853, whips; "Strange Duels" 1927, golf; "A strange duel . . ." 1890, cannon).

In the nineteenth century there are many references in the press and publications more generally to fights between individuals with poison; a form of combat, which as we will see, was commonly described, but rarely actually carried out. Here, for instance, is a description of a British play:

> Another new burletta, entitled *An Affair of Honour*, was also produced during the week at the theatre. The main interest of the piece turns upon the ludicrous scene between Keeley and Liston, who, as two officers of dragoons, quarrel about a lady, and fight a duel by the novel mode of each of them swallowing a pill, which they draw by lot from a box containing two pills perfectly alike in appearance, but one of them a deadly poison, the other innoxious. ("Olympic" 1835)

The poison duel commonly appeared in the theater and in short stories in the nineteenth century ("The Mohawks" 1900 for the play *Taking a Pill*; short stories include "The Poisoned Draught" 1888; "His Only Duel" 1895).

Why would men duel with poison rather than swords? One reason, probably the one in the lost script of *An Affair*, was that both men wanted the duel to end with a killing: "It must be a battle to the death" ("A Terrible Duel" 1883). But in some cases, it was to provide equality between a soldier and a nonmilitary man.

> An apothecary had refused to resign his seat at a theatre in Vienna to an officer, who feeling himself insulted sent him a challenge. The apothecary was punctual at the meeting, but observed he had to propose a new way of settling the dispute. He then drew from his pocket a pill-box, and taking there from two pills, thus addressed his antagonist: "As a man of honour, sir, you would not wish me to fight on unequal terms. Here are therefore two pills, one composed of the most deadly poison, the other perfectly harmless. We are, therefore, on equal ground if we each swallow one; you shall take your choice, and I promise faithfully to take which you leave." ("An Apothecary's Duel" 1851)

These unequal duels often ended without the pills being taken: the man of science had twitted the military man, who had perhaps forgotten that he was to fight only with members of his class. In the case of the dispute over the theater chair: "It is needless to add that the affair was settled by a hearty laugh" ("An Apothecary's Duel" 1851). In other cases, neither pill had poison, and much was made of suggestibility, how a combatant could kill himself just through belief (e.g., "His Only Duel"; see further **"Downie's Slaughter"**).

The duel itself was fought according to different rules. The classical poison duel was a simple random choice, with both parties knowing that one of the pills was deadly: "You gentlemen will cause four capsules to be prepared. Three shall be filled with water, the fourth with hydrocyanic acid, the deadliest poison known to science" ("Strange Southern Duel" 1895). The duelists chose according to a coin toss. Some other form of chance, or on one memorable occasion a game of dominoes ("Duelling Extraordinary" 1882), was also used to decide who should knowingly drink poison. Here, the loser was expected, effectively, to commit suicide.

> A singular duel has just taken place at Berlin between a journeyman silversmith and another artisan. The arms selected was that whichever of the two adversaries threw the lowest with dice should swallow the contents of the fatal phial. ("A Duel and a Farce" 1867)

There was then the animal challenge. The duelists went into rooms full of tarantulas or poisonous snakes, and the last to leave the room won ("A Horrible Duel" 1887; "Tarantulas for Two" 1892, *CW*; "A Duel with Snakes" 1896, *CW*). In one duel between a Mexican and an American, the Mexican comes out declaring that he has been bitten, but "the Mexican had not been bitten at all, but had scratched his hand on a protruding nail in the wall and had thought it a spider's bite" ("Tarantulas for Two" 1892).

Most of these reports are simple journalistic fantasies, with personal details lacking. However, there are some exceptions. There really was a dominoes poison duel in Warsaw in 1882 ("Duelling Extraordinary" 1882).[25] We also have one fascinating early nineteenth-century account where a proposed poison duel entered legal record in the United States. Here one of the men was disabled, so a normal duel was not possible ("American Duelling" 1823).

How old is the poison duel? The folklore motif lists have H223: "Ordeal by Poison." It is interesting that in some pre-nineteenth-century sources the combatants are doctors. In the eighteenth century the Italian occultist Cagliostro challenged a Scottish Dr. Rogerson in Russia. The doctors are expected to poison each other, and the winner will be the one who can cure the poison he has taken: Rogerson, however, refuses (Photiadès, *Count*, 119–20). A twelfth-century duel from the Arab world has exactly the same conceit (Prioreschi 2001, 443–44). Here the poison duel is a battle of skill, not of chance.

50. PRAYERS AND THE THIEF

Summary: A burglar enters a woman's bedroom and is reformed after praying together with her. Earliest Attestation: 1872 (Britain and the US). Motif: N/A. Secondary Literature: N/A.

An unusual number of unsourced stories about single women confronting single male burglars circulated in the later 1800s. There was necessarily danger in narratives of this type and also a frisson of sex. A strange man, after all, was in a woman's most intimate space, and there was "the universal feminine uneasiness respecting 'a man in the room'" ("Aspasia" 1882, *CW*). One Victorian story has a burglar promise not to look while his victim got out of bed and dressed ("Raggles" 1880); there are two stories about a burglar and a woman marrying ("A Queer Story" 1896 and "The Romance" 1873; see also the interwar story Norris 1923). Many burglar-and-lady stories are heavily larded with comedy: we know of an early twentieth-century music hall sketch entitled simply "The Lady and the Burglar" ("The Lady and the Burglar" 1905).

In some lady-and-burglar yarns, the woman cleverly traps the burglar (in one way or another) so that the police can arrest him (e.g., "A Terrible Quarter of an Hour" 1881). There is also the story of the woman courageously reforming the thief with prayers: this was perhaps a more common and certainly a more stable narrative. The classic story is best given with an example. In 1895 this version appeared in a British newspaper. The prayer referred to is, I assume, the Lord's Prayer

> Pluck equally striking, and perhaps of a higher quality, was shown by the elderly English lady who when about to recite her nightly prayer detected a man under her bed. She neither fled nor changed countenance, but she changed her form of petition, and instead repeated a prayer which is almost as common as the English tongue, and goes up nightly from thousands of baby lips. When she had finished she heard a voice begging her not to be frightened, and assuring her that she should not be harmed. The man, so runs the tale, crept from his hiding-place, and, with tears in his eyes, told her that he had repeated that prayer at his mother's knee. He had neither uttered it nor heard it for years, but it had reached the one tender spot, which the optimist assures us remains even in the hardest hearts. ("Stories about Burglars" 1895, with a byline from a Chicago paper)

Another version of this "religio-sensational narrative" appeared in many British newspapers in October 1872. It seems to have come from a correspondent in

Sheffield, though it was set in the south of England ("A Burglar Story" 1872). There was a longer and a shorter version; there follows the abbreviated one. It includes a *coda* that crops up in many versions.

> A lady who lived at an old-fashioned home in a southern county, upon retiring to her room one night at the witching hour, found a man under her bed. She feared to go to the door, lest she should be intercepted, so, with admirable presence of mind, she sat down, took her Bible, opened it by chance at the Parable of the Prodigal Son, and read at the man under the bed. At the conclusion of the chapter she knelt down, and after praying for her own safety, besought forgiveness for others who might have been tempted into ill-doing, winding up her petitions with the prayer that, even that night, some such sinner might, like the Prodigal, be made penitent. She then rose from her prayers and went to bed. The man got up noiselessly as he could, and said: "I mean you no harm ma'am; I am going to leave the house, and thank you for your prayers," and vanished. This is sufficiently notable, but the sequel is eminently wonderful. The lady, whilst recently visiting a friend in the North of England, was asked to go and hear a Dissenting minister, who was a reformed character. She went, and to her astonishment heard the preacher relate all the incidents previously stated. After the service she hastened into the vestry and asked the minister who had told him the story, when, after some very excusable hesitation he said that he was the burglar, but that ever since that night he had lived a reformed life. ("A Burglary Story" 1872; a longer version "The Lady and the Burglar" 1872; I counted 12 in the BNA from 15–31 Oct 1872)

The journalist responsible for abbreviating the text above writes:

> The story may, or may not, be true, but we cannot help thinking that it wants what is technically called a tag. By all the rules of effective composition it should have ended with the union of reformer and reformed. ("A Burglary Story" 1872)

Again the sexual frisson. In an 1873 version from San Francisco a journalist corrected that failing: "So they met for the first time face to face, and they are supposed to have lived happily ever afterwards" ("The Romance" 1873). In an 1890 version the woman is already married, closing down any possibility of future romance with the preacher ("Reformation" 1890). The story was common enough to be parodied. In a beautifully written 1882 story an ugly woman leaves a ladder for a thief to come into her room and a note on her bedside table instructing him to wake her so that he can be reformed. The man, however, on seeing the woman's face flees in terror and reforms himself ("Aspasia" 1882). Often the woman pretends not to have seen the burglar; this is the heart of the narrative. Similar stories appeared, though, where the woman immediately called out the thief: in a news report in 1913 (a burglar made the mistake of entering the house of a female Salvation Army captain, "Prayer" 1913); and in 1916 in a short story (a son comes to burgle his father's house but is reformed by an old flame, Swan 1916). I have also found a report about an American clergyman taking a burglar, with a gun, to his most precious objects: his two sleeping children. The burglar is moved and reforms ("The American Clergyman" 1863).

51. THE RED HAND!

Summary: A wealthy family is ready to pay for someone to undergo a terrible underground ordeal on their behalf. Earliest Attestation: 1827. Motif: N/A. Secondary Literature: N/A.

An aristocratic house has a terrible mark placed against their name. Because of a past crime, they have to carry a bleeding red hand on their heraldic stemma. However, if the family is able to convince a man to do penance for them in an underground place for seven years, then they will be able to remove the hand (and its associated dishonor) from their escutcheon. Indeed, for anyone willing to go into the cellar or a cave and live in the dark for seven years, they will pay a thousand pounds. Fiction? Certainly. But there is a hint that a belief like this was current in England in the earlier nineteenth century and that people were prepared to act upon it. The story is taken up in 1827 in a letter sent to William Hone's *Table Book*. The author preferred to remain anonymous and the letter-writer or the editor made it difficult to place this nightmarish account. Possibly we are outside Seckington in Warwickshire.[26]

> One December evening, the year before last, returning to T . . . , in the northern extremity of W . . . , in a drisling rain, as I approached the second milestone, I observed two men, an elder and a younger, walking side by side in the horse-road. The elder, whose appearance indicated that of a labourer in very comfortable circumstances, was in the path directly in front of my horse, and seemed to have some intention of stopping me; on my advancing, however, he quietly withdrew from the middle of the road to the side of it, but kept his eyes firmly fixed on me, which caused also, on my part, a particular attention to him. He

then accosted me, "Sir, I beg your pardon." "For what, my man?" "For speaking to you, sir." "What have you said, then?" "I want to know the way to S . . ." "Pass on beyond those trees, and you will see the spire before you." "How far is it off, sir?" "Less than two miles." "Do you know it, sir?" "I was there twenty minutes ago." "Do you know the gentleman there, sir, that wants a man to go underground for him?" "For what purpose?" (imagining, from the direction in which I met the man, that he came from the mining districts of S . . . , I expected that his object was to explore the neighbourhood for coals.) His answer immediately turned the whole train of my ideas. "To go underground for him, to take off the bloody hand from his carriage." "And what is that to be done for?" "For a thousand pounds, sir. Have you not heard anything of it, sir?" "Not a word." "Well, sir, I was told that the gentleman lives here, at S . . . , at the hall, and that he offers a thousand pounds to any man that will take off the bloody hand from his carriage." "I can assure you this is the first word I have heard on the subject." "Well, sir, I have been told so"; and then, taking off his hat, he wished me a good morning. I rode slowly on, but very suddenly heard a loud call, "Stop, sir, stop!" I turned my horse, and saw the man, who had, I imagined, held a short parley with his companion, just leaving him, and running towards me, and calling out, "Stop, sir." Not quite knowing what to make of this extraordinary accost and vehement call, I changed a stout stick in my left hand to my right hand, elevated it, gathered up the reins in my left, and trotted my horse towards him; he then walked to the side of the road, and took off his hat, and said, "Sir, I am told that if the gentleman can get a man to go underground for him, for seven years, and never see the light, and let his nails, and his hair, and his beard grow all that time, that the king will then take off the bloody hand from his carriage." "Which then is the man who offers to do this? Is it you, or your companion?" "I am the man, sir." "O, you intend to undertake to do this?" "Yes, sir." "Then all that I can say is, that I now hear the first word of it from yourself." At this time the rain had considerably increased, I therefore wished the man a good morning, and left him. I had not, however, rode above a hundred and fifty yards before an idea struck me, that it would be an act of kindness to advise the poor man to go no further on such a strange pursuit; but, though I galloped after them on the way I had originally directed them, and in a few minutes saw two persons, who must have met them, had they continued their route to S . . . , I could neither hear anything of them, nor see them, in any situation which I could imagine that they might have taken to as a shelter from the heavy rain. I thus lost an opportunity of endeavouring to gain, from the greatest depths of ignorance, many points of inquiry I had arranged in my own mind, in order to obtain a development of the extraordinary idea and unfounded offer, on which the poor fellow appeared to have so strongly set his mind. ("The Bloody Hand" 1827)

The old man had determined to undertake the dread task himself and had traveled a good way to do so: he did not know the area. There are several British traditions of red hands on heraldic symbols being placed there as a mark of a dishonor against this or that aristocratic family: one of these was the Holts of Aston Hall, Warwickshire (Westwood and Simpson 2005, 808–9). It is to some such tradition that we should relate this bizarre letter. In the late nineteenth century there are other references to seven years of penance for the red hand. The earliest two that I have found date to 1895, some seventy years after the old man walked towards S....

> You were called upon to pass seven years in a cave without a companion and possibly that proved hard enough for the flesh. But when added to that there was the prohibition to be shaved! what spirit could stand that? Yet did other terrors remain for those that dared to brave the terrible "red badge," and wished to wipe it out. The years of penance had to be passed in a cave without uttering a single word! (Free Lance 1895)

In that same year there is a short reference to a custom in the Welsh borders.

> There is locally an interesting bit of folk-lore attached to the common belief that the coat of arms contains a bloody hand. It is said that if a man would spend seven years in one of the dungeons, and be fed by one of the servants, and never speak, the bloody hand would disappear. It is added that one man once almost completed the ordeal but failed at last. (Bonum 1895)

The notion of a terrible ordeal resulting in a reward can be found elsewhere in nineteenth-century publications, including ten years spent in a dark cell in London ("Two very strange stories..." 1871, done for a ten-thousand-pound bet in an aristocratic circle). Or consider the following hoax story concerning a Russian princess's will. It appeared in the *Daily Tribune*, in 1893.

> A curious will contest, according to Paris papers, is about to be tried in the Seine courts. Five years ago, a Russian princess died, leaving a large fortune. There was great surprise among her relatives when the testament was opened. By one of its clauses, she left 5,000,000 francs to the person who would remain a year in the chapel to be erected above her grave in the Pere-la-Chaise. The body of the princess, according to the legendary report, lies in a crystal coffin, in a wonderful state of preservation. No one of her relatives has been able to remain longer than two or three days in the chapel. What will become of the 5,000,000 francs is the question. ("Singular Provision" 1893)

Many American readers volunteered their services, yet the story was a fantasy dreamed up by a Chicago journalist (Woodyard 2015).

We might also compare this with the lottery of death, an idea circulated in the papers in mid nineteenth-century Britain.

> The Polish and German peasantry have given the authorities at Posen considerable trouble by their inquiries respecting a "Rothschild's Lottery." They have been led to believe that the "great Rothschild" has been sentenced to be beheaded; but that he had been allowed to procure a substitute, if he can, by lottery. For this purpose a sum of many millions is devoted, all the tickets to be prizes of 3,000 thalers each, except one—that fatal number is a blank—and whoever draws it, is to be decapitated instead of the celebrated banker! Notwithstanding the risk, the applications have been numerous. There is nothing surprising in the number of applications for these shares. Every man who enters the army in war times takes out a ticket in a similar lottery. ("Lottery of Death" 1852)

The story seems to have first appeared in Britain in *The Times* ("The Authorities ..." 1852). There are thirty-four instances in the BNA, accessed 11 March 2019, from April to August 1852 (see, too, later "Queer Hoaxes" 1858).

52. THE RETURNED WATCH

Summary: A pickpocket, on realizing that he has stolen a watch from a famous person, sends it back with apologies. Earliest Attestation: 1870. Motif: N/A. Secondary Literature: N/A. Compare with: the "**Pickpocket's Ring.**"

There is a well-known modern legend (the "Helpful Mafia Neighbor") where a couple move in next door to an elderly man, lose all their property in a burglary, and then arrive home one day to find that all the stolen objects have been returned. Their elderly neighbor, a mafia *capo*, had intervened on their behalf (Brunvand 2012, I, 293–94). The following two stories may be ancestors. In both a celebrity is robbed, and in both, criminals returned the stolen objects, with expressions of esteem. The first concerns Charles Dickens (1812–1870).

> Charles Dickens, during one of his visits to Paris, had his watch stolen from him at the theatre. This watch had been given to him by the Queen and was therefore very much prized by him. On returning to his hotel, Mr. Dickens found a small parcel waiting for him, to which was pinned the following note: Sir, I hope you will excuse me but I assure you that I thought that I was dealing with a Frenchman, and not a countryman. Finding out my mistake, I hasten to repair it as much as lies in my power by returning you here the watch I stole from you. I beg you to accept the homage of my respect, and to believe me, my dear countryman, your humble and obedient servant, A PICKPOCKET. ("Charles Dickens..." 1881)

I wonder whether there were other versions where a thief returned objects simply because his or her victim was a co-national? Dickens's celebrity seems to have counted for little here. An 1881 version claims that this narrative was "one of Dickens' after-dinner stories" ("A Discriminating Pickpocket" 1881: Dickens had appeared in court against a pickpocket in London, "Dickens and the Pickpocket," 1870; the pickpocket accused Dickens of being a fence!) If this is Dickens's anecdote, it came to us by a circuitous route. The earliest British version I have been able to find dates to 1870 and the days after Dickens's death and ascribes the story to "the theatrical *chroniqueur* of the *Gaulois*" ("Charles Dickens and the Pickpocket" 1870).

An even more pleasing story concerns Lord Shaftesbury (1801–1885) and his watch. Again, this appeared just after Shaftesbury's death, though it is supposed to be an "old story."

> There crops up an old story concerning the late Lord Shaftesbury which is worth telling the younger generation of newspaper readers. It is well-known that the noble earl was in the habit of spending a great deal of his time in the slums of London, and his philanthropy in such missions took the widest possible form. Of him, as of the village parson in the "Vicar of Wakefield," it could truly be said, "His pity gave ere charity began," and the roughs, pickpockets, and loungers of The Dials, The Cut, and other interesting centres of habitation were not slow in recognising the benevolent side of the good man's character. They gave many proofs of their gratitude, one of the oddest being when they returned him his watch, which a young urchin had stolen from him in The Cut thoroughfare running out of the Westminster Bridge Road. The lad did not know Lord Shaftesbury, but one of his tutors happened to see him commit the robbery, and was half inclined to thrash him on the spot for "easing" the common friend. Punishment was, however, inflicted upon the gamin the next night. He was thrust into a sack with the watch tied round his neck, and deposited on the door-step of his lordship's residence. The bell was rung, and when the butler opened the door the sack and the living

freight tumbled into the hall. On a card suspended from the watch was the following exhortation to Earl Shaftesbury: "Lock 'im up, mi lord, he's a disgrace to our profession; he orter known how yer lordship was free of the wud [*sic*]; giv' 'im five years 'ard. Yer Friends." Lord Shaftesbury took his watch, and, instead of prosecuting the thief, turned him into an honest shoeblack. ("Pickpockets and the Late Lord Shaftesbury" 1885)

53. SELLING SOVEREIGNS

Summary: A bet is laid on a man standing on London Bridge for a day and failing to sell a single sovereign for a penny. Earliest Attestation: the mid-1820s. Motif: N/A. Secondary Literature: N/A.

The earliest *full* version of "Selling Sovereigns" known to me dates to 1832:

> A gentleman laid a wager to a considerable amount, that he would stand for a whole day on London Bridge with a trayful of sovereigns, fresh from the Mint, and be unable to find a purchaser for them at a penny a piece. Not one was disposed of. (Chambers 1832 II, 633–35; for an earlier allusion: "Thames Police" 1830)

The story points to the cynicism of people, perhaps particularly those living in a big city. "Suspicion," in the words of a roughly contemporary writer, "is ever ready to mar good fortune, and whispers in the ear of every passer-by, 'all is not gold that glitters'" ("Strong's Sonnets" 1835). Or, in more concrete terms, from a summary of the narrative published in 1908, "the offer was too good to be true, and [those going by] laughed at the idea of being able to buy sovereigns at a penny a time" ("It will cost you nothing" 1908).

Where did the story come from? One London swindler, who knew it well, reported, circa 1850, that it involved Captain Barclay (1779–1854), a celebrated Scottish walker, who was famous in the late eighteenth and early nineteenth century for his pedestrian challenges made for large sums of money. Here the bet is mixed up with anti-Semitism.

> Captain Barclay, and another of the same sort, bet a wager, that one of these Jew-boys could not dispose of a certain number of real sovereigns in a given time,

supposing the Jew-boy cried out nothing more than "here's sovereigns a penny a piece." The number he was to sell was 50 within the hour, and to take his station at London Bridge. The wager was made, the Jew-boy procured, and the sovereigns put into the pot lid. "Here are real sovereigns a penny a piece, who'll buy?" he cried; but he sold only a few. The number disposed of within the hour, I have heard, was seventeen. (Mayhew 1851, I, 353)

There are other references connecting this wager to Captain Barclay, including a court case from 1830, when a "young man" in the dock claimed that he had been, previously, "engaged by Captain Barclay to sell sovereigns at a penny a piece at the end of London Bridge, when the celebrated wager was laid" ("Thames Police" 1830). The "young man," a street seller and political radical, does not inspire trust as a source for oral history. Barclay's name is again associated with the bet in 1903 ("Sovereigns at a Penny a Dozen" 1903). However, there are other contenders including a Captain Smith and Captain Brown ("Sovereign Gulls" 1840, 213), the Marquis of Waterford ("Two men…" 1840), "three sporting gentlemen" ("Gulling" 1885), "a fabulously rich marquis" ("The Strangest of Wagers" 1895), and, in 1917, it was even claimed that it was a "psychologist" who had laid the bet ("The Value" 1917)! There is a persistent, and I imagine groundless, tradition that the bet took place in 1809 or 1810 ("Carlisle Races" 1859; "Gulling the British Public" 1885; the nineteenth-century sovereign was minted for the first time in 1817; perhaps the coin in question was originally a guinea?) London Bridge, which recurs again and again as the setting is redolent with English folklore (Gomme 1908, 22–32).[27]

What *is* clear, in all this, is that the story went hand-in-hand with swindling. The reason that members of the public did not want to buy the cut-rate sovereigns was that they were used to swindles where they were invited to pay a penny for something that was apparently valuable but that was actually worthless. This included "sovereigns." At Southampton Races in 1840, one "young fellow" was trying to sell sovereigns at "half-crown a piece." "We did not hear how much counterfeit money the fellow got rid of, but his wager was repeated more than once" ("Southampton Races" 1840). In the same year a similar trick was reported from central London about two men selling sovereigns for a sixpence ("Two men" 1840). Then, also in 1840, the swindle was played out in the suburbs of London. Here the swindler's patter is preserved.

Fifty golden sovereigns at three-pence each, to decide a most important wager … Fifty golden sovereigns at three-pence each. The wager is, that in the short space of half an hour I shall dispose of fifty golden sovereigns at three pence each. ("Sovereign Gulls" 1840)

By 1859 the story-telling and scamming had aligned perfectly. At Carlisle Races in that year a "fellow dressed as a livery footman," trying to sell "gold" rings spoke thus:

> You will remember, gentleman, the celebrated wager made in 1810, when a man stood upon London Bridge selling sovereigns for pennies and saw the crowd go by without believing him. ("Carlisle Races" 1859)

Mayhew's swindler, circa 1850, offered some historical perspective: "The wager between the two sporting noblemen has been a long time settling. I've been at it more than fifteen years" (1851, I, 353). This takes us back into the 1830s. There is a court case from 1825 ("Sentences" 1825). Mayhew's swindler believed that the swindle had been inspired by a real bet. I suspect—though, I have no proof—that the swindle inspired the story.

"Selling Sovereigns" had a fascinating afterlife in the early twentieth century in advertisements. It was used for selling notepaper in 1902: "You know the story of the man who tried to sell sovereigns on London Bridge for a penny each" ("One Shilling for a Pound" 1902). In 1908 it was used to advertise a prize draw: "You may have heard of the man who stood the whole of one morning on London Bridge" ("It will cost you nothing!" 1908). Then in 1909 it was used by a printer in Workington: "The man who attempted to stop the traffic on London Bridge [?] by selling sovereigns, succeeded in selling one" ("The man who ..." 1909). In 1917 it was trotted out to sell silver ("The Value").

54. SEWER MONSTERS

Summary: Monsters live in the London sewers. Earliest Attestation: a possible reference in the eighteenth century, well established by the midnineteenth century. Motif: N/A. Secondary Literature: Brunvand 2012, I, 15–16; a fundamental web resource for these questions is http://sewergator.com/ [accessed 7 May 2019], which has a full archive of nineteenth-century references to sewer monsters from the United States.

Crocodiles and alligators in sewers are among the most celebrated twentieth- and twenty-first-century urban legends (Brunvand 2012, I, 15–16; Reid 1991,

184–85). However, there were already nineteenth-century accounts from London about animals trapped in the sewers there. These included numerous cats, dogs, a hedgehog, horses, and even a seal (for dogs, cat, seal and hedgehog, see Hollingshead 1862, 70–71; for horses, see "Sewer Accident" 1852). But there were also less pleasant creatures hiding in the shadows. The most important sewer monster in the 1800s was, of course, the rat. There can be no doubt whatsoever that the sewers of London hosted large rat populations. The toshers (London's sewage scavengers, see **"There's Gold in Those Sewers"**) and the sewage workers claimed that these rats, on occasion, killed anyone foolhardy to go into the underground tunnels alone.

> Stories are told of sewer hunters beset by myriads of enormous rats, and slaying thousands of them, till at length the swarms of the savage things overpowered them, and in a few days afterwards their skeletons were discovered picked to the very bone. (Mayhew 1851, II, 150)

Or in the vivid words of a tosher: "They've pulled men down, and worried 'em, and picked their bones as clean as a washed plate" (Kirwan 1871, 402–3). These stories seem to have been known not only among toshers, but also among the general population. Take these rat horror stories from a tosher interviewed by Mayhew. The tosher assumed a general knowledge about rat atrocities (my italics):

> I know a chap as the rats tackled in the sewers; they bit him hawfully: *you must ha' heard on it*; it was him as the watermen went in arter when they heard him a shouting as they was a rowin' by. (Mayhew 1851, II, 154)

> *Do you recollect* hearing on the man as was found in the sewers about twelve year ago? *Oh you must.* The rats eat every bit of him, and left nothink but his bones. (Mayhew 1851, II, 154)

A particularly celebrated case came, circa 1843, when a tosher's skeleton was found underground ("Life" 1845; I take this to be the case alluded to Mayhew 1851, II, 154, where the death is definitely ascribed to rats). His fellow toshers became convinced that their colleague had been eaten alive by rats. The official line was that the man had had a fit, which had killed him, and that only then had the rats moved in to devour his flesh ("Life" 1845).

Associated with these sewer rats there may have been the Queen Rat:

[T]here was a kind of spirit down the sewers who would invisibly follow the men about, and if she saw one she liked, she would listen to his conversations with his mates, find out what kind of ladies he fancied, and the turn herself into a woman that matched his particular tastes, and appear next to him when he was out enjoying himself. (Thompson 1995a; see also Thompson 1995b)

Unfortunately, the Queen Rat is only attested from the mid-1990s, in a series of memories handed down in a London family. I'm skeptical about these memories for three reasons: (i) the survival of these kind of folk memories in a working-class London family over almost a century and a half; (ii) the transmission of quite explicit sexual details in these stories over that same period; (iii) the lack of easy British parallels. Jacqueline Simpson (1995), however, finds the legend credible.

There was certainly, in the nineteenth century, a belief in a number of feral hogs in the sewers near Hampstead. Mayhew wrote in 1851:

The story runs, that a sow in young, by some accident got down the sewer through an opening, and wandering away from the spot, littered and reared her offspring in the drain, feeding on the offal and garbage washed into it constantly. Here it is alleged, the breed multiplied exceedingly, and have become almost as ferocious as they are numerous. (Mayhew 1851, II, 154–55; see also Pettitt 1995b and Ingemark 2008, 157–62)

Note that rats were particularly associated with areas below slaughterhouses and elsewhere that flesh and blood poured into the sewers (Kirwan 1871, 330; Hollingshead 1862, 66). Mayhew continues:

This story, apocryphal as it seems, has nevertheless its believers, and it is ingeniously argued that the reason why none of the subterranean animals have been able to make their way to the light of day is, that, they could only do so by reaching the mouth of the river at the river side, while in order to arrive at that point, they must necessarily encounter the Fleet ditch, which runs towards the river with great rapidity, and as it is the obstinate nature of a pig to swim against the stream, the wild hogs of the sewer invariably work their way back to their original quarters, and are thus never to be seen. (Mayhew 1851, II, 155)

Had Mayhew been tricked into printing a "bull" by one of his tosher informants? It seems not. In 1859 the *Daily Telegraph* ran with an editorial including labored allusions to a "monstrous breed of black swine" in the Hampstead sewers, "which have propagated and run wild among the slimy feculence, and whose ferocious snouts will one day up-root Highgate archway" (Boyle 1989, 204[28] dated 10 Oct. 1859—I have not been able to check the original. Pettitt 1995b, argues that this report is independent of Mayhew; it certainly is not passively copied from that author.) In 1871 another "shore worker" referred to the same dread creatures: "They do says there's wild pigs almost as big as bears in some shores [sewers]" (Rowe 1871, 402). We also read that about 1850—though I have found no contemporary reference—a man captured a pig in a London sewer, which desperately resisted attempts to bring it above ground. The pig "was exhibited, during six months, in a show by his captor, who charged so much admission for a sight of this sewer-prodigy, by which he made a great amount of money" (Morwood 1883, 188). It may be possible to trace the sewer pig legend back to the early eighteenth century. In 1736 a "boar" escaped into the Fleet Ditch sewer, lived there for five months and then emerged rather larger than when it had gone in: "improved in price from ten shillings to two guineas" ("Tuesday" 1736). Could yarns about these sewer pigs perhaps have been used to explain the occasional body parts found floating in the sewer run-offs? (Hollingshead 1862, 70, 79–80).

We might even be able to track the sewer crocodile back, at least in part, to Victorian London. In 1892 a medical man had the idea of introducing crocodiles into the Thames. These crocs were to be brought to London, stamped with the city seal, and then allowed to feast on "all the unpleasant stuff that the once-lauded silver stream contains" ("The Crocodile" 1892; five instances in the BNA, accessed 7 May 2019; the article was credited to *The Medical Press and Circular*. I have not been able to examine the original. Was it perhaps an April Fool's joke that got out of hand?). After the Thames was cleaned, the crocodiles would be introduced into the London sewers to clean them out. This was a hypothesis rather than a legend, and a fairly bizarre hypothesis at that. But it might have spawned stories in the British capital and helped the establishment of the sewer crocodile in the United States. The earliest reference to an alligator in an American sewer dates to 1873 in Atlanta ("The New Sensation" 1873; a factual event?).

55. SHE'S MY DAUGHTER?

Summary: Children, separated from family members early in life, accidentally marry parents or siblings in adulthood. Earliest Attestation: antiquity. Motif: N365 "Incest unwittingly committed"; missing from Baughman 1966, 372. Secondary Literature: Ashliman and Duggan 2005. Compare with: "**Do You Know Her?**"

Cases of incest were covered in nineteenth-century British and American newspapers and frequently ended in prosecutions: usually these were minors being sexually abused by parents or elder siblings (a useful study for North America is Sacco 2009, 19–52). However, there were also narratives about accidental incest, a well-known folk motif dating back to Oedipus (Ashliman and Duggan 2005). These were established in British folklore, although scant attention has been paid to this story type by scholars. In an example from the seventeenth century (Hall 1654, 389–91, which seems to be British, with German authorities also cited), a mother deliberately has sexual relations with her son (although he does not realize), and later the son unknowingly marries his daughter/sister. For the nineteenth century, at Martham there was "a gruesome story of a man who was unwittingly married to his own mother. According to the inscription on a stone now decently covered over, the parties were buried in the church!" ("At Hickling" 1908).

There follows a very generic English example from 1899:

> The facts are that a widower fell in love with a married a lady much younger than himself. They enjoyed their married life for about a year, when the gentleman made the awful discovery that he had married his own daughter. It appears that she had been lost when very young, and her parents had given her up for dead: but she had been adopted by some lady, and was living under another name. However, the gentleman took it to heart so much that he committed suicide, and his daughter (and wife) died from a broken heart. ("Oddities" 1899)

This story type depends on a credible trauma, the loss of a child, and a scarcely credible coincidence: the father and daughter (or sometimes the brother and sister) later meeting and falling in love. Naturally, these unbelievable but all too readable coincidences were often found in the press. There follow some examples from the turn of the century when such reports were most common.

In 1894 a young Hungarian woman had gone to America and met there an older Hungarian whom she married. On returning together to Hungary, they discovered the terrible truth that they were daughter and father ("Married His Own Daughter" 1894). In 1897 a man committed suicide in London after discovering that he had married his sister: both had been stolen by gypsies from the same squire's family ("Truth" 1897; "Mr. Wyatt ..." 1897 for the falsehoods in this report). In 1900 there was a report of how Adam Cordiff had "nearly" married his own daughter. This forty-five-year-old from Ohio had been courting a young woman in West Virginia. Luckily, before the wedding his wife-to-be had shown him a photo album with her mother in it ("Nearly" 1900). In 1907 an almost identical story was set in Japan ("Father's Dilemma" 1907). In 1908 a German woman went to America, married an older man, and then they came back to Bromberg (their home town): "On their arrival ... it was discovered that the husband was none other than her own father, who, while in the United States, had changed his name" ("Amazing" 1908).[29]

There are also some cases of one of the married pair knowing and the other being ignorant of their blood relations.

> In Milan, in 1874, an Englishman of wealth and position became the father of an illegitimate daughter. The mother married and lived elsewhere, while the child was carefully and liberally educated in France and Italy by the father, who represented himself as her guardian, and brought her to live in Littlehampton, unknown to his wife and family. In 1890 his wife died, and within a few months, he proposed marriage to the ward who was also his daughter. The marriage took place privately in London, unknown to his friends and relatives. In 1892 a child was born, and in July the mother then aged eighteen learnt the true facts of her relationship. She at once withdrew from the house and took refuge with a clergyman, by whom, we understand, measures are being taken suitable to deal with the case, though the matter may be arranged privately. ("Another Scandal" 1892)

There is no longer any remarkable coincidence, and stories such as this are all too credible. This is particularly so, when one considers the interesting but ill-established psychological principle of "genetic sexual attraction": siblings or parent/children separated early in life may feel sexual attraction on being reunited in adulthood (Greenberg and Littlewood 1995; Paul 2010 wrote that while "the data [for GSA] are as yet scanty, they are well documented").

56. SHOOTING AT A GHOST

Summary: Daring young man agrees to wait in a haunted room; he fires at a (fake) ghost, and the ghost throws bullets back at him. Earliest Attestation: 1833. Motif: N/A. Secondary Literature: N/A.

The following story was published in the United States in 1889.

About six years ago there was studying at a noted eastern medical university an extremely bright and promising young fellow from Tennessee. He was distinguished among his fellows for his absolute fearlessness. Many a ghastly joke have they put up on him to shake him from his pinnacle of courage, but he remained undaunted. They resolved to give him a mighty test. They dared him to sit alone through the night in the dissecting room in the presence of a corpse. He accepted the challenge. The dissecting room was a long, narrow chamber with a door at each end, with several suggestive tables in the middle and ranging shelves of surgical instruments on the walls. Into this room was brought the body of a man who had committed suicide a couple of days before. The body was laid on a slab at one end of the room. At the other end was a table, with a student's lamp in the center and covered with books. Two loaded revolvers were laid on the table side by side. The student had placed them there as a precautionary measure. But the men who were testing his nerve took the bullets out of the revolvers and replaced them with blank cartridges. Early in the evening the student entered the room, examined the corpse, lit his lamp and sat down at his table and began to read. He became deeply absorbed in what he was reading and was oblivious to his surroundings. His fellows, who were watching him through a crack in the door at the other end of the room, took advantage of his absorption and one of them, clad in a long white robe, quietly entered the room and took the corpse from the slab and placed it underneath a table. He then lay down on the slab in the place of the corpse. The student, intensely interested in his book, heard nothing and did not look up. He read on for another half hour, when he heard a slight noise. He looked up and he turned white as he noticed one arm of the corpse slowly moving. He was totally unsuspicious of any trick. The supposed corpse slowly sat bolt upright. After a moment it rose to its feet and stood perfectly still. The fellows, who were watching through the farther door, noticed that the student was deathly pale and seemed dazed. But he did not lose his nerve. He jumped up, seized a revolver in either hand and faced the supposed corpse. The corpse took a long step towards him, then slowly advanced. The student commanded it to stop. No response, but the corpse kept advancing. Again the student, evidently crazed at the sight, commanded it to halt. No attention was paid to his demand, and the corpse was gradually nearing him. The youth, who was enacting the part of the corpse, raised his hand, pretended to catch the bullet (he had a hand full of them), and threw it back at the student. Again the latter fired, and again and again, until he had discharged the twelve cartridges. After each shot the bullet was tossed back at him. The pistols fell out of the student's hands and he dropped dead. ("About six years ago . . ." 1889, *CW*)

The earliest version I know is from Britain and dates to 1833 ("Fatal Frolic"). Two much longer British versions were published in 1886: one set in Germany ("A Wager" 1886), the second in the Crimea in the dragoons during the war ("The Spectre Monk"). In all four there is a wager or a challenge given to a fearless man; in all four cases the ghost throws the bullets back in the fearless man's face; in two of the three versions—the one set in America and the one set in Germany—the man dies of fear.

57. THE SHOPLIFTER'S DILEMMA

Summary: A wealthy female shoplifter is caught and given a choice between being handed over to the police or being whipped; she chooses a whipping. Earliest Attestation: mid 1840s (possibly Scottish origin). Motif: N/A. Secondary Literature: N/A.

The shoplifter's dilemma is well told in a newspaper story from 1846.

> A young lady, whose name, on account of her respectable connections, we forbear to hint at, lately called upon a milliner in Edinburgh, and, having made some trifling purchase, was about to depart, when one of the assistants whispered to her mistress that she had observed the lady secrete a valuable lace collar. The milliner instantly charged her customer with the theft. She denied it, and the milliner insisted on her being searched, when the missing article was discovered in her muff. "Now madam," said the milliner, "you have been guilty of a most disgraceful act, and I am determined you shall not escape unpunished. I give you the choice of two things—either I will have you given up to the police, or you must submit to receive a sound whipping." After many vain attempts to mollify the

anger of the dressmaker, the fair thief at last, with no very good grace, consented to submit to the latter alternative. A servant having been despatched for a pair of taws, with which she quickly returned, and all obstacles having been removed, the milliner proceeded to administer the well-merited punishment, which she did with a heart and a will, in the presence and much to the entertainment of the assembled workwomen, who, in turn, "took" the taws. All parties being tired with the exercise, the lady, whose complexion was considerably heightened, was permitted to withdraw, and stepping into a noddy in which she had come, was driven home, having got a lesson which she will not soon forget, and which will operate as a warning to those ladies who cannot distinguish between *meum* and *tuum*. ("Lynch Law" 17 Jan 1846; this story is credited to the *Edinburgh Chronicle*, but mainly circulated in Ireland)

The "extraordinary story" was not a first for another journalist noted that "a prototype . . . , stating the occurrence to be in London, went the round of the papers, a year or two" before ("Lynch Law" 21 Jan 1846). This is the remarkable "A Tale of a Lady Thief" (1845, *FG*) in which a woman is whipped by one "John Thomas" in a London baby-linen shop: it is the only example known to me where a man carries out the punishment on a woman. In the *Daily Telegraph* in 1869, an "Edinburgh shopkeeper" is given a "private whipping" ("Lady Shop-Lifters" 1869). Then, from 1897, I have come across several versions. In that year "a Westend Shopkeeper" began "a novel course of procedure." A wealthy shoplifter was given the customary choice and gave the customary answer:

> Two stout birch rods were produced. The proprietor retired, and the sister [of the proprietor?], with the assistance of the manageress of the establishment, proceeded to administer to the lady corporal punishment in the orthodox method practised at our public schools. ("A Cure for Kleptomania" 1897)

In 1903 the same newspaper reported that this shopkeeper had confided that some "twenty ladies have accepted the ordeal" ("Birch for Lady Shoplifters" 1903). In reaction to the story, a woman wrote to the letter's page about being whipped in a Glasgow establishment. The punishment "was not with a cane or a birch, but with her hand in the orthodox style, reminiscent of my earlier days, and in the presence of my twelve-year-old daughter" ("The Birch for Lady Shoplifters" 9 Feb. 1903). She felt the punishment had done her good. Another woman who worked in a firm on Princes Street in central Edinburgh described, in a letter to the paper, that she had stolen some trifling objects from her workplace. She was given the choice of being handed over to the police or being punished. She chose to be caned. "The manageress is a tall, muscular person, while I am about the medium height, though well built. She lifted me in her arms and laid me on a table, removing my clothes" ("The Birch for Female Shoplifters" 28 Feb 1903). A Princes Street firm subsequently wrote in to "absolutely and flatly contradict the scene of the outrage." "We regret that there is some foundation for the report that such an atrocity took place in Edinburgh, but the street dishonored by it was not Princes Street, nor was the firm implicated a Princes Street firm" ("A Vindication" 1903).

In 1904 the practice was reported in London:

> Two lady assistants were called into the room. The door was locked, and the wealthy thief was placed at one corner of the table, and her ankles strapped to the table legs. Then she was bent over on the table face down, and her wrists were strapped to two of the remaining corners. Thus trussed she was vigorously belaboured with a yard measure. ("Drapers Who Cane" 1904)

In 1913 a related story has a couple of suffragettes vandalize a golf course. Only one is caught, by a brother and two sisters, and the captured suffragette, after begging not to be taken to the police—she was about to be married—was given the choice of being whipped (like a naughty child) or having her head shaved (like a lunatic). She chose to be whipped. The siblings blindfolded her, took her to their home, and the two sisters gave her "a dozen strokes" there ("Pretty Suffragette's Punishment" 1913). In 1915, a letter-writer describes how, around 1911, one West End drapery offered a thief "the alternative of being handed over to the police or of being turned over the sofa and receiving correction with an improvised birch" (Agony 1915). As in all the cases above, the thief chose corporal punishment.

There was clearly some satisfaction for newspaper readers in seeing thieves, particularly the wealthy, being punished for their crimes. Indeed, there was so much interest in wealthy shoplifters in the 1840s that newspaper stories were invented about them ("Shoplifting" 1845; to be read with "Frauds on Newspapers" 1845). One short story from the 1890s has a wealthy shoplifter commit suicide after being caught ("A Terrible Fall" 1895; for another example of the shame of shoplifting among the wealthy, see "A Delicate" 1843).

Did the beatings described really happen? The number of references suggests either a widespread form of vigilantism, which has so far eluded social historians, or a Victorian urban legend. I personally find it hard to believe that thieves—particularly wealthy thieves—would be whipped in back rooms. I admit, however, to being shaken by the two letters to papers from women who claimed to have undergone the experience: even if one of them was an employee rather than a customer ("The Birch for Lady Shoplifters" 9 Feb 1903;

"The Birch for Female Shoplifters," 28 Feb 1903: note neither could be classed as "wealthy"; in the second case, the victim is not a customer who has stolen, but an employee who is furious about the way in which she has been humiliated by her manageress).

Was there also a latent sexual element in the story, at least for some readers? Consider this report from 1933, from a date when writers were freer to express themselves in these matters than in the 1870s. It reads like an S&M fantasy.

> Some time ago a girl of 15 and two handsome, charming ladies—Mrs Y, aged 23, and Mrs Z, aged 36, were birched by two strong young women for shoplifting, one of whom recounted the incident. The girl of 15 received eight strokes and the two women 24 strokes each. The former must have suffered a good deal for she shrieked very loudly with pain after each stroke, and was a long time getting over it. The two women, however, were much braver, though Mrs. Y could not withhold her cries for long, and was begging for mercy towards the end. Mrs Z. a very beautiful women [sic], displayed unusual fortitude at first, although the two girls used long fresh birch rods and whipped her with all their might in a slow cadence. When the second dozen was about to begin, however, Mrs. Z could stand no more and writhed and squealed pitifully beneath each subsequent stroke. Instead of relenting the girls, biding their time, birching the victim with even greater force so that when it was over Mrs. Z was quivering all over and sobbing as if her heart would break . . . I may add that the culprits were always tied and received the punishment on the bare flesh. (W. C. 1933)

A hidden sexual element was maybe lurking behind the earlier reports—most dramatically "A Tale of a Lady Thief" (1845) with its sexual innuendo[30]—and was perhaps one of the reasons that they seem to have disappeared for most of the second half of the nineteenth century. I would, in any case, be inclined to characterize the "Shoplifter's Dilemma" as an urban legend that surfaced briefly in the 1840s in British and Irish newspapers, but that became too risqué for the press to cover in high Victorian England. The story then re-emerged in the newspapers in the very late nineteenth century and, in the twentieth century, its ability to titillate was fully exploited.

58. THE SKELETONS THAT ELOPED

> Summary: A young couple are believed to have eloped from a party; later their skeletons are found showing either that they did not elope or that they died as soon as they set off from home. Earliest Attestation: 1866. Motif: N/A. Secondary Literature: N/A. Compare with: "**Hollow Tree Death**"; "**Immured Lovers**"; "**Mistletoe Bride**."

Elopements were a staple of nineteenth-century newspapers. Perhaps the only other Victorian institution to bring editors and readers such glee was the duel (see the "**Poison Duel**"). The fact of a couple running off together was "romantic"; they also had occasional comic value. Here, just to give a sense of the potential of a nineteenth-century elopement, is a brief summary of some six months of newsworthy elopements from 1882:

> An elopement at Louisville was frustrated by a small boy, who with a well directed snowball knocked off the coachman's hat. While he was recovering his hat the train the unhappy couple were endeavouring to reach started, and the pursuing parents came up. In Illinois a young lady ran away barefooted; her lover insisted upon stopping to buy a pair of shoes. The delay proved fatal. A lover at Winona was so impetuous that he did not even wait for the young lady's consent, but lassoed her as she was going to church, and was dragging her away to a justice's office when help arrived.... One elopement ended in a tragic manner. The lady was pursued by her mother down the railroad track. The old lady, in her excitement, failed to notice the approach of a locomotive, which ran over her and killed her. ("Eccentric Elopements" 1882)

There was, however, a formulaic elopement story whose origins probably ran back into early modern European folklore. Typically, a young man and woman disappeared and were assumed to have eloped: they often disappear from a party ("Romantic" 1866, wedding party?; "A Remarkable Story" 1884, wedding party; "A Warwickshire Ghost" 1914, Christmas party). Several years later, two skeletons are found in the vicinity and are identified as the young couple. The explanation at this point differs. Sometimes we have an elopement gone wrong—the couple had fallen down a mine shaft, say; sometimes they had been murdered. Here is a French instance of an elopement gone wrong, which appeared in the British newspapers in 1866:

M. de R___, having acquired a fortune in business, retired to a handsome property he possessed near Fontainebleau. Soon after, his daughter Julie, 21 years of age, was asked in marriage by a gentleman in the neighbourhood, and in spite of her opposition and avowed repugnance, the wedding took place. In the evening the bride was missed, and the result of the researches made was only to find that the groom's man, who had been a friend of the young lady's from infancy, had likewise disappeared. The father, like everyone else, believed in an elopement, and all the usual means were employed to trace the fugitives, but unsuccessfully. This occurred five years ago, and M. de R___ having lately purchased some adjoining property on which was a quarry long out of use, set some men to work, who found at the bottom of an old excavation two skeletons, which from the remains of the clothes and the jewels were recognised as the missing bride and her lover. ("Romantic" 1866)

There are also examples of murders dressed up as elopements. For instance, in Russia in 1900, David O. ("the full surname is suppressed, *noblesse oblige*, in the official register") was given a ten-year penal sentence: he had killed his elder brother and his fiancée and "caused it to be bruited about the neighbourhood" that the two had eloped. Their skeletons were later discovered, and the murdered brother was identified by a ring. Justice followed ("Romantic Story" 1900).

Here is another variant that originated in the French newspapers in 1884. It builds on a supposed wedding scandal in 1867, for which I can find no proof:

On January 17, 1867, M. Augoit married Mdlle. Marie Domadier. During the wedding breakfast at the Palais Royal a waiter informed the bridegroom that a coachman wished to speak with him on a matter of importance. M. Augoit excused himself to his guests and left the table. Several persons saw him enter a cab, bareheaded, in his wedding suit, with a serviette tucked in his breast. Since then his relations and the police have made every endeavour in their power to solve the mystery, but in vain, and the unfortunate bride resumed her maiden name and went to live with a sister at Neuilly. Two or three weeks ago, Senor Perez Urrigaray, whilst chamois hunting in the mountains near Seo d' Urgel, in Spain, was obliged to descend to the bottom of a deep crevice in search of an animal he had killed. There he came upon a skeleton to which some remnants of clothing were still adhering, and on returning to Seo he gave notice to the authorities. ("A Remarkable Story" 1884)

Augoit's body had been found. "It is rumoured that Augoit's marriage had aroused the jealousy of a woman who entrapped him into eloping with her to Spain, and there hurled him over the precipice on his stating his intention to return to his wife" ("A Remarkable Story" 1884).

This story type was familiar in British versions too, but it typically appeared, when set there, as fiction not pseudo-news. Take this from a storyteller who, in describing a psychopathic local family, wrote a brief summary (recalling in some way the "**Immured Lovers**"):

> There was a lady who had given her squire cause of jealousy with a handsome cousin; the pair were believed to have eloped from a Shrovetide merry-making; the squire went abroad, leaving his heir and lands in the care of a faithful steward, and died fighting in the Low Countries; but years after, two skeletons were found locked up in a deep and long-disused wine cellar. ("The Unhired Servant" 1859)

Consider, likewise, this story from 1891, which ends with the discovery of two skeletons: "Yes, she and Clymer disappeared together the night Massing killed himself, and people all think they eloped" (Fields 1891).

The story apparently had roots in British folklore. We have a record of skeletons of an eloping pair being dragged from a pond at Bulkington (Warwickshire) in the early nineteenth century. Here a young couple had been said to have eloped from a Christmas party but had actually committed suicide together. A haunting caused the bodies to be turned up and the mystery of their disappearance to be resolved ("A Warwickshire Ghost" 1914). In 1922 the discovery of two bodies at a mine working at Castleton in the Peak District led to much excitement in the area. Local tradition had it that two eloping lovers, Allan and Clara, had been murdered there, around 1760, by some drunk and avaricious miners and then been buried in secret. It was thus suggested that these bodies proved the tradition to be correct ("Skulls and Bones" 1921). However, a guidebook described how the lovers' skeletons had already been discovered several decades before (quoted in "Skulls and Bones" 1921).

59. THE SPANISH PRISONER

Summary: A letter from Spain describes a treasure buried close to the recipient's house: as soon as a small sum of money is paid, then the treasure can be retrieved. Earliest Attestation: mid-1870s. Motif: N/A. Secondary Literature: Marco 2018; Lincos 2018.

This letter understandably came as a surprise to the householder in Arbroath, Scotland, who received it in the spring of 1879. The writer, a complete stranger, was in the "Prison of Madrid," and he wrote in broken English of buried treasure near Arbroath.

Dear Sir. I take the liberty to address you this letter fur speak to you of an affair of the greatest importance. I was Colonel in the army of the King Charles the 7th when the last civil war in Spain, and in February 1876 I was commissioned by the Chief General, the Count of Caserta, for to conduit and deposit in the Bank of England the sum of six millions of pesetas (Spanish shillings). With this sum I come out from Pena Plata, but they were so many the dangers of this commission that it should be too large to tell you all in this present letter till the moment that for to put in salvation the said sum was obliged to bury in the earth in the environs of your town the little iron box, where into were the funds, in bank notes. Immediately as I do the occultation [hiding] I sign a typographical plan the place where the Box was buried, this plan I put it into a secret of my bagagges, unknow of some an other person then [than] I. I retourn in Spain for given account of my mission and take new orders, and arrive to Santander I was done prissoner and conduit [brought] here to Madrid, where I am now in this prisson, and my bagagges were taken by Tribunal, who has my process [trial]. Now, I am sentensied to 12 years of prisson, and the Tribunal has notified to that if I not pay the costs of the prosess my bagagges shall be sold in public auction. In this situation I desire to recover the buried Box and with gold to be free, but for that I must recover bagagges for obtain the original plan, and I necessity of an honorable person, who do the advanse of the requited sum by Tribunal, and after this same person with the original plan in the hand to find treasure and await my instructions. During the court [short] instance [stay] at your town I have obtained very good references upon your honorability and good position, and I in the complete conviction that you will help me in this important affair, and I will given you the third part of the contains [contents] of the buried Box for your service. I have to your disposition important document by which you shall see that all what I tell you now is true and veritable. As I can not receive myself your letters in this prisson, you shall put it into tow [two] enveloppes, the interior to my name and the exterieur at the address here under who is friend of complete confidence, who will bring to me all your letters. Allso for precaution you shall not sign your letters with your name: you shall put only "T. W. O." Waiting your reply very soon, I am, Dear sir, your faithfully, Pedro Miguel. Address: Spain. Sr. Dn. Alfredo Crespo Sagarra, Comisionista, Madrid. ("The Buried Treasure Swindle" 1879)

Lest there be any doubt as to the letter's content, Pedro Miguel had buried some treasure near Arbroath. Unfortunately, Pedro was in prison, and the treasure map was in some luggage that had been confiscated by the court who had sentenced him. Pedro, then, wrote to an Arbroath local asking for help. As soon as the Arbroathian paid to release the luggage, Pedro would forward the map and the local would take, as payment, a third of the contents of the treasure trove. Everyone would win.

Welcome to the "Spanish Prisoner" scam. Here we have the grandfather of the modern email scam; a "Nigerian" requests an advance to help him get a large sum of money out of his home country, money that he is prepared to share with his generous benefactor. The buried treasure scam was both more convincing and more expensive to run than email equivalents. The treasure was not in a Swiss bank account or a safety deposit box in Tanzania, but in a field just a couple of miles from the correspondent's home. The problem for the crooks was that letters cost money (although I know of one case, "That Buried Treasure" 1894, where the "mark" received a letter without a stamp and was expected to pay 5d postage!), and it was also necessary to scout out people in a given locality who would be likely to have the necessary funds. This operation was run out of Spain, probably from Barcelona ("The Empress Eugenie's Jewels" 1882). According to one source, the first letters appeared in France in 1870 ("The Empress Eugenie's Jewels" 1882; but Lincos 2018 points to an Italian version from 1765; and Marco 2018, 77–80, notes antecedents—without a letter—in Arab-Spanish folklore). The earliest I have been able to find from Britain dates to 1872 ("Jewels" 1872). The group was ambitious, though, and would eventually send letters to North America and even to Indian princes ("An Old Swindle" 1898; "The Spanish Treasure Swindle" 1898). Their persistence is demonstration enough that the scheme worked. We know of one British mark who sent 700 pounds and of another legal case launched against the operation ("The Buried Treasure Swindle" 1894; "Treasure Seekers" 1879; Marco 2018, 84 talks of 4% of contactees falling for the swindle).

The first record of this ruse I have been able to uncover in Britain dates to 1872. In that year one "José Toreno" contacted a Mr. James Thomas of Cardiff, informing him that he had been obliged to bury some 8,000,000 francs-worth of treasure near the Welsh capital ("Jewels" 1872). One of the most bizarre aspects of the scam is the notion that rich Carlists were rushing around the British countryside burying their valuables on the edges of second- and third-tier urban centers, including Buckfastleigh, Bungay, Leith, Goole, Jedburgh, Kirk Hallam, Otterton and Tavistock. In 1875 the scam could still be described as a "Novel Attempt at a Swindle." But this would change. In 1888 a journalist spoke wearily of "another ingenious Spanish swindle" ("A Buried Treasure"); by 1893 a newspaper article about the hoax was entitled "The Old, Old Story"; and by 1905 a Scottish writer talked of how the "impecunious occupants of the military prisons of Spain still continue to plead for help to generous-hearted merchants and professional men" in Perthshire ("Spanish Swindle Again" 1905).

The scam was, of course, all about money. But as the newspapers showed, by publishing the letters, it also became a story shared by Victorians of all classes. There was the wealthy Spaniard with his hoard thrown into prison. But there was also the British correspondent who, according to temperament, either squandered his fortune or recognized the "dirty" foreign trick for what it was. Local newspapers often made much of the fact that *their* readers were too smart to fall for such nonsense: for example, "We fancy, however, [the swindlers] failed to make any marked impression upon hard headed cautious Yorkshiremen: at any rate we never learned that any one in this district was victimised" ("The Buried Treasure Swindle" 1894). The evil geniuses behind the scheme recognized the importance of a good yarn. Scamming is, after all, a form of narrative: "se valieron de la imaginación literaria para construir nuevos mundos ficticios que dejaron absorbidos a muchos de sus seducidos lectores" (Marco 2018, 75; Marco, 80–83 also makes the case that the *Count of Montecristo* was a partial inspiration for the Spanish version of the scam). As a result, the letter evolved, being sharpened over the years. In the 1870s there was the treasure and the Spanish prisoner. By the 1890s the prisoner had a daughter who would bring the treasure map north ("Buried Treasure Near Arbroath" 1892; some thirteen years after "The Buried Treasure Swindle" 1879 in the same location). In this way money and a hint of Mediterranean romance were mixed together into the formula.

60. THE SUICIDE CLUB

> Summary: A club in which members, chosen randomly, were expected to commit suicide. Earliest Attestation: 1750s. Motif: N/A. Secondary Literature: Ancery 2019.

In suicide clubs, members were submitted to a semiregular trial. The club president chose, publicly and at random, one of those in the club, who was then given a certain period of time to end his or her life. The origins of this peculiar and largely legendary institution are difficult to trace. The Last Guinea Club operated in Britain and Ireland in the early 1700s. Members who no longer had any money to live their dissipated lives were expected to put a bullet in their brains. Its motto was: "A short life but a merry one" ("Causes of the Increase" 1755; "Traditions" 1871). A suicide club was, it has been claimed, in operation in Berlin in the 1810s. It came to a lonely end in 1817 when the last member shot himself (Hawkins 1829, 165). A suicide club of twelve was said to be operating in Paris in the 1820s (Hawkins 1829, 171). In 1831 there was news of a suicide club in Prussia ("Frédéric Kregler" 1831).

Dante Gabrielle Rossetti wrote in 1848, jokingly, of a "Mutual Suicide Association," "by the regulations whereof any member, being weary of life, may call at any time upon another to cut his throat for him" (Rossetti 1895, II, 42). There is a record of a suicide club in Britain in the 1850s, although it is unclear whether members actually killed themselves or whether, according to our one account, they just experimented with half hanging (allowing themselves to almost die in the noose, "A 'Suicide Club' 1855 is . . ."; recirculated in the 1880s, "What Hanging is Like" 1885). In 1873, a French newspaper ran a story about an English suicide club: "On sait que les Anglais sont les gens les plus excentriques du monde." Apparently, once a year, members met for a wonderful feast, and one of the pieces of cake contained a poisoned portion—signaled by the presence of a *fève* or bean ("Le Club des Suicidés" 1873). A later British author seems to refer to this or to a similar tradition when he writes: "There is a thrilling French story of a Suicide Club the members of which dined together every week, one dish on the table being seasoned with a deadly poison" ("The Horrors" 1884).

The most important development in the history of the legend of the suicide club came in the late 1870s. In 1878 Robert Louis Stevenson published a short story entitled "Story of the Young Man with the Cream Tarts" in a small-circulation magazine entitled *London*. The "Story" details how Prince Florizel infiltrates a suicide club in the capital and dismantles that organization. Members had to regularly draw playing cards, and the man who drew the ace

Figure 16 'A Ladies' Suicide Club' (1898). Note the 'Rules', presumably club rules, on the wall behind.

of spades was sentenced to death, while the man who drew the ace of clubs had to do the killing. The "Story" was part of a triptych known collectively as "The Suicide Club." These three only became really well-known when they were published together in Stevenson's *New Arabian Nights* in 1882 (Stevenson 1915, 3–92). Stevenson seems to have based the "suicide club," in terms of setting, on his own experience at the Savile Club (Abrahamson, "'Here . . .'" 2015). As to the idea of agreed killing and self-killing, Stevenson may have come up with this himself. But it is more likely that he picked up an earlier reference in print or talk to suicide clubs, such as those mentioned in the previous paragraph ("Suicide Clubs" 1898 suggests that Stevenson was inspired by the Bridgeport Suicide Club. The inspiration, if anything, ran the other way; see below). Whatever the case may be, references to suicide clubs became much more common in the English-speaking press after 1882. Stevenson may not have borne moral responsibility for what followed, but he was, as several contemporary writers recognized, the material cause of a change (e.g., "In view of the fact" 1894).

In fact, "suicide club" became part of the language and culture of the English-speaking world. It was used to refer not just to organizations as defined above, but to suicide pacts (for instance, three adolescent males agree to poison themselves together ("Boy's Suicide Club" 1903; see also "A Suicide Club" 1883) and extremely dangerous situations ("The Suicide Club" 1915; the term was used frequently by the British in relation to the Great War; it is not to be found in the longer *OED*). The "suicide club" appeared in jokes ("Finnegan" 1896) and in other stories and novels in English (most famously Barrie's "Society for Doing Without Some People," which combines a murder with a suicide club, Barrie 1888; see also Hulme-Beaman 1899; "The Suicide Club" 1901, set in Chicago).

Suicide clubs were reported widely in the British press at the end of the 1800s and in the early 1900s. There was a rich women's suicide club in San Francisco ("Women's Suicide Club" 1903); the Round Robin Club in New York (which chose victims with a roulette wheel, "A Suicide Club," 17 June 1895, South Wales); another suicide club in New York whose members were called "fellow da se" (get it?) ("The suicide of . . ." 1892); a suicide club in a Romanian military school ("A Suicide Club" 1892); the Hoboken Christmas Day Suicide Club (members chose who was to die at a Christmas day meal, "American Suicide Club 1900); a girls' suicide club in Terida Spain ("Women's Suicide Club" 1904); the Order of the Black Veil in Chicago (the unlucky member received a black veil, gloves, and stockings in the post, "Members" 1908); the St. Petersburg's Suicide Club, which had a portrait of Schopenhauer on the clubhouse wall ("Un 'Club'" 1912); and many, many more. As one British contemporary put it about the reporting of suicide clubs in the United States (although this is equally true for much of the Continent in the period): "One has naturally great doubts as to the authenticity of sensational news telegraphed from America, since pressmen there go on the principle that if piquant items do not evolve themselves from the social congeries they must be invented" ("A Suicide Club" 17 June 1895, Yorkshire).

Sometimes we are clearly dealing with invented reportage. Consider this news about a suicide club based in Vienna, which was apparently rocking the Austro-Hungarian Empire to its foundations in 1897, and that never appeared again in print:

> At a recent sitting no fewer than four of the members drew fatal lots, the result being that they were solemnly pledged to put an end to their lives before the Easter festival. Three out of the four have carried out their oaths—namely the Grand Duke of Mecklenburg, who killed himself at Cannes on April 10th; Count Ernest

Paul Hugel, who shot himself at Gras with a revolver on April 13th; and Count Guido Zich, who put an end to his life by the same means in Hungary on the 15th, two days afterwards. The suicide of the fourth unlucky member may be expected any day, although it is believed that he lacks the courage which his brethren evidently possessed. Failure to perform self-immolation means expulsion from the club; but refusal to perform the terms of the oath is not uncommon. ("A remarkable story..." 1897)

This chatty interview with the girls of the Harlem Suicide Club in 1897, likewise, is surely invented:

Thirteen Harlem girls... have formed a suicide club. They are not tired of life, they have met with no hard luck, their friends have not deserted them, nor are they perishing with hunger. But all last winter they met to read Shakespeare, and when the spring came they had nothing else to do, so they banded themselves together with 13 ties on the 13th day of March to meet every thirteenth month thereafter on the thirteenth day thereof to take 13 ballots to see which girl should kill herself in one of 13 ways. This much is stated on the authority of the president and secretary of the club, Misses Lyle Jay and E. Gervaise Morrissey, orphan sisters, well endowed with earthly goods, who live under the protecting wings of a duenna, at 213 East One Hundred and Eighteenth Street. "You see it was this way," said the President enthusiastically. "We thirteen girls had been reading Shakespeare, and we got to talking about superstitions, and then the suicide club was started." "See we've got a ring for a badge" broke in the secretary, bound to have her say. She pointed to the little finger of her left hand, where there was a turquoise surrounded by 13 diamonds. "Why not an opal?," asked the reporter. "On no," they both cried, "that would be unlucky." They then went on to tell about all the plans of the club. The next meeting will be held 13 April, 1898. When the girl is chosen who must kill herself she may choose one of 13 ways in which to do it, one of which is marriage. "One might as well be dead as married, you know," explained the president. ("Girls' Suicide Club" 1897)

In some cases, clubs seem to have been real institutions. The most famous of these genuine clubs is the Suicide Club of Bridgeport (Connecticut, aka Bridgport), which appeared in the press for many years. This organization made up originally of German immigrants had a meal each year at which one member was chosen to commit suicide by lottery and then given a year to do so ("A Suicide Club: Its History and Rules" 1891). There is much inaccuracy in reporting about the Bridgeport club: for instance, its last member was said to have died in 1895, 1904, and 1905 ("A Suicide Club" 30 Nov 1895 and a statement the last member was about to die; "Last of the Suicide Club" June 1904; "The Record" April 1905); while one member, Wendel Baum was reported as dying in 1890 and then again in 1895 ("A Suicide Club" 9 Apr. 1890; "A Suicide Club," 30 Nov. 1895). There is also much intentionally black comedy: a member thoughtfully invented a suicide burial to combine the two necessary last acts ("Suicide 'De Luxe'" 1896). But the Bridgeport organization existed. To what extent suicide or jokes were its primary aim is a nice question. Ideally a Connecticut historian would look at the history of this organization.

Suicide clubs continued to appear in the news through the first decades of the twentieth century and were often the product of conspiracy theories. For instance, after two women had shot themselves on a transatlantic liner, the Lucania, in 1909, other passengers convinced themselves that a suicide club was at work ("Suicide Club" 17 Apr 1909). It is likely that many suicide clubs were cobbled together by the press or the public seeing patterns in local suicides. Indeed, "[w]henever a mysterious suicide occurs, for which there is no apparent motive, the idea [of the suicide club] is revived . . ." (Rose-Soley 1897, *CW*). In 1935 Miss Edith May Cameron complained to a Judicial Committee about "anti-Christian and seditious forces' in central London, including 'Jews' and a local 'suicide club'" ("A 'Suicide Club'" 1935).

61. SWALLOWED UP

Summary: A man is swallowed up to his chin in the ground for his godlessness. Earliest Attestation: medieval. Motif: H1573.1.1 Heathen swallowed by earth. Compare with: "**Devil Take Me.**"

The Victorians very much believed in a benevolent deity who could turn nasty. There are a number of nineteenth-century stories where God strikes sinners down. For instance, a speaker breaks a blood vessel after uttering profanities ("Curiosities" 1882; then there are occasional lightning bolts, "The Awful Fate" 1886, *CW*). The later 1800s may have been a more metaphysical age, but God could appear with frightening immediacy in legend. Consider this miracle story from 1860:

> A letter received from a non-commissioned officer at Aldershott [sic], dated August 26, contains the following remarkable passage: "A most extraordinary

transaction has just occurred within six or seven miles of this place. A farmer, when going over his crops, accompanied by some of his neighbours, was so grieved at witnessing the injuries inflicted by rain, &c, prayed to God that he may be struck asleep until the fine weather would come. He had only uttered the prayer when he fell to the ground at full length fast asleep, and so firm in the earth that he could not be removed. A shed has been built about him, and hundreds are daily going to see him; he breathes as natural as is [*corr.* if] he was lying asleep on his bed. ("Remarkable Incident" 3 Sep 1860)

This belongs to a long tradition of stories about blasphemers being punished, typically being swallowed by or glued to the ground. These were much in evidence in seventeenth-, eighteenth-, and nineteenth-century chapbooks (Rollins 1927, 62–67 "A most wonderful and sad judgement," 1661; Ashton 1882, 65 "God's Just Judgment on Blasphemers," 1700s; Hindley 1871 "Wonderful, Just and Terrible Judgement on a Blasphemer," 24, mid-nineteenth century?). Such stories can be traced back further to medieval hagiography (e.g., Henken 1987, 328–29, 353, 358). It is perhaps surprising, though, to find them as contemporary belief legends in the midnineteenth century.

The 1860 story is credited to the *Limerick Chronicle*, but the relevant issue seems not to have been scanned. Before the report be rejected as an Irish paragraph-filler, consider this. The story was widely excerpted by the British press: the BNA has 36 versions from the autumn of 1860. Some newspapers put distance between themselves and the story: for instance, the *Buxton Herald* had it under the headline "Remarkable Incident (Very!)" (6 Sep 1860). However, the *Bristol Daily Post* included instead the comment: "This curious tale ... was the original property of the good people of Bridgwater," which suggests that there was an equivalent yarn in the Severn Valley ("Remarkable Incident" 5 Sep 1860). Presumably, thinking of the story's connection with Limerick, an Irish soldier had written home from Aldershot, an important British military base, with mess talk.

That very same autumn a similar narrative was bruited about by another paper:

> Then we have the story which the many-tongued [i.e., rumor] has localised in our neighbourhood, but which has been known and believed in many districts—of the impatient and blasphemous farmer, who, for cursing the weather, was stricken into the earth, and remained imbedded up to his chin in the middle of the field, for an indefinite number of days, and had to be fed there with a spoon ... there are still a few who aver that the unfortunate gentleman remains in the same unpleasant position, and that his afflicted friends have erected a tent over him, to

protect him from the inclement weather. It is not said why they do not dig him out. ("Marvellous Tales" 1860)

The common elements are the shed and tent and the reference to the weather in both accounts.

The locality of this remarkable event is variously stated. The generally received opinion is that it occurred at Sydenham, or Aldershott, or Ireland, or Norwich; while some have had the temerity to insert some additional letters between the two syllables of the last, and say North Woolwich; but this was suicide, and shook the faith of perhaps half the believers ... ("Marvellous Tales" 1860)

The story might be too supernatural, too "medieval" in some respects, for modern tastes in urban legends. It may also have been rather baroque for some Victorian newspaper writers. However, these reports suggest that the narrative was believed and that it was circulating in 1860.

62. THE TELL-TALE EYE

Summary: A murder victim's eye catches an image of the murderer on the retina allowing for justice to be done. Earliest Attestation: 1856. Motif: N/A. Secondary Literature: Campion-Vincent 1999; Evans 1993; Lanska 2013; Bondeson 2018, 52–66.

From about the mid-1850s to the Second World War, there was the popular idea that "the last thing seen at the moment of death remains imprinted upon the retina of the eye" (Evans 1993, 341). This, as we shall see, had a basis in science, where such images are termed "optograms." There was also a far more dubious and far more popular notion: the "Tell-Tale Eye." If, it was suggested, a person had, say, been strangled, then they might have captured an optic "photograph" of their murderer's face, allowing the miscreant to be arrested, tried, and punished. This "persistent nineteenth-century urban legend" (Lanska 2013, 56) has been carefully studied by modern scholars. Here is, in fact, one of the few stories in the corpus of Victorian belief legends where there is a tradition of modern academic writing to draw upon (Campion-Vincent 1999—the phrase "Tell-Tale Eye," inspired by Poe, is hers, 13; Evans 1993; Lanska 2013; Bondeson 2018, 52–66).

The earliest reference to the "Tell-Tale Eye" known to me dates to the autumn of 1856—not, as has previously been suggested, 1857 (Lanska 2013, 56; Evans 1993, 359). A Chicago paper reported,

> A series of experiments have recently been made by Dr. Pollok, an oculist of this city ... to test the truth of an article published some time since by a celebrated physician in England, which alleged that the last scene viewed by a dying man would remain impressed upon the retina as does the impression upon a daguerreotype plate.[31]

No trace has been found of this "celebrated physician in England" and still less of his article. Physician and article may just have been invented by an American journalist. Alternatively, an English physician may have given a speculative aside in a medical piece.

The origins of the "Tell-Tale Eye" and an explanation for its almost immediate popularity are likely to be found in the Victorian vogue for photography, "the powers of which were exaggerated in the nineteenth century because its technical processes were then more complex and solely in the hands of professionals, so were not properly understood by the public" (Campion-Vincent 1999, 15; I am reminded of another inspiration from early photography, namely, the idea that images from nature or the supernatural could be caught on glass panes and mirrors, Allen 1982). There was also in the background the invention of the ophthalmoscope in 1850, which allowed doctors to look deep into the eye (Evans 1993, 359). In the BNA there are five references to the ophthalmoscope for 1855; thirteen for 1856; twenty-nine for 1857; fifty-seven for 1858; and twenty-nine for 1859: the instrument was gradually becoming part of national consciousness in just the period that the "Tell-Tale Eye" appeared. Campion-Vincent makes an interesting connection to the medieval custom of "cruentation" whereby suspected murderers had to touch their alleged victim to see whether the corpse bled, so proving their guilt: the body accused the murderer, just as the "Tell-Tale Eye" did (Campion-Vincent 1999, 22).

Whatever the origins of the "Tell-Tale Eye" were, it quickly became embedded in Victorian culture. As early as 1865 one writer could refer to it as a "very old hoax." Indeed, the author in question complained how "A few days ago I heard two sensible-looking men discussing, and fully convinced of the truth of this latest grand discovery. It was no use to tell them it was all humbug" (A Physician 1865). A writer in *Popular Science* noted, in the same year, that the "Tell-Tale Eye" was used chiefly by newspapers "on the score of the merit it possesses of filling a stray corner when other more important matter is not handy or come-at-able" ("Photographing from Dead Eyes" 1865). In 1882 one journalist trotted out in rather world-weary tones:

> We have all heard something of the sensational story of the likeness of the murderer photographed on the retina of his victim and the conviction that followed the ultra-scientific proceeding by which the picture was developed and fixed. ("Pictures in the Eye" 1882)

The idea died hard. Brian McConnell, born in 1928 reported that "my parents, other relatives and their contemporaries impressed upon me . . . that the 'Tell-Tale Eye' was ingrained in folkloric or superstitious belief at the time" (McConnell 2000, 118; I take this to mean that McConnell was encouraged not to believe).

The claim that optograms could solve crimes was there in the earliest reports. In the 1856 Chicago article reference was made to a photograph of the retina of the murdered man J. H. Beardsley ("Important Discovery" 23 Oct. 1856). In 1860 it was suggested that the technique be used in the most famous British murder case of that decade, the killing of Francis Kent ("The Road Murder" 1860; for the case generally, see Summerscale 2009). In 1863, after the murder of Emma Jackson, a photographer wrote to the detective in charge of the case and suggested that Emma's eyes be photographed. The detective, James F. Thomson, replied—clearly open to the technique—but giving reasons why it would not work in this case (Lanska 2013, 57–59; Bondeson 2018, 52–56). In 1864 and January 1865 an investigator in Florence (Italy) demanded the use of the technique in a series of homicides in the city. In the first two murders, his superiors refused him permission, but in the third, a photograph was taken. The photograph was greatly magnified, and the image was traced by an artist and compared favorably to the suspected murderer (who was prosecuted on the basis of other evidence) ("Italy" 1865).[32] Hiram Powers, the celebrated American sculptor, then resident in Florence, suggested that the photograph (which he had seen) represented "mere accidental changes of forms of or on the optic nerve" ("Judicial Application" 1865). Demands for optograms in murder cases were regularly made in the next years and appeared, all too predictably, in relation to the Whitechapel murders in 1888 (Monk 2010). Indeed, demands were still being made for murder optograms as late as the 1920s (Lanska 2013, 80–81).

One writer in 1865 hoped that "this piece of folly and wicked nonsense" would "not get into our 'sensation novels'" (A Physician 1865). A vain wish! The first "Tell-Tale Eye" story known to me had already appeared in 1864 in *Once a Week* ("From Darkness," *CW*). In 1867 Villiers de l'Isle Adam used the "Tell-Tale Eye" in a short story (later expanded into a novel) "Clair Lenoir" (see Evans 1993, 344–46 for discussion and full references). In 1891 Rudyard Kipling borrowed the optogram for his horror story "At the End of the Passage"

Figure 17 Verne, *Les Frères Kip*, 445. 'Eux!... eux!... les assassins de mon père!'

(Kipling 1931, 244–69). In 1893 *Scarabæus: The story of an African beetle* opens with an optogramic experiment by a young photographer on the body of a murdered man (Lanza 1892). Jules Claretie wrote *L'Accusateur: L'Oeil du Mort* in 1897 (Claretie 1897). Jules Verne depended on optograms to catch a killer in the final chapter of *Les Frères Kip* in 1902 (Verne 1903, 440–51; see figure 17). Thomas Dixon Jr. had a professor, a microscope, and a dead woman's eye identify a "black devil" in *The Clansman* (Dixon 1905, 312–14; see also Evans, "Optograms," 347–49; *The Clansman* was the inspiration for D. W. Griffith's film *Birth of a Nation*). The "Tell-Tale Eye" makes it into a Joycean stream of consciousness in 1922 in *Ulysses*: "Wrongfully condemned. Murder. The murderer's image in the eye of the murdered. They love reading about it" (Joyce

1994, 105). Arthur Evans, meanwhile, has argued, plausibly that the "Tell-Tale Eye" is the origin of science fiction brain scan stories, where memory films and photographs are recovered from the dead (Evans 1993, 350–56).[33]

What is the science behind the Tell-Tale Eye? The great breakthroughs in optometry made by two Germans, Franz Christian Boll and Wilhelm Kühne, in the late 1870s and early 1880s gave the story a flimsy foundation in fact. Their studies showed that optograms were possible: Kühne used the retinas of various animals and, on one occasion, of a guillotined criminal and retrieved extremely crude images (Lanska 2013, 59–74; William Warner, a British photographer, allegedly carried out experiments with an ox eye, "Wonderful if True" 1863; Bondeson 2018, 53–54). Kühne was only able to do this, however, by creating unusual conditions, which precluded any kind of forensic application. In the words of Arthur Evans, photographing an approximate image from the retina of a dead person "is possible ... if the individuals stared for a few minutes at a brightly lit object before dying, if they closed their eyes immediately upon death and remained in a darkened room, if their eyes were rapidly excised and the retinal tissue removed and bathed in an alum solution ..." (Evans 1993, 357–58).

There was skepticism about the "Tell-Tale Eye" from the beginning. For instance, in the very first Chicago report a British editor added these thoughts:

> We give this "important discovery" as it is reported by our transatlantic contemporary—and merely as a specimen of the hoaxes that, with a grave style and imitation of scientific phraseology, can pass current for truth among Western readers, with no less ready acceptance than by the benighted population of the Old Country. ("Important Discovery" 10 Nov. 1856)

The first determined scientific attack on the "Tell-Tale Eye" dates to 1865 (A Physician 1865). In 1866 this was followed up more forcefully in *Notes and Queries* under the heading "Photographic Canard" (Quin 1866). By 1882 news was feeding through into the British press about the experiments in Germany, and skepticism was expressed about any legal applications for optograms ("Pictures in the Eye" 1882). It also perhaps began to be understood that for an optogram to be taken, the eye would have to be removed. This was not just a question of photographing the surface of the face, but of desecrating the body. The vast majority of cases given here (legal and fictional) involve photographing the surface of the eye. They do not envisage the retina being removed. When in 1888 the request was made to photograph the eye of the Ripper's murder victim, even amateur scientists were capable of pointing, in the newspapers, to the hopelessness of any such procedure (Hodges 1888). Yet well into the twentieth century we have cases where eyes were removed from victims by criminals, allegedly to stop optograms being taken (e.g., "10 'Shock' Police" 1936, see also Evans 1993, 344 and Campion-Vincent 1999, 18–19).

63. TICK TOCK

Summary: A thief steals a clock and is found by its ticking. Earliest Attestation: 1871. Motif: N/A. Secondary Literature: N/A. Compare with: "**Pickpocket's Ring**."

An 1871 news report describes an Indian thief who steals a music box and while trying to open the box sets off a tune and risks detection. The journalist writes:

> The story bears a resemblance to the older one of the thief who stole a bag full of watches, but could not take them through the town because they were ticking so he waited all night, cold and hungry, in a wood until they ran down. ("A good story..." 1871)

A decade later a reference is a made to a similar tradition, this time from the United States:

> Stories are told of the detection of thieves in a crowd by the watches they had abstracted striking the hour at a *malapropos* moment. ("Curious Time" 1881, 40)

We have two allusions then, but the closest I have come to a full version dates to 1912 and is from the United States. The restaurant of one A. Covillo in Chicago had been robbed. The police are on the job.

> As a clew in their quest, the detectives wrote a list of the articles stolen and they included two alarm clocks. Several hours after they had started on their thief hunt the detectives approached Halsted and West Madison streets. Suddenly they heard a long drawn out but muffled sound. "Ding-a-ling-a-ling" it started and continued for two minutes. Newman [the burglar], who was standing on the corner, began to run when the alarm went off. The detectives ran too after him ... Later in the morning Newman was arraigned before Municipal Judge Caverly. He

Figure 18 'Alarm Clocks' 1912.

evidently was considering a plea of "not guilty," despite the finding of the clock in his pocket, when there was a disturbance in the court-room. "Ding-a-ling-a-ling" and so on it went. It was the second stolen clock. Newman looked perplexed, then downcast. He knew pleas of innocence would avail him nothing, so he stepped up and received his sentence. ("Alarm Clocks" 1912, *CW*)

There are other close relations. Here are two from, or at least set in, France.

In the pit of the old French opera, one of the audience suddenly discovered that his watch was gone. The evening's entertainment had not commenced, and the owner of the property mounted a bench, stated the loss, which could not have occurred above two or three minutes, and begged those around him to remain perfectly quiet, as his watch struck the hours like a clock, and, it then being on the stroke of seven, the watch would speedily indicate into whose possession it had fallen. There was a dead silence; but the eye of the proprietor detected an individual who was trying to edge away from the vicinity, and immediately denounced the skulker as the thief. The latter was seized, and the watch was found upon him; and as the owner quietly put it in his pocket, he remarked, "The watch does not strike the hours, but I thought my assertion that it did would enable me to strike out the thief." ("In the pit . . ." 1867, *CW*)

The next story dates to 1884.

The other day a lady, having paid her hotel bill, sent away her boxes on a cab and sallied forth on foot. No sooner had she departed than the landlord discovered that the clock had disappeared from the mantelpiece of the room which his late lodger had been occupying, though he remembered to have seen it there subsequent to her trunks being despatched. Convinced that she must be the thief, he rushed out in hot pursuit, and overtaking her, he charged her with the robbery and gave her into custody, the lady meanwhile protesting loudly against the traducer. She was, however, taken before the *Juge d'Instruction*, to whom she resumed her torrent of indignant denial with the extraordinary volubility peculiar to the daughters of Gaul. Her indignation was at its height when, lo!, 12 o'clock rang forth in clear tones from the region of madame's dress improver [i.e., a bustle]. The expression of consternation depicted upon the fair pilferer's countenance, together with the appositeness of the quaint phenomenon, were too much for the gravity of the officials, who burst into a fit of uncontrollable laughter. Five minutes later a female warder returned the tell-tale timepiece to its owner. ("A Queer Hiding Place" 1884)

64. THERE'S GOLD IN THOSE SEWERS

Summary: Vast amounts of money are to be found in the sewers. Earliest Attestation: midnineteenth century. Motif: N/A. Secondary Literature: N/A. Compare with: "**Sewer Monsters.**"

"Hidden in the bosoms of the sewers of every Great City lies a world of romance" (Kirwan 1871, 330). Principal of the stories told about large urban sewers, particularly those of London and New York, was the unimaginable wealth supposed to be gathered there. Coins lost in the streets, rings accidentally washed down the sink, even valuables ditched in drains by criminals could all easily find their way into the sewers. Certainly, in London, a number of men—usually called "toshers"—went into the sewers and, illegally (Kirwan 1871, 330), lived off the objects that they found.

Our sources suggest that there were between two hundred and three hundred of these sewer scavengers in the British capital in the midnineteenth century (Mayhew 1851, II, 152; "200" some years before, Mayhew, II, 150).[34] They tracked through the subterranean labyrinths in groups of three or four. Stories soon emerged about the extraordinary valuables that these toshers turned up: for instance, a purse containing two hundred sovereigns (Kirwan 1871, 333–34). Henry Mayhew, who was not easily gulled, had been informed, and seems to have believed, that a tosher could make about two pounds a week—far more than the average clerk (Mayhew 1851, II, 152). Mayhew also worked out that, for this number to be correct, each household in London would have to lose one shilling, four pence into the sewer every year: something that suggests that two pounds was rather optimistic (Mayhew 1851, II, 152, particularly given that only a fraction of lost possessions would be found).

More reliable as a guide to the treasures below might be the list of objects that one late nineteenth-century municipal sewage worker described finding in his career:

> We've found lots of German silver and metal spoons; iron tobacco-boxes; nails, and pins; bones of various animals; bits of lead; boys' marbles, buttons, bits of silk, scrubbing-brushes, empty purses; penny-pieces, and bad half crowns ... We've found false teeth—whole sets at a time ... and corks; how about corks? I never see such a flood of corks, of all kinds and sizes, as sometimes pours out of this sewer into the Thames. (Hollingshead 1862, 71)

There is an interesting passage where a Glaswegian tosher describes how he once, exceptionally, found eighteen shillings in a day, "but on coming to the level or day light, he found to his bitter disappointment that the most of it was bad money [i.e., clipped or forged]" ("Life in the Glasgow Sewers" 1848). A London sewer worker talks of those who thought that the sewer was full of wealth:

> Some of 'em creep down the side entrances when the doors are unlocked ... under the idea that they're going to pick up no end of silver spoons. They soon find out their mistake. (Hollingshead 1862, 72)

A mystique grew up around the toshers, not least because their profession was so dangerous. The toshers had to avoid not only the police, sewer rats, and wild sewer pigs (see **Sewer Monsters**). They also had to climb through tiny spaces, risk drowning in mud, suffocating in pockets of sewer gas, and worst of all they feared getting caught by the tide: the Thames flowed in and out of the London sewers. Why would anybody do a job like this unless there was remarkable compensation?

Occasionally stories leaked out of British and American newspapers and books about the kind of treasures enjoyed by the brave Cockney toshers and their equivalents in other urban centers. There were reports from mid-nineteenth-century London of "conglomerates": "iron, nails, various scraps of metal, coins of every description, all rusted into a mass like a rock, and weighing from a half hundred to two hundred weight altogether" (Mayhew 1851, II, 152). These conglomerates were so heavy that they typically could not be moved. They would stay there, in the opinion of one tosher, "till the world comes to an end" (Mayhew 1851, II, 154).

In the early 1860s, an immigrant named Schwartz was said to have made some 27,000 dollars from one trip into New York sewers. "So great, however, were the difficulties and dangers which he encountered that nothing could induce him again to visit 'New York underground'" ("Treasures in Sewers" 1867). In 1862 a story appeared in an Irish paper suggesting that someone had found their way from a drain into the vault of the Bank of England, which takes "sewer treasure" to an all-new level ("A Strange Story" 1862; the subterranean passage into a treasure vault perhaps deserves a study of its own, e.g., "Sewer Thieves" 1894). In 1863 a poor family in Dover lost a half-sovereign down a grate. On going to retrieve the coin, they found not only the coin but also "several pieces of silver" ("Dover" 1863). In 1867 two young men and a woman retrieved, on an expedition into New York sewers, about 3,000,000 dollars-worth of valuables, but one of the young men died ("Treasures in Sewers" 1867). The pattern of audacity, reward and tragedy repeats itself in these legends.

In 1869 another American paper report described how a certain John W. Crane became possessed "with the hallucination that treasures untold are imbedded in the sewers of Boston, New York and Philadelphia." He was, after almost drowning, arrested on leaving a sewer with a carpet bag full of valuables ("Treasure-Seeking" 1869). In 1880, in Greenock (UK), police had to be brought in to clear a crowd who had come to rummage through sewer diggings brought onto the street: some coins and valuables had been found there ("Money and Valuables" 1880). In 1885 boys ventured into a Philadelphia sewer, and one almost died: "The boys believed an old story to the effect that about middle-way up Dock Street there were deposited great quantities of gold" ("A Week" 1885). In 1899 at Barnard Castle a sewer was cleaned and, according to one newspaper, "19 sovereigns, a host of coins of lesser value, silver spoons, a diamond ring, and other valuables were discovered" ("Sovereigns in the Sewer" 1899). In 1900 a sewer treasure story did the rounds in Kensington, London. A laborer working in sewer mud there had come across "a funny looking stone" that turned out to be a valuable diamond ("Diamond" 1900). Narratives like these (some based on fact, others simple fantasies) continue up until the Second World War both in Britain and in the United States, although by this time the day of the toshers was long past.[35]

65. TUNNEL KISSING

Summary: A young man on a train takes advantage of the dark in a tunnel to kiss a young woman in the same carriage. There are many variants with different outcomes. Earliest Attestation: early 1840s. Motif: N/A. Secondary Literature: N/A.

Trains were places of sexual danger in Victorian Britain. If left alone in carriages, young couples could take their pleasure ("Lovers' Kiss" 1873), or predatory men might leap onto unchaperoned young women (Walter 1888, vol. 9, XIII; for the most famous Victorian court case, that of Valentine Baker, see Beckett 2003, 78–79; for a rare predatory female, see Bradley 2015, 186–87). Abraham Solomon's controversial 1854 painting ("First Class" see figure 19) brilliantly captures the kind of situation that might arise. There was such an outcry when "First Class" was exhibited that Solomon felt obliged to repaint the piece with the woman sitting demurely on the other side of her guardian (Tennant 2016, 60). There is also, from about the same time, the ballad "The Charming Young Widow I Meet [*sic*] in the Train." The "widow" flirts with a male passenger, gives him her baby to hold while she runs to talk to an acquaintance, and vanishes—having picked his pockets: the swaddled baby is a piece of wood. "Somewhere behind all these cases is an obvious truth: that close confinement with another is a matchless incubator of desire" (Bradley 2015, 187).

Tunnels were particularly perilous because passengers were plunged into darkness—when, as often happened, lights were not provided: "'Oh good gracious! What shall we do? I declare I never saw such culpable misconduct. We are entering a tunnel, and they have neglected to put in the lamp.' 'Abominable!' said my next neighbour gravely. 'Somebody ought to write a letter to *The Times*'" ("A Kiss in a Tunnel" 1854). There was, above all, the danger that members of the public would embrace in the pitch black. It is worth recalling all this when reading about a bizarre British rumor from 1843.

Figure 19 'First Class: the Meeting... and at First Meeting Loved', Abraham Solomon, 1855.

> There is a remarkable lie travelling through England at the present moment, to wit, that the Great Western Railway Company have determined to take the top off the Box tunnel to unbox it, and to make it no tunnel at all.... ("The Box Tunnel" 1843)

The reporter went on to state that this was untrue: he had talked to the Great Western Railway Company's engineers. Why, though, we might ask, would an unexciting rumor of this type pass around the country? The full rumor—it was given in an edited form here—was probably that the tunnel would be unroofed to prevent illicit coupling along its almost two miles of length. Certainly, from when the Box Tunnel was opened in June 1841—at that time the world's longest tunnel[36]—it had been associated with kisses, stolen or otherwise.

As one "poet" put it, just a month after the tunnel had been put into use: "And the Box tunnel full of noise and hiss, / Tends but to drown the impassioned, furtive kiss" ("The Railroad Essay" 1841).[37] In later Victorian sources, which discuss such matters with extreme reticence, there are further references. In 1849 a sculptor impudently kissed a woman in the Box Tunnel and ended up before a magistrate ("Gross Outrage" 1849; in 1933 an ex-MP likewise found himself in front of a magistrate for unwanted kisses in the tunnel "Sir Leo Money" 1933).

In an 1856 short story, a man falls in love in the tunnel when a woman accidentally kisses him ("A Kiss in a Tunnel" 1856).[38] In 1859 a joke story about a kiss in the Box appeared in *Chambers's Journal* ("A Dangerous Experiment" 1859). Then in 1860 a short story was published where a kiss in that tunnel ended in an unlikely marriage. Before entering the tunnel, the future husband, a dragoon, gauchely tells a story to the woman who will become his wife (what he calls "a gentleman's joke"):

> A lady and her husband sat together through the Box Tunnel. There was one gentleman opposite, and it was pitch dark. After the tunnel had been passed through, the lady said, "George, how absurd to salute me going through the tunnel." "I did no such thing!" "You didn't." "No! Why?" "Why because somehow I thought you did!" ("The Box Tunnel" 1860)

Lovers of Victorian prudishness will note the reluctance to even use the word "kiss" ("salute") in this delicate passage, where a soldier is flirting with a middle-class woman.

The story of the cuckolded husband in the tunnel became a Victorian staple and was associated with railway tunnels everywhere, not just the Box. There are examples from as early as 1859 ("A Dangerous Experiment" 1859, a slightly more complicated version, as the husband pretends to be the other man in the carriage; "A Mystery" 1891) and by 1904 it was so well known that it could be subverted in a variant that required knowledge of the original:

> Mrs. Hunnemune (as the train emerges from a long tunnel): "Dear me, John, did you kiss me just now in the dark?" Mr. Hunnemune (glancing round to find the perpetrator of the outrage): "No, indeed! I wonder who dared to!" Mrs. Hunnemune (simply): "Nobody. But you missed a splendid chance, John." ("Mrs. Hunnemune" 1904)

Other versions of the kiss in the tunnel ("a dark mystery," in the words of one British newspaper; "Wit and Anecdote" 1889) abounded. Indeed, so popular were these stories that different variants were collected ("Tricks in a Tunnel" 1884; Bombaugh 1876, 273–320, is dedicated to "The Kiss in Humorous Story," and 278–81 are given over to "Tunnel Stories") and at the end of the century there were even two British silent shorts *The Kiss in the Tunnel* or the *Tunnel Kiss* (1899, Smith; Gray 2019, 185–93) and *Kiss in the Tunnel* (c. 1899 Bamforth and Company, Gray 2019, 191). The first film was, according to a contemporary, "Carefully managed so that the picture may be shown to any audience without giving offence" (Gray 2019, 185).

Some examples of tunnel-kiss stories follow. A wife sits opposite her husband on a train, tries to kiss him in the dark, but accidentally kisses another man: her husband had shuffled along as a passenger had left the carriage

(Bombaugh 1876, 279–80). A young man exits a carriage and comes back in the dark of the tunnel and makes the mistake of kissing a young and beautiful widow instead of his wife ("The Kiss in the Tunnel" 1895). In a "well-known" incident, a woman has a piece of "court-plaster" on her upper lip going into a tunnel, but on leaving the plaster was on the lip of a handsome man sitting opposite: "Curious, was it not?" (Bombaugh 1876, 278). A newlywed American was asked why she and her husband had chosen a particular train route. She replied saucily: "Because it has so many tunnels!" ("On the Marseilles..." 1881, *CW*). Back in England, the entire carriage makes fun of a couple who have noisily kissed in the dark ("A Kiss in the Dark" 1855).

Sometimes the stories can get rather convoluted. Two girls travel together, and one of them pretends to be her friend's fiancé—sitting opposite—by kissing her friend in the dark: "The young couple," after an argument, "were reconciled, married and the other young woman was not invited to their wedding" ("Tricks in a Tunnel" 1884). A woman hits two men traveling with her in the tunnel, and the two vow to beat each other up, not realizing that they had been slapped by the woman ("The train..." 1869).[39] In an American version, a lieutenant offers to kiss a married woman in a tunnel; she assents, but she then changes places with her "coloured nurse" in the dark. Once the train leaves the tunnel, the "Lieutenant looked like a sheep-stealing dog..." and quickly escaped ("A Kiss in the Dark" 1888). In one of several tunnel-kiss short stories, a woman tries to kiss her brother's cheek but accidentally locks lips with a stranger ("A Kiss in a Tunnel" 1854). In yet another version, two male friends, one of them "bashful," find themselves with a beautiful young woman in a carriage.

> While going through a tunnel [his male] friend knocked off the bashful young man's hat, forced his fingers through his hair, kissed the back of his hand, and then slapped his own face violently. ("A Mystery of the Tunnel" 1891)

That kiss on the back of the hand brings us to the most satisfying of the tunnel-kiss stories. This was published as early as 1868, where it was widely circulated in the British newspapers ("The Kiss in the Tunnel" 1868; told in the beginning of Horace Vernet 1789–1863, "the eminent French artist"; this story appeared 68 times in the BNA in Oct. and Nov. of that year; there is a version about a "Western youth" in Bombaugh 1876, 278 and a generic version "A Kiss in the Dark" 1895). Perhaps the best version, though, dates to 1903:

> A distinguished French novelist, whose works are extremely popular with the fair sex, recently found himself travelling in a railway carriage with two very talkative women. Having recognised him from his published portraits, they both opened

fire upon him in regard to his novels, which they praised in a manner that was unendurable to the sensitive author. Fortunately the train entered a tunnel and in the darkness the novelist, who understood women, lifted the back of his hand to his lips and kissed it soundingly. When light returned he found the two women regarding each other in icy silence, and, addressing them with great suavity, he said, "Ah! madames, the regret of my life will hereafter be that I shall never know which one of you it was that kissed me." ("Kissing in a Tunnel" 1903)

Many modern readers will be familiar with the following version—still popular today. It apparently began to circulate in the Second World War. I have found no example earlier than 1942:

A young woman, her mother, an Italian officer, and a Nazi trooper were in an Italian train. It came to a tunnel. As soon as darkness enveloped the compartment a kiss was heard—followed by a hard slap. When the train emerged into sunlight, the passengers' thoughts were these. The Nazi: "Those mad, romantic Latins. How dare he kiss that girl. How cowardly to try it only in the dark." The Girl: "The nerve of him trying to kiss my mother. I am glad she was able to defend herself." The Mother: "So they'd my kiss daughter, eh? Well, I brought her up properly, and I'm glad she took proper action." The Italian: "It was worth kissing my hand, just for chance of slapping that Nazi." ("Day by Day" 1942)

66. THE VANISHING LADY

Summary: Mother and daughter go to a hotel; in the morning the mother has vanished, and the hotel insists that she was never there. Earliest Attestation: 1897. Motif: N/A. Secondary Literature: N/A.

The journalist covering this remarkable story for *Pall Mall Gazette* in 1913 only needed to summarize the narrative in "a few brief sentences" as "by this time everyone knows the story" ("Disappeared" 1913). Indeed, "Over the dinner-table last night and at luncheon again to-day all London has been discussing it."

An Englishwoman and her daughter on the conclusion of a tour in the Near East, arrived at a Paris hotel at the time of the Exhibition. They were given separate rooms, one above the other. After resting a few hours the daughter went to see her mother. Her room was empty and entirely altered. In great agitation, she called the maid and then the manager. "You are under a delusion," he told her, "when you arrived at this hotel you were quite alone." "But," said the bewildered girl, "we signed our names in the visitors' book, my mother and I." The visitors' book was brought. Above the daughter's name, where the mother had signed, was the signature of an entire stranger. Not till a year after did the daughter learn that her mother had died suddenly of plague, and that in order to save Paris from unutterable panic and the Exhibition from absolute ruin it was hurriedly agreed by the authorities that the death should be completely hushed up, and that the daughter should be made to believe, by the repeated denials of hotel servants, hotel manager, and cabman, and by the proofs of the changed room and the altered visitors' book, that her unfortunate mother never reached the hotel. ("Disappeared" 1913)

The Exhibition in question was presumably the 1900 Exposition Universelle in Paris. But it could have been the 1889 Paris world fair. One-time prime minister Arthur Balfour (1848–1930) was said to have "guessed the solution" as soon as he had heard the first part. How? It was suggested that "he had heard something about it when he was in office" ("Disappeared" 1913). Balfour was "in office" in both 1889 and 1900. And was the story true? One collector believed it to be true "because it is very much easier to believe that it happened than to suppose that it was invented" ("Disappeared" 1913). A dangerous sentiment where legend is concerned.

The story itself is certainly older than 1913. Bonnie Taylor-Blake and Garson O'Toole have traced it back to 1897 (Taylor-Blake and O'Toole 2010; Taylor-Blake and O'Toole 2011).[40] In November 1897 "Dropped out of Existence; A Strange and True Mystery of the French Capital" appeared in the American Press, and it was associated with a minor American author and journalist, Nancy Vincent McClelland. The only important difference from the story above is that in McClelland's version there are *two* daughters, the family is American, and the legend is presumably told in relation to the 1889 Exposition Universelle. There is also, in what appears to be McClelland's original, a forthright claim: "Editor's Note. The following remarkable story is true. The writer is personally acquainted with the persons [the daughters?] who participated in the scenes which are described" ("A Mystery of Paris" 1897; this Utah version is also credited to Nancy V. McClelland; see Taylor-Blake and O'Toole 2010, 9). "Alternatively, [McClelland] may have used the powerful skills of invention displayed in her short stories and her later successful careers to craft the compelling tale" (Taylor-Blake and O'Toole 2010, 10). Twentieth-century versions tend to have one surviving relative, which is more successful in narrative terms because it allows real doubt as to whether the disappearance of the mother is a fact or a mental aberration; one of the reasons perhaps that the "Vanishing Lady" has so often appeared in the cinema (Smith and Hobbs 1992). It might be worth adding that, as readers of this book will have seen, fantastic stories in British and American newspapers were often set in Paris.

67. WATCH THE CLOCK

Summary: A landlord takes on a bet to watch a clock for a certain period of time without his attention straying: while he does so, his house is burgled. Earliest Attestation: an "old story" in 1875. Motif: N/A. Secondary Literature: N/A

In 1882 a British publication included a story about two young men who bet a landlord in "a hotel in Richmond" that he couldn't beat his forefinger in time with the clock for an hour, saying, all the time "here she goes, there she goes." The landlord determined to win the bet. Various people tried to distract the landlord, including his wife and a doctor whom she had fetched, both of whom believed the landlord had gone mad. Once the hour was up, the landlord had won the bet, but the two young men were nowhere to be seen. They were thieves and had made the most of the landlord's distracted state to rob him and decamp: "a couple of swindling sharpers, with wit to back them" ("The Old Clock" 1882; recycled in "An Unlucky Wager" 1888).

This is not a new narrative. An 1875 report talks of "the old story"

> of a thief who, engaging the landlord of a country tavern in a bet that he could not sit in front of a clock for half hour, beating time with his hand in harmony with the movements of the pendulum, improved the half hour so secured to him in robbing the house, and making off with all the portable valuables. ("A New Trick" 1875)

The journalist in question compares this "old story" with a "new trick." The following report is probably an invention—the French press had a reputation for romantic and unlikely stories in the nineteenth century—and the similarity with the older clock trick is striking.

A robbery of a very similar and equally ingenious character has just been brought under the attention of the Paris police. Count M. Marchadier, a gentleman of independent means living at Courbevoi, had as a neighbour a Pole known by the name of Koratt. M. Marchadier had one day the idea of asking Koratt to photograph him in the garden, and the apparatus was accordingly arranged for the purpose. The Pole, having directed M. Marchadier to fix his eyes immovably on a given point, and not to stir until he gave him the word, slipped into the house and commenced to make up a hasty packet of any articles of value he could find about. ("A New Trick" 1875)

FG has informed me that the clock story was also established in Poland in the nineteenth century. An 1877 story from that country begins: "Mr. Raczek was once visited by two gentlemen (both unknown to him) who got him into the half-an-hour-sitting-in-front-of-the-clock bet" (Mr. Raczek was from Racibórz, and the story, *FG* tells me, was published in the *Katolik* weekly in 1877).

PB has turned up a similar story in the Netherlands ("Het Goudvischje" 1892). The story was also recorded in Dallas (Texas) in the midtwentieth century among German immigrants under the name "The Journeyman and the Clock" (Mankin 1961, 261–62, *FG*).

68. WILD THING

Summary: A man lives in the wild, often taking on animal characteristics. Earliest Attestation: the medieval mild man, though there are also antique parallels. Motif: N/A. Secondary Literature: vast (e.g., Bernheimer 1952; Bartra 1997; Pouvreau 2014) but nothing for nineteenth-century wild men.

In 1831 a traveler was passing through the countryside of New Hampshire when he encountered a "wild man." This strange being was "in a state of perfect nudity, bronzed by the wind and sun, and leaping about the wood with all the playfulness of an ourang outang."

When called to [the wild man] seemed frightened, and ran off, for the space of 50 yards, with a long free step. After showing himself in the edge of the woods and among the tall bushes he finally disappeared altogether. He appeared to be about 25 years of age, and his movements indicated the possession of quiet and graceful strength. Subsequently the writer ascertained that he is a lunatic—a harmless good natured fellow, who has wandered about for years in the woods. They put clothes upon him, but he tears them off and escapes out into the open air, and gambols about among the green trees and the flowery shrubs, picking berries, chasing butterflies, and playing bo-peep with some children day after day. Yet there is danger to be apprehended—his bodily strength is believed to be prodigious, and it must be so, if we may judge by his stature and the beautiful proportions of his limbs: for symmetry is always a sign of strength. ("A Wild Man" 8 Oct. 1831)

By "wild men," nineteenth-century writers did not mean—as some modern writers assume—a race apart of sasquatches or other hominids (for confusion Arment 2006). It is likewise unsatisfactory to assimilate the Victorian wild men listed here too closely to the medieval and early modern myth of the wild man (e.g., Bernheimer 1952; Bartra 1997; Pouvreau 2014; or, indeed, Asian or African instances e.g., Forth 2008).[41]

For the Victorians "wild men" were members of their own society, who had for reasons of mental health, temperament, poverty, or necessity headed off into the woods. In the nineteenth century, there were hundreds of such individuals dwelling on the edges of communities. Take the man named Goings who took to the woods near Florence (Alabama). When he was finally captured, he presented a picture "of abject misery and squalid wretchedness." He begged to be left alone but was forced to go home ("The Wild Man of Alabama" 1853). There was Jean Sayce, a French national who had lived in Shooter's Hill Wood (Kent, UK) in the winter of 1882. He had come to Britain for work, lost his money, and was so horrified by his one night in a workhouse that he had taken to the countryside. He hoped to return to France in the summer ("Wild Man of the Woods" 4 Feb. 1882). In 1892 in Australia the police found a "wild man of the woods" at Paratoo. He was almost naked and was unable to communicate properly, though he said his name was "Knox" ("The South Australian police …" 1894). The reality of the wild man's life was doubtless far less pleasant than the idealized view reported from New Hampshire.

The reports of Goings, Sayce, and Knox sound factual and can probably be trusted. However, it is clear that these wild men, and others like them, attracted folklore material to themselves. A good British example of this is Simon (aka Tim) Goodwin (aka Goodman) (c. 1780- c. 1840) who lived for most of his life in the woods at Bletsoe in Bedfordshire. Goodman stayed apart, after a disappointment in love, and came to be associated with the devil, in whose company he was said often to be found (Hurst 1878, 63–74; "A Local Legend" 1933).

The simplest way in which we see the mythologization of the Victorian wild man is in his "wilding." By staying away from other humans, he became like the animals, much as Nebuchadnezzar, who, in biblical tradition, ate grass (Daniel 4, 25). For instance, one wild man captured in Tennessee had been a bankrupt shoemaker. But after a prolonged absence from civilization, his body grew scales, and his eyes doubled in size ("A Wild Man of the Mountains" 23 Nov 1878; there were plans to exhibit him, which is perhaps the explanation for the story). The wild men sometimes began to scurry along on hands and feet. The Ogle wild man, for instance, "has long grey hair which covers his shoulders, and a disagreeable habit of walking on all-fours and groaning and growling like a bear" ("A Wild Man in Illinois" 1874; hair or fur was typical in medieval accounts and imagery, Pouvreau 2014, 23–61). An Irish wild man in Pennsylvania went, in 1871, "on his hands and feet ... with the fleetness of a wild tiger" ("An Irish Wild Man!" 1871). There were wild women, where much was made of their lack of clothes (e.g., "Without a Rag" 1895, *CW*). In other cases, wild men only ate raw meat. In 1851 a wild man in Co. Limerick (Ireland) lived naked and stole sheep "which he devours ravenously in a raw state"—the "general belief of the people" was that he had escaped from a "menagerie or exhibition" in Liverpool ("A Wild Man of the Woods" 1 Nov 1851). A wild man in Kent allegedly ate a horse carcass raw ("The 'Wild Man' Again" 1868). Then there were charges of cannibalism: the wild man of Flint Hills (Kansas), an escaped convict, had killed and eaten, it was said, sixteen human beings ("An American 'Wild Man of the Woods'" 1886).

Most curious perhaps are the jumping abilities of these wild men (for parallels in medieval Irish wild man tradition Sailer 1997, 200–204). A Green County wild man (Arkansas), in 1851, "ran away with great speed, leaping from 12 to 14 feet at a time" ("A Wild Man of the Woods" 24 June 1851). This wild man is the least human of all the accounts gathered here, yet the journalist says: "The general entertained idea appears to be that he was a survivor of the earthquake disaster which occurred in 1811. Thrown helpless upon the wilderness of that disaster [*sic*], it is probable that he grew up in his savage state, until he now bears only the outward resemblance of humanity" ("A Wild Man of the Woods" 24 June 1851). A Missouri wild man, in 1857, was able to escape from court by jumping over some policemen: "He made a sudden spring over the heads of those who surrounded him, and darted away with the speed of the reindeer" ("Capture" 1857). A Yorkshire wild man in 1864 "ran with wonderful speed sometimes leaping into the air" ("A Wild Man in Yorkshire," 25 Aug 1864). The Ogle County wild man was said to have been able to carry out "extraordinary leaps" ("A Wild Man in Illinois" 24 Aug 1874). The 1879 St Joaquin wild man jumped "over the bushes in his path like a deer" ("A Reported" 1879). A wild man in Berkshire was seen "leaping over hedges" ("Wild Man of the Woods" 30 Mar 1923). Why were wild men so often seen in the air? Possibly jumping represented the wild man's dubious freedom. Perhaps it signaled, as suggested above, them becoming animal-like. But it is also tempting to think of Spring-heeled Jack and other extraordinary beings from the nineteenth century (Bell 2012; Dash forthcoming).

69. THE WRONG BED

Summary: Someone (often a newlywed) accidentally gets in the wrong bed, usually with an attractive member of the opposite sex. Earliest Attestation: 1859 (commonly associated with America). Motif: N/A. Secondary Literature: N/A.

In Ohio in 1859 a young bride went into the wrong hotel and ended up in bed with a merchant from Indiana ("In the Wrong Bed!" 1859; ten versions in the BNA). In 1862 a bride (in an article published in Britain but of uncertain provenance) entered a hotel room. However, a "gentleman commercial in the tobacco trade" was already in the bed who claims he only awoke, "though few believe him," when the undressed bride was about to get under the sheets. She mistook him for a ghost ("A Real Ghost" 1862). In 1868 a young man accidentally walked into the wrong house and into the room of a young woman while she was "all unready": they later married ("Getting" 1868). The same article details how a drunk Irish soldier ended up in bed, quite accidentally, with a wife and her husband: "The next time they retire to rest, they should bolt the front parlour window" ("Getting" 1868). In 1869 in Pittsburgh a sister accidentally got into her brother-in-law's bed: they subsequently married ("Popping" 1869, *CW*). In 1874 an Iowa merchant found himself in the wrong bed and witnessed a newlywed wife undress: "there was a surging of white lace and tumble of orange blossoms; there were snappings of stays" ("In the Wrong Bed" 1874, *CW*).

The following example from 1869 is the most sexually explicit. Once more we have the newly-weds:

> An extraordinary matrimonial contretemps transpired in Williamson co., on Christmas night. A double marriage occurred in the same house, and the

Figure 20 'In the Wrong Bed', front page of *Illustrated Police News* (1 Mar 1890).

wedding festivities were celebrated in the old fashioned style ... prompted by Christmas and the blissful event which made a double couple happy. About midnight both brides retired to rest, and half an hour after the newly-made husbands followed. By some strange mistake, each gentleman found his way to the wrong room. The mistake was not discovered until daylight, when one of the ladies shrieked her surprise after a vigorous fashion. A general hubbub was the result, and at last accounts the brides were disconsolate, on account of the scandal created. All sorts of schemes of reparation were proposed, but it appears that no tangible plea for undoing the double mistake was arrived at. The above episode actually transpired as narrated. ("An extraordinary matrimonial ..." 1869, *FG*)

In a version of this story from 1889, the brides, after a night of accidental lovemaking, exchange husbands and remarry ("A Strange Mistake" 1889). These stories were, for the most part, too strong for the strait-laced British press: or at least they had to be set outside the country; the concentration on the United States is striking.

70. THE WRONG TROUSERS

Summary: A man comes home and, finding his wife in bed, undresses: she convinces him to go out and buy something, which he does only to find that the trousers he has on are not his own. Earliest Attestation: 1871. Motif: N/A. Secondary Literature: N/A.

Wrong Trousers is the only Victorian urban legend known to me that deals with infidelity. Here is the earliest collected version set in Scotland.

> In a suburb of Dundee a golden discovery was recently made by a husband, who had hitherto manifested the most unqualified confidence in the fidelity of his wife. It seems that he had been from home one day recently, and had returned rather unexpectedly late at night. On arriving, he found that his wife, who had not previously evinced any symptoms of illness, complained of having been suddenly seized with spasms. The danger was no more serious, however, than that the wife thought a little whisky would remove it, and there being none in the house she earnestly urged her spouse to procure the same. The good man had undressed for the night, but was not proof against her entreaties, and having hastily put on what he supposed to be his trousers, proceeded to a public house in the neighbourhood. The keeper, on hearing his complaint, gave him a gill of whisky, for which he laid a coin on the counter. The publican asked if the man hadn't a shilling, and [the man] said he had given him one. The keeper, however, told him it was sovereign, and [the man] expressed his astonishment, he was not aware that he had any gold in his possession. Again putting his hand into his pocket he pulled out a number of gold pieces, and the third time he plunged with a similar result, having taken out all about twenty sovereigns. He was perfectly dumbfounded [sic] by this auriferous discovery, and astonishment was greatly increased when on looking he ascertained that his trousers were further adorned with what appeared to be gold stripes down the side of each leg. Imagining that some kind fairy had been at work and bewitched his trousers, he took a closer inspection of them, but a terrible thought crossed his mind when he found the stripes were like those worn by defenders of our country. The affectionate husband immediately rushed from the shop and made the best of his way home in the hope that would yet be in time to find the owner of the pantaloons. The bird, had flown, and the melancholy spouse, determined to make the best of the matter, drowned his sorrow at the expense of his rival. ("Curious Discovery" 1871)

In 1884 a detailed version of this story was set in Baltimore and involved Henry Clark, "a conductor in the employ of the Baltimore and Ohio Railroad." The trousers "were several inches too short for him," and there was a roll of bills "amounting to $250" ("Got on the Wrong Trousers" 1884, *FG*). Henry sent the trousers to the "gay Lothario's wife" and started divorce proceedings against his own spouse. In 1900 another version appeared in Australia and was set "in a southern city's suburbs" ("A 'Sovereign' Remedy" 1900, *FG*).

Notes

Preface and Acknowledgments

1. Filip Graliński is presently working on a technology to take this method forward for newspaper archives (though the applications are clearly broader; Graliński 2019). Filip's search engine can be taught, with some user interaction, to recognize the type of story that the researcher is looking for. The search engine focuses on salient words, phrases, and sentences in target texts.

2. The skill is the same as that needed in finding a good tabloid headline. My stepfather, Philip Round, an exceptionally fine journalist, died as this book was being planned (20 Jul 2018). I often felt his absence while trying to come up with memorable names.

Introduction

1. Note that the 1866 version sweeps away the theory of Bonaparte (1941, 109–14), that the dead passenger is a sacrifice for a good outcome (e.g., the death of Hitler). However, Bonaparte (1941, 121) and our Dutch author, Fr. v. R. 1934, both guess correctly that the legend was older. Bonaparte (1941, 121): "Probably a similar myth of a corpse in a horse drawn carriage ... was circulated in England or on the continent at the epoch of Napoleon for the purpose of predicting the death of the 'Corsican Ogre'"; Fr. v. R. (1934): "Heeft men hier te doen met een vertelling, die misschien *een eeuw oud* is en die, waardoor dan ook, in modernen vonm oververteld wordt, of is er een positief, concreet geval, dat er aanleiding toe was?" [my italics].

2. Dégh 1996, argues that *all* legends involve belief, and that therefore the word "belief" in "belief legend" is redundant; I would argue that the word "belief" is redundant but *useful*, particularly in the present phase of study. Note, too, Hansen for "belief legends" as stories about the supernatural (Hansen 2017, 16–18).

3. "Urban legend" suggests a legend restricted to urban areas; see also translations in other European languages such as the Italian *leggende metropolitane*. Many of the stories collected here, for example, "Death in the Car(t)," were recorded in the countryside; others had a rural setting, for example, **"Eagle and the Baby"**; **"Hollow Tree Death."**

4. Why start distinguishing between stories that are set in the past or the present? Pettitt (1995a, 97), makes a crucial point when he asks, "Could [the story] happen to [those

who listen or read it], to people like them?" *CW* reminds me of M. R. James's similar comment from 1904 (2011, 406): "The setting [of a ghost story] should be fairly familiar and the majority of the characters and their talk such as you may meet or hear any day. A ghost story of which the scene is laid in the twelfth or thirteenth century may succeed in being romantic or poetical: it will never put the reader into the position of saying to himself, 'If I'm not very careful, something of this kind may happen to me!'" One of the many important insights of those extraordinary scholars who founded "contemporary" legend studies in the 1980s and 1990s was that industrial and postindustrial societies are more likely to set stories in the present.

5. I would distinguish "legend chasing" from the historical-geographical school of folklore studies (Frog 2013). "Legend-chasers" are, in my experience, as much historians as they are folklorists. Legend-chasers also look at a far greater range of source types and (necessarily) put less emphasis on oral collection. Finally, they are interested in genealogies, but they have no or little interest in the illusory search for origins (as some of the early proponents of the historical-geographical school most certainly did). Note that half of the legends in this volume could easily be extended into full-length "legend chasing" articles; a handful could usefully be studied in monograph-length works.

6. I have lived, for ten years, in an Italian village of some eight hundred in the Apennines. When COVID-19 arrived in the village in the spring of 2020, it took about two days for the news to reach me by word-of-mouth transmission. I suspect that in 1900 the news would have circulated in every family in this village within hours. Physical (as opposed to virtual) modern Western communities no longer have the social capital necessary to sustain a proper gossip network by word of mouth alone.

7. My impression is that there has been an informal convention whereby the subject of orality is handed over to scholars of literacy after 1800 (e.g., Vincent 1989). The most important studies on modern British orality, for example, Fox 2000 and Fox 2020, draw to a close before 1800. A historian of Victorian orality is badly needed.

8. Search with 'aloud' 1800–1849 and 1850–1899 in the UK RED database https://www.open.ac.uk/Arts/reading/UK/ [accessed 3 Mar 2020].

9. For comments on American journalism see "A Tall Story" (1867 or 1891), "The wealth . . ." (1898) and "Baby Carried" (1888): "Sceptics may, indeed, reply that the story is an American" story; i.e. that it is untrue. For French journalism, see the comments in "The French Press" (1873), 411. My experience of these two journalistic traditions is that American journalists were often self-consciously hoaxers and jokers; French journalism, meanwhile, had a different understanding of truth (Birch 2018, 26–39).

10. More typically an American journalistic strategy. For instance, the *Sun* kicked off its infamous moon story (Goodman 2008, 136) with reference to a nonexistent piece in the *Edinburgh Courant*. It was dangerous to use invented clippings from British newspapers in this way within Britain. Britain was a small country with good infrastructure. Narratives could be quickly checked (e.g., "Hoax" 1815). But it is possible that some apparently foreign clippings were dreamed up by British journalists.

The Nail in the Skull and Other Victorian Urban Legends

1. Note Flanders 2011, 231, suggests that the broadside depended on Reynolds. It is more probable that they both drew on a well-known oral story.

2. Ogden 1840, 235: "The benevolent Mrs. Montague, author of the 'Essay on the Writings and Genius of Shakspere,' was in the habit, during the latter part of the last century, (this lady died in 1800), of giving an anniversary dinner to the Sweeps, on May-day. It was commonly reported that the repast was bestowed in remembrance of her long-lost son having been found in the employment of a Sweep, and happily restored to his friends. In this particular, however, we have an additional specimen of the mode in which truth and fiction are commonly confounded in traditionary legends. It was, in fact, Edward Wortley Montagu, son of the witty Lady Mary, who eloped from his parents, and voluntarily took upon himself the sable garb of sweephood: in this state, he was accidentally met in the street by a friend of his family, and taken back to the fearful pains of cleanliness and opulence." Needless to say, there is nothing of this in Grundy 2004, "Montagu"; see further, for this myth-making, Joshua 2007, 91–93 and (*PB*) Roud 2008, 94–95 and 98–99. Note that a Dutch report, "Als eene" 1901, reports how "each year the British ambassador [in Germany] throws a party for the Berlin chimney sweeps. This has been instituted by the British ambassador Sir E. Malet, in remembrance of a 'romantic but completely true' incident involving his mother's family. A boy was abducted and taken to Orleans, where he was sold to a chimney sweep. Working in a castle near Orleans, the boy finds gold coins he recognizes as English. This in turn alerts the owner of the castle to the fact that the little chimney sweep is British and eventually he is reunited with his family. This is why the Malet family throws an annual party for chimney sweeps" (summary and reference *PB*).

3. Pers. comm., 1 Jul 2019, *FG* writes, "The riot was real, if you believe reports published in Polish newspapers, which were shocked that 'even intelligentsia' believed the rumors. The mother was allegedly a Jewish ten-year-old—foreign newspapers specified her name: Anna Dybek or Dybeck, though I have been unable to find this name in Polish papers. It's hard to say whether she actually existed, probably not."

4. Another American devil dance story came from New Jersey. There a priest had to give a disclaimer—it would be interesting to see whether these devil narratives were more common in Protestant or Catholic communities. "The story has been growing and growing until it is talked of everywhere. I belong to a big club not far from here, and we members have had the greatest amount of sport comparing the different devil stories [i.e., variants]. We have tried to trace it to its source, but so far have been unable to do so" ('Saw the Devil' 1893 *CW*; see also in the same article: "Oh, you have come about that devil story, have you?' said Father Mooney, with a smile. "Well, I've heard that story in several different forms. It seems to have gone all over the country)."

5. Brunvand 2012, I, 181–82 and C12.5.3(a): "Girl says she will go to dance even if she has to go with devil. The devil escorts her." Baughman 1966, 381 references; Q386.1 "Devil punishes girl who loves to dance" for parallels from the Arab Middle East, Braccini 2018, 127-30. Brent C. Augustus (pers. comm., 10 July 2019) described the different outcomes of the Devil in the Dance Hall from contemporary Newfoundland tradition: "Sometimes the dancers find that in the presence of the stranger they cannot stop dancing and all the people on the dance floor are supernaturally forced to keep dancing regardless of exhaustion and pain until the local priest is called to chase away the devil. Sometimes during the dance the girl drops her handkerchief and when bending to pick it up discovers that her handsome stranger has one cloven hoof instead of a human foot and shoe. These variants tend to end with the devil fully manifesting after being discovered and running off or disappearing in a puff of sulphurous smoke, sometimes taking the girl with him. There are some local legends where the parish hall itself, situated on a cliff, then falls into the sea and locals claim that on

certain night, if you stand on that cliff, you can still hear dance music playing." Valk 2001, 200, has no reference to dancing devils for Estonia.

6. Note that Hobbs (1973) makes reference to "Murder by Jest," *Beeton's Boys Own Magazine* 3 (1859), which I have not been able to check. I assume that this too belongs to (D).

7. An Object (1843) is set at St. Mary's College in an unnamed Scottish town. The most famous St Mary's in Scotland is at St. Andrew's, but Sandy Hobbs points out to me that King's College, Aberdeen, was originally St. Mary's and "this dedication was sometimes recalled over the centuries." As no city is mentioned in the text, St Mary's may just be a likely sounding "generic" name.

8. This mythical case is often quoted in such studies. It should be included with N384.4(a) "The initiate dies from supposed loss of blood. The members blindfold him, run a piece of ice across his arm and start water dripping at the same time. They leave; when they return several hours later, he is dead" (Baughman 1966, 374).

9. There is also this related story from 1927, "'Grim Tragedy': 'Priest Murdered While Watching Corpse. ASSAILANT IN COFFIN. (Received 11 a.m.) ODESSA, December 6. A rich Ural landowner's body was placed in the church and watched throughout the night by a priest and a choir boy. When the church was opened in the morning the boy was found unconscious, and the priest strangled. The boy declared that the corpse rose up at midnight and seized the priest, and he then collapsed and saw no more. The police found the corpse still in the coffin, and suspected a local undesirable, who, when arrested, said the priest had refused to repay him five roubles which he had borrowed, and he (the arrestee) hid in the church and took the corpse's place in the coffin and murdered the priest" (*CW*).

10. Were there stories about Victorian "roofies"? "The Alleged Outrage" 1891: "After some further conversation, he said he would not wrong me like some scoundrels, who would think I was just the sort of girl who might be very easily drugged. I said no one could drug me because I never entered a public-house. To that he said that there were a lot of men walking about who were thinking of nothing but how they could get innocent girls and drug them." See also Burger 2014, 127–30, to which might be added Walter (1888), VI, chap. 4, which has a passage where a girl was possibly drugged; see also II, chap. 1 (where Walter believes that a virgin he has bought has been drugged).

11. Note also that the escaped baby became known as "the Eagle," something common in eagle-and-child legends. Are these just etymological stories? See also Michell and Rickard 1982, 142. Hannah's story appeared later in newspapers and in school readers.

12. See also "'An eagle stole a baby and took it to Hoy" (1969); http://www.tobarandualchais.co.uk/en/ fullrecord/64344/9;jsessionid= 7E3179C5A908D354DB9698E57B7506EC; "Am pàiste a thugadh air falbh le iolaire" (1960); http://www.tobarandualchais.co.uk/en/fullrecord/54270/9;jsessionid= 7E3179C5A908D354DB9698E57B7506EC; "A baby girl was snatched by an eagle" (1970); http://www.tobarandualchais.co.uk/en/fullrecord/68213/9 [all accessed 31 May 2019]).

13. Pers. comm., 29 Oct 2017; in a subsequent email, where she gave me permission to publish this account, Carina writes that her nan passed in November 2018. For other modern examples, see Michell and Rickard 1982, 138–43.

14. My father, an ornithologist writes to me (pers. comm., 31 May 2019): "One thing I've seen is the way that several species of big birds, from sparrow-hawk upwards, can try to lift something to carry it off, rise up a bit, then have to let go, possibly dropping down a bit in height first. They think they can do it but find in practice it's too heavy. Maybe some of the

stories start like this but get embellished." The best documented "real" case—a fascinating and well-documented account—is discussed in Rickard 2011. Note that the victim apparently has no memory of the flight.

15. Ruth, a reader of strangehistory.net, corresponded with Gaynor in March 2017, after I had printed the Kirwan King egg-ring story there: http://www.strangehistory.net/2017/03/16/victorian-urban-legend-egg-ring/ [accessed 23 Mar 2019].

16. We are dealing here, of course, with a question that fascinated nineteenth-century writers, particularly in guillotine-using France: Does consciousness survive decapitation? See further: "Death by Decapitation" 1834 and Bondeson 2018, 30–51.

17. I find it remarkable how many histories take the Wheeler narrative seriously. As of 1 May 2019 the world's most popular source for information on the mutiny reports: "At the time a story circulated that [Miss Wheeler] had killed the sowar and several members of his family and committed suicide, but this was later discredited and she is believed to have married the sowar and lived in Cawnpore for another 50 years." https://en.wikipedia.org/wiki/Hugh_Wheeler_(East_India_Company_officer).

18. "Set" does not, of course, mean that these stories are really medieval or early modern. I have found several British versions of the barber story set in Paris before Lurine (e.g., Porter 1902 for an 1824 article; Watts 1825, 268-69; "Terrific Story" 1827), but nothing French. Several British sources also refer to an account in Fouché's "Archive of the Police" (or some such), for example, Pengelly 1922. Fouche's work seems not to exist: I have found no reference in Peuchet, *Mémoires tirés des archives de la police de Paris*.

19. This story, uniquely, combines with the "**Nail in the Coffin**." It continues, "Chit-Chat" 1861: "He could not move: a hand strong as death held him fast, and in his fright he fell back dead from the sudden shock. His cloak had been caught by the falling coffin-lid, and his imagination did the rest. The narrator forgets to say how it was that the lady did not escape, but probably died of fright also."

20. The houses are Ridley Hall and Chipchase; as in Hogg the house belonged to a "Colonel Ridley"; numerous online sources associate the story with a long gravestone in the local graveyard: https://en.wikipedia.org/wiki/Bellingham,_Northumberland [accessed 2 Jun 2019]; for another candidate, Swinburne Castle, see Richardson 1841–1846, III, 11.

21. One author recalls how the postal mark to "obliterate" the stamp was, at that time, in red. In the very early 1840s: "[A black cross] continued to be used on the introduction of the one penny black stamp; but in some cases the black ink was found not to obliterate the stamp sufficiently, so was altered to red. Shortly after this change was made, the stamp itself was changed to brown; and the red mark, being again found not to obliterate properly, was altered to black" (Whymper 1863, 77).

22. The earliest million-stamp chain letter in D. W. Arsdale's extraordinary paper chain letter archive (www.silcom.com/~barnowl/chain-letter/archive/%21content.html, accessed 14 Apr 2019, dates to 1900 and is the New South Wales hospital letter "Snowball" 1906.

23. Hallowes returned to this theme some years later: "The instinct of a dog has discovered murder before this, the wad of a gun that was fired at a victim has found out the murderer [I am not familiar with this story], 'a nail in the skull of a man long since buried has found one out" ("The Rev. J. F. T. Hallowes" 1886).)

24. The text begins "A few weeks ago, the public journals contained an account of a benevolent lady in Philadelphia"; note that the passage appeared in a speech (Everett 1879, III, xiv "Charitable Institutions and Charity: An Address delivered before the Boston Provident Association on the 22nd of December, 1857").

25. I rely on *FG* (pers. comm., Sept 2014): "the unfortunate duellist's name was Julian . . . Dawert." We have Dawert's death record and a Polish account: "the winner was called Aleksy (Aleksander) Borowicz—actually it was not a quarrel, Aleksy and Julian were close friends—the problem was they both fell in the love with the same girl, their boss' daughter . . . Borowicz was arrested after the duel and brought to trial. He was sentenced to two weeks—counsel for the defence claimed that it was Dawert (as the older of the two) who organised the duel . . . and legally it was not a duel."

26. The pointers in the text are "returning to T . . . , in the northern extremity of W . . ." and "I want to know the way to S . . ." When I placed this text on the Beachcombing Blog, 25 June 2016 "Matt" responded: "That's a pretty specific set of conditions [described in the letter], but surprisingly there is a candidate that fits all of them. The town of Tamworth was formerly divided between Warwickshire and Staffordshire, and about four miles away from Tamworth, down what's now the B5493, lies the village of Seckington—which is in a (former) coal mining area, has a grand old manor house, and also has a church with a very prominent steeple which is easily visible from the main road, as described in the story."

27. I know of only one example of the action being shifted to Westminster Bridge (Strong's Sonnets 1835) and an American version on Brooklyn Bridge ("20 Dollar" 1908, *CW*).

28. Note that Boyle's book, entitled *Black Swine in the Sewers of Hampstead*, offers many excellent insights into "Victorian sensationalism," but it has nothing else on the sewer pigs.

29. These stories have been revived with the arrival of the internet. As I was finishing this volume *BC* sent me a file of modern incest legends. Headlines included: "Online love, then a shock for Dad"; "Man Dates Gal on Internet for Six Months and it Turns Out She's His Mother"; "Sarah went online to find a lover . . . and ended up on a blind date with her long lost brother."

30. The whipping is carried out by John Thomas (slang for the penis; www.greensdictofslang.com/entry/rjedumy, accessed 6 Sep 2020). John "had quite a colour when the performance was over—so had the fair delinquent. Whipping no doubt, sends the blood to the head!" Note also "We would be more minute in our 'interesting particulars,' but for reasons which we shall keep to ourselves." Is it even possible that in oral transmission the "Shoplifter's Dilemma" involved sex?

31. The British article "Important Discovery" (10 Nov 1856) refers to "the *Chicago Press* of the 17th ult." The earliest scanned American version appears to be "Important Discovery" (23 Oct. 1856) from Illinois, *CW*. *CW* writes (pers. comm., 20 May 2019): "The *Press* is what the Chicago paper is called in the British accounts. There is no such paper. There was a *Chicago Democratic Press* which lasted from 1852–57." *CW* also notes that 'Dr. Irving J. Pollok, Occulist and Aurist, from St. Louis has ads in the *Chicago Tribune* in May of 1856, stating he's permanently relocated in Chicago. His assistant struck out on his own in August, 1856 and referred to "the celebrated Dr. Pollok's Eye and Ear Institution." *FG*, meanwhile, found a slightly different report from 11 Oct.: "Interesting Examination" about Sandford's attempt to solve a murder at Auburn (Alabama). This report was folded into the Chicago article.

32. This is, I think, the first case where we can be absolutely sure that the technique was used by a police force; Bondeson 2018 has, for earliest, a freelance case from 1870 and a police case from 1877.

33. For other modern examples, see Campion-Vincent 1999, 18; for a cross-over, see the film *Horror Express* (1972), in which Christopher Lee and Peter Cushing examine the retina of an alien creature, and it reveals the image of a prehistoric Earth seen from space.

34. In "former times . . . this custom prevailed much more than now" (Mayhew 1851, II, 150); Kirwan (1871, 331) talks of "two or three hundred" toshers. Note that Mayhew (1851, II, 152) states that tosher leaders are 60–80 and had worked as toshers their whole lives; this implies that the profession was already established back in the mid to late eighteenth century.

35. When did toshers vanish? Hollingshead (1862, 71–72) claimed that there were fewer toshers than before. "London Sewers" (1892) claimed that the toshers "are no more." Later reports, for example, "London's Queerest Workers" (1896), continue to describe the toshers, but these could be based on earlier writing (Mayhew etc.), rather than present practice.

36. "When the line was open these old wives' tales as to the dangers of the tunnel had a considerable effect on timid passengers, for they left the trains at the stations each side of the tunnel, and posted by chaise to the next station on the other side, where they regained the later trains" ("The Great Western" 1895).

37. This was a very approximate translation from a Latin composition; the "furtive kiss" and Box Tunnel are not in the original "A Railroad Essay" 1841; that the author decided to slip them in suggests that the potential of the tunnel was being talked of then.

38. The Box is not mentioned, but as the author claims, the tunnel was three miles long, and as the Box was the only tunnel approximately that length in southern England, I presume this is what the author had in mind.

39. At least this is how I interpret the following poem, "The train . . .": "The train soon pass'd the tunnel through,/ And came again to light—/ Exposed their faces in a view –/ It was a sorry sight!/ With swollen nose and watery eyes,/ Each vowed in right good sooth/ He would the other well chastise,/ And beat him without ruth./ The train soon to a station came,/ At which the lass got out,/ And, having much enjoyed the game,/ Said, with a pretty pout:/ 'Good night, kind sirs; to you I wish/ A very pleasant ride;/ And counsel you, when next you fish,/ To see how runs the tide./ Let this to you a warning be –/ As to each loving spark –/ If girls won't kiss you when they see,/ Don't try it in the dark!'"

40. Several sources claim that this tale can be traced back to 1889; this, as Taylor-Blake and O'Toole 2010 note, was caused by "a simple transposition of numbers" for 1898, when one version of the story had been published in Detroit; the confusion was possibly helped along by the date of the most recent Exposition Universelle in 1889.

41. Having said that, there are some striking parallels between nineteenth-century and earlier wild men: a synthesis of these different wild man traditions is needed.

Bibliography

A. "Begging Children," *Hull Advertiser* (21 Aug 1846), 6.
A. A. "Collecting Postage Stamps," *Notes and Queries* 4 (1857: 2nd series), 500.
A. B. M. "Collecting Postage Stamps," *Notes and Queries* 4 (1857: 2nd series), 329.
"A Black Snake in a Man's Stomach," *Essex Standard* (7 Jun 1834), 4.
"A Blundering Devil," *Leeds Times* (8 Mar 1851), 7.
"A Burglary Story," *Eastern Morning News* (17 Oct 1872), 2.
"A Buried Treasure Swindle," *Kirkintilloch Herald* (19 Dec 1888), 2.
"A Child Attacked by an Eagle," *Cheltenham Chronicle* (31 Jul 1886), 4.
"A Chloroform Panic," *The Medical Times* (15 Nov 1862), 535.
"A Chloroform Robbery," *The Advocate* (11 Sep 1850), 4.
"A Clever Swindle," *The Weekly Republican* (18 Jan 1895), 8.
"A Condemned Sermon," *Globe* (9 Sep 1831), 3.
"A cracking good find," *Sunday Independent* (18 Mar 2001), 47.
"A Cricklewood Divorce," *Hendon and Finchley Times* (3 Nov 1922), 3.
"A Cure for Kleptomania," *Eastern Daily Press* (25 Feb 1897), 8.
"A Curious Egg Story," *Arbroath Herald* (12 Aug 1897), 2.
"A Curious Story about Marshal Ney," *Lancaster Gazette* (17 May 1879), 2.
"A Curious Thief Story," *Ross Gazette* (16 Feb 1899). 5.
"A Dangerous Experiment," *Chambers's Journal* 11 (1859) 78–79.
"A 'Day Out' with 'Busmen,'" *South London Press* (1 Sep 1866), 12.
"A Dead Body Found in the Trunk of a Tree," *Grantham Journal* (16 Jul 1870), 3.
"A Delicate Investigation," *Taunton Courier* (17 May 1843), 3.
"A Discarded Lover's Resolve," *South London Press* (19 Jan 1867), 3.
"A Discriminating Pickpocket," *Aberdeen Evening Express* (4 Jan 1881), 4.
"A Duel and a Farce," *Paisley Herald* (20 Apr 1867), 3.
"A Duel with Snakes," *Globe* (23 Sep 1896), 3.
"A False Rumour," *Leicester Journal* (1 Apr 1853), 3.
"A Fellow-De-Ce-Ived," *Newcastle Chronicle* (3 Sep 1864), 3.
"A Funny Story," *Sonoma County Journal* (10 Jun 1859), 1.
"A Garotte Story," *Leeds Intelligencer* (20 Dec 1862), 3.
"A Ghastly Fraud," *Ohinemuri Gazette* (16 Jul 1892), 9.
"A Ghost," *York Herald* (13 Jan 1838), 2.
"A Ghost in Wirral," *Cheshire Observer* (29 Oct 1887), 8.
"A Ghost Nailing a Visitor in Westminster Abbey," *Stroud News* (17 Mar 1871), 6.

"A Glance Over Selby's *Ornithology*," *Blackwood's Edinburgh Magazine* 20 (1826), 657–80.
"A good story...," *Leeds Times* (29 Apr 1871), 7.
"A Gruesome Find," *Jackson Sentinel* (18 Jul 1919), 1.
A Handbook for Travellers in Durham and Northumberland with Travelling Map (London: John Murray, 1864).
"A Hard Road to Travel," *All the Year Round* 20 (1868), 235–40.
"A Horrible Duel," *Donegal Independent* (3 Sep 1887), 4.
"A Horrible Story," *London Daily New* (19 Aug 1846), 3.
"A Horrible Story," *Hull Packet* (4 Sep 1846), 7.
"A Horrible Story," *Chicago Tribune* (19 May 1867), 1.
"A Horrible Story," *Dublin Evening Post* (18 Jun 1867), 4.
"A horrible story...," *Dundee Courier* (8 Nov 1869), 4.
"A Horrible Story," *Northampton Chronicle* (11 Feb 1892), 1.
"A Horrible Story and Its Moral," *Liverpool Echo* (15 Sep 1885), 3.
"A Horrible Story from India," *Bristol Times* (30 Nov 1869), 3.
"A Horrible Story from Ottawa," *The Scotsman* (25 Aug 1890), 9.
"A Horrible Story, If True," *Dundee Advertiser* (30 Aug 1864), 5.
"A horrible story that...," *Nantwich Guardian* (10 Jan 1883), 8.
"A Husband's Predicament," *Bradford Observer* (18 Nov 1847), 7.
"A Kiss in a Tunnel," *Coleraine Constitution* (7 Oct 1854), 4.
"A Kiss in the Dark," *Leicester Chronicle* (1 Sep 1855), 2.
"A Kiss in the Dark," *Leigh Chronicle* (14 Sep 1888), 13.
"A Kiss in the Dark," *Lichfield Mercury* (18 Nov 1895), 6.
"A Ladies' Suicide Club," *Illustrated Police News* (30 Jul 1898), 7.
"A Little Hard," *Tit-Bits* (12 Nov 1881), 5.
"A Little Too Fishy," *Weekly Freeman's Journal* (23 Jul 1887), 9.
"A live frog...," *Shepton Mallet Journal* (18 Apr 1862), 2.
"A Local Legend: The Hermit Of Lawn Wood And His Burial," *Bedfordshire Times* (14 Jul 1933).
"A Local Legend," *Bedfordshire Times* (14 Jul 1933), 10.
A Londoner, "Newspaper Folklore," *Notes and Queries* 1 (1852), 221.
"A lot has been written...," *Weston-super-Mare Gazette* (15 Aug 1896), 12.
"A Lottery of Death—Freemasonry and War," *Dundee Evening Telegraph* (5 Mar 1881), 4.
"A Major Buried Alive," *Gloucester Citizen* (30 Apr 1887), 3.
"A Man with a Living Snake in His Stomach," *Paisley Herald* (10 Apr 1869), 3.
"A Manchester Ghost Scare," *Manchester Courier and Lancashire General Advertiser* (4 Feb 1886), 3.
"A Melancholy Occurrence," *The Monthly Anthology* 6 (1809), 164–65.
"A Minnesota Monstrosity," *The Rolla Herald* (22 Jan 1891), 2.
"A Modern Jonah," *St. Louis Globe-Democrat* (28 Jun 1891) 22.
"A Modern Jonah," *Sunderland Daily* (20 Feb 1892), 4.
"A Modern Jonah," *Carrickfergus Advertiser* (12 Aug 1892), 3.
"A Modern Miracle," *Lloyd's Weekly Newspaper* (11 Jan 1885), 6.
"A Monster," *Reading Mercury* (17 Jun 1843), 3.
"A Mystery of Paris," *Salt Lake Herald* (15 Nov 1897), 5.
"A Mystery of the Tunnel," *Hull Daily Mail* (7 Jan 1891), 4.
"A New Danger to Railway Travellers," *Lancashire Evening Gazette* (1 Apr 1897), 4.

"A New Trick," *Globe* (9 Aug 1875), 1.
"A new version ...," *Manchester Courier* (19 Jun 1886), 11.
"A paragraph has appeared ...," *Berkshire Chronicle* (22 Jul 1843), 4.
A Physician, "A Science (so called) vs. Religion," *Morning Advertiser* (28 Jan 1865), 3.
"A pickpocket ...," *The Scotsman* (4 Feb 1869), 7.
"A Pinch of Snuff," *Yorkshire Evening Post* (1 Apr 1897), 2.
"A Queer Hiding Place," *Worcestershire Chronicle* (20 Dec 1884), 3.
"A Queer Story from Hull," *Hamilton Herald* (24 Jul 1896), 3.
"A Queer Story," *Peterhead Sentinel* (27 Oct 1865), 3.
"A quick-witted ...," *South Wales Echo* (4 Feb 1891), 4.
"A Railroad Essay," *Bristol Times* (17 Jul 1841), 4.
"A Real Ghost," *Bedfordshire Mercury* (31 May 1862), 8.
"A Remarkable Incident," *Aberdeen Evening Express* (4 Oct 1888), 3.
"A Remarkable Incident—Is It True?," *Aberdeen Evening Express* (2 Oct 1888), 2.
"A Remarkable Story," *Derby Mercury* (5 Nov 1884), 6.
"A remarkable story ...," *Daily Gazette for Middlesborough* (10 Feb 1893), 4.
"A remarkable story ...," *Buckinghamshire Examiner* (14 May 1897), 2.
"A Remarkable Story," *Bromyard News* (24 Jan 1901), 2.
"A Reported Wild Man," *Huddersfield Chronicle* (19 Sep 1879), 4.
"A Ridiculous Story," *Glasgow Evening Citizen* (24 Aug 1889), 3.
"A Roadside Romance," *The Southern Reporter* (19 Mar 1891), 4.
"A Romance of the Rebellion," *Falkirk Herald* (5 Jul 1860), 2.
"A Romantic Story," *Cork Examiner* (14 Jun 1871), 4.
"A rumour that ...," *Salisbury and Winchester Journal* (25 Apr 1868), 6.
"A Sad Sell," *Herts Gaurdian* (24 May 1856), 8.
"A Scotch Laird's wife ...," *Tit-Bits* (31 Dec 1881), 1.
"A Sensation Story," *Edinburgh Evening Courant* (15 May 1869), 7.
"A Sheffield Paper ...," *Worcestershire Chronicle* (24 Feb 1858), 1.
"A Shilling in a Hen's Egg," *Swindon Advertiser* (30 Apr 1892), 6.
"A Shocking Discovery," *Kirby's Wonderful and Eccentric Museum* 1 (1803), 130–31.
"A Skeleton Hunter," *National Police Gazette* (22 Apr 1882).
"A Skeleton in a Tree," Salina *Daily Republican* (2 Mar 1892), 2.
"A Skeleton in a Tree Trunk," *Miners Journal* (17 Mar 1893), 2.
"A Snake Yarn," *Cornishman* (2 Jun 1881), 6.
A South Londoner, "A To the Editor," *Croydon Advertiser* (16 Nov 1872), 3.
"A 'Sovereign' Remedy," *Truth* (1 Jul 1900), 1.
"A Splendid Yarn," *Driffield Times* (16 Apr 1892), 4.
"A St Petersburg Ghost Story," *Yorkshire Evening Press* (3 Jan 1891), 3.
"A Startling But True Story," *The Englishman* 1 (1874), 121.
"A Startling Statement," *Northern Daily Mail* (13 Aug 1907), 2.
"A strange duel ...," *Daily Gazette* (11 Sep 1890), 4.
"A Strange Mistake," *Sedalia Weekly Bazoo* (17 Sep 1889), 8.
"A strange story ...," *Stamford Mercury* (4 Feb 1831), 4.
"A Strange Story," *Northern Star* (Apr 1841), 3.
"A Strange Story," *Manchester Courier* (29 Nov 1856), 4.
"A Strange Story," *Cork Constitution* (5 Sep 1862), 2.
"A Strange Story," *Congleton and Macclesfield Mercury* (1 Feb 1868), 3.

"A Strange Story," *Paisley Herald* (6 Sep 1873), 3.
"A Strange Story," *Weston-Super-Mare* (24 Mar 1877), 3.
"A Strange Story," *Wetherby News* (25 Oct 1877), 5.
"A Strange Story," *Globe* (31 Jan 1879), 2.
"A Strange Story," *Melton Mowbray Mercury* (25 Jan 1883), 2.
"A Strange Story," *Nottingham Evening Post* (2 May 1888), 2.
"A Strange Story," *Sheffield Daily Telegraph* (25 Sep 1891), 5.
"A Strange Story of Faith Healing," *Western Mail* (25 Nov 1892), 7.
"A Strange Story of the Dice," *Worcestershire Chronicle* (22 Apr 1882), 3.
"A Suicide Club," *Portsmouth Evening News* (2 Jun 1883), 3.
"A Suicide Club," *Dublin Daily Express* (9 Apr 1890), 4.
"A 'Suicide Club,'" *Gloucester Citizen* (2 Mar 1935), 7.
"A Suicide Club," *Nottingham Evening Post* (5 Apr 1892), 2.
"A Suicide Club," *South Wales Echo* (17 Jun 1895), 3.
"A Suicide Club," *Yorkshire Evening Post* (17 Jun 1895), 2.
"A Suicide Club," *Pateley Bridge and Nidderdale Herald* (30 Nov 1895), 7.
"A 'Suicide Club' is . . . ," *Luton Times* (23 Oct 1855), 8.
"A Suicide Club: Its History and Rules," *Gloucester Citizen* (18 Jul 1891), 4.
"A Tale of a Lady Thief," *Blackburn Standard* (5 Feb 1845), 3.
"A Tale of the Mutiny," *Homeward Mail* (29 Nov 1869), 4.
"A Tall Story," *Maidstone Journal* (28 Dec 1867), 3.
"A Tall Story," *Daily Gazette* (9 Feb 1885), 2.
"A Tall Story," *Bristol Mercury* (5 Oct 1891), 5.
"A Tall Story," *Newry Reporter* (10 Sep 1897), 3.
"A Tall Story of a Pugnacious Owl," *Dundee Evening Telegraph* (6 Jul 1886), 2.
"A Terrible Duel," *Leeds Times* (13 Oct 1883), 6.
"A Terrible Fall," *South Wales Echo* (16 Apr 1895), 4.
"A Terrible Quarter of an Hour," *Tit-Bits* (17 Dec 1881), 2.
"A Throw for Life," *Tit-bits* (29 Oct 1881), 9.
"A Tipperary Man a New Zealand Chief," *Globe* (27 Jun 1846), 3.
A. V. "The Trade of Begging," *Tadcaster Post* (16 Sep 1869), 3.
"A very extraordinary story . . . ," *Western Daily Press* (26 Nov 1872), 2.
"A Very Nice Mixture," *Ashburton Guardian* (13 Aug 1900), 1.
"A Very Strange Story," *Pall Mall Gazette* (22 Oct 1869), 3.
"A Very Strange Story," *Berkshire Chronicle* (26 Sep 1874), 7.
"A very strange story is related . . . ," *Cambridge Independent Press* (24 Apr 1880), 3.
"A Very Strange Rumour," *Leamington Spa Courier* (8 Feb 1851), 4.
"A Very Unlikely Story," *Hereford Times* (16 Aug 1862), 12.
"A Vindication of Princes Street," *Edinburgh Evening News* (5 Feb 1903), 2.
"A Wager," *Newcastle Evening Chronicle* (31 Jul 1886), 4.
"A Warwickshire Ghost," *Banbury Advertiser* (1 Jan 1914), 7.
"A Week in a Sewer," *Dundee Courier* (9 Jan 1885), 7.
"A well-known gentleman . . . ," *Newcastle Journal* (9 Feb 1893), 8.
"A well-known Kansas citizen . . . ," *Otago Witness* (5 Jan 1893), 40.
"A Whole Medical Staff Anæstheticised," *Coventry Standard* (31 Dec 1847), 3.
"A Wild Man," *Waterford Mail* (8 Oct 1831), 2.
"A Wild Man in Illinois," *Edinburgh Evening News* (24 Aug 1874), 3.

"A Wild Man in Yorkshire," *Caledonian Mercury* (25 Aug 1864), 3.
"A Wild Man of the Mountains," *Tamworth Herald* (23 Nov 1878), 4.
"A Wild Man of the Woods," *Newry Telegraph* (24 Jun 1851), 4.
"A Wild Man of the Woods," *Tralee Chronicle* (1 Nov 1851), 2.
"A Wild Rumour," *Dundee Evening Telegraph* (24 Feb 1888), 2.
"A woman in Cape Town ...," *Hull Daily Mail* (19 Feb 1902), 1.
"A Wonderful Story," *Manchester Evening News* (23 Sep 1875), 4.
"A Yell man rescues baby girl from an eagle's nest," www.tobarandualchais.co.uk/en/fullrecord/31904/1, (1955) [access. 25 Mar 2021].
Abbott, Geoffrey. *Execution: A Guide to the Ultimate Penalty* (Chichester: Summersdale, 2005).
Abhba. "A Lady Restored to Life," *Notes and Queries* 11 (1855: 1st series), 146.
"About six years ago ...," *The Kansas City Gazette* (21 Mar 1889), 4.
Abrahamson, Robert-Louis. "'Here gather daily those young eaglets of glory': Robert Louis Stevenson, the Savile Club and the Suicide Club," *Cahiers victoriens et édouardiens* 81 (2015), https://journals.openedition.org/cve/1964 [acc. 14 May 2019].
"According to ...," *Pall Mall Gazette* (15 Sep 1870), 4.
Ache. "The Throw for life or death," *Notes and Queries* 9 (1860, 2nd series), 434.
Adamson, William. *Salmon-fishing in Canada, by a resident* (London: Longman, 1860).
Addams, Jane. "The Devil-Baby at Hull House," *The Atlantic* (Oct 1916), https://www.theatlantic.com/magazine/archive/1916/10/the-devil-baby-at-hull-house/305428/.
Adeline, Genevieve. "Competing Narratives of Crime and Punishment in Nineteenth-Century Street Literature," (ed.) David Atkinson and Steve Roud, *Street Literature and the Circulation of Songs* (London: Ballad Partners, 2019), 75–85.
"Adventures of a Diamond Ring," *Aberdeen Evening Express* (3 Sep 1892), 4.
Agony, M. S. "Dear Sir," *Sporting Times* (14 Aug 1915), 8.
"Alarm Clocks Trap a Robber," *Escanaba Morning Press* (10 Aug 1912), 7.
"All the world ...," *Penny Satirist* (20 Jan 1838).
Allan, Sue. "Penurious Poets and Ballad-Mongers: Some Nineteenth-Century Ballad Singers in Cumberland and Westmorland," (ed.) David Atkinson and Steve Roud, *Street Literature and the Circulation of Songs* (London: Ballad Partners, 2019), 17–33.
"Alleged Outrage on Hotel Book-keeper," *Northampton Chronicle* (1 May 1922), 4.
Allen, Barbara. "The Image on Glass: Technology, Tradition, and the Emergence of Folklore," *Western Folklore* 41 (1982), 85–103.
"Als eene eigenaardige gewoonte ...," *Nieuwe Tilburgsche Courant* (13 Jan 1901), 2.
Altick, Richard D. *The English common reader: a social history of the mass reading public, 1800–1900* (Columbus: Ohio State University Press, 1998).
"Amazing German Story," *Sheffield Evening Telegraph* (27 Jul 1908), 3.
"American Duelling," *Warwick and Warwickshire Advertiser* (12 Jul 1823), 2.
"American Suicide Club," *Nottingham Evening Post* (26 Dec 1900), 4.
"Amusing Breach of Promise Case," *Falkirk Herald* (25 Jul 1878), 8.
"An American Wild Man of the Woods," *Aberdeen Press* (30 Sep 1886), 2.
An Anti-Garotter, "War To Garotters," *The Times* (11 Nov 1856), 12.
"An Apocryphal Story," *Bell's Weekly Messenger* (5 Jul 1862), 6.
"An Apothecary's Duel," *Canterbury Journal* (12 Jul 1851), 4.
"An East Anglian Miracle," *Banbury Beacon* (11 Mar 1899), 3.
"An Egg Wins a Husband," *The [Philadelphia] Times* (23 Nov 1890), 14.

"An English Green-Room Story," *Rhode Island Press* (21 Jul 1877), 1.
"An Englishman's Valuation of His Life," *Penny Magazine* (1835), 22.
"An Englishman's Valuation of His Life," *Tit-bits* (21 Jan 1882), 13.
"An Exchange of Babies," *Tit-Bits* (10 Dec 1881), 8.
"An Extraordinary Incident," *The Scotsman* (6 Feb 1888), 9.
"An extraordinary matrimonial . . . ," *The Native Virginian* (8 Jan 1869), 2.
"An Infant Murderer," *Good Health* 27 (1892), 153.
"An Irish Wild Man!," *West Somerset Press* (19 Aug 1871), 6.
An Object, "An Owre True Tale," *Fraser's Magazine* 28 (1843), 237–41.
"An Old Hoax," *Weekly Irish Times* (21 Jun 1890), 3.
"An Old Swindle Revived," *New York Times* (20 Mar 1898).
"An Unlikely Story from the Hill Country," *Sheffield Independent* (3 Apr 1866), 7.
"An Unlucky Wager," *West London Observer* (22 Sep 1888), 5.
Ancery, Pierre. "L'étrange prolifération des 'clubs du suicide' aux XIXe et XXe siècles," https://www.retronews.fr/societe/echo-de-presse/2019/01/07/les-clubs-du-suicide (7 Jan 2019) [acc. 14 May 2019].
Anderson, Clare. *Subaltern Lives: Biographies of Colonialism in the Indian Ocean World, 1790–1920* (Cambridge: Cambridge University Press, 2012).
Anderson, Graham. *Greek and Roman Folklore: A Handbook* (London: Greenwood Press, 2006).
Anderson, Olive. *Suicide in Victorian and Edwardian England* (Oxford: Clarendon Press, 1987).
Anderson, Seonaid Morag. "Gassed and Robbed: An emerging motif?," *Contemporary Legend* 10 (2007), 52–73.
Anglo, Michael. *Penny Dreadfuls and Other Victorian Horrors* (London: Jupiter 1977).
"Another Alleged Robbery by Chloroform," *Morning Advertiser* (7 Mar 1851), 2.
"Another Scandal in High Life," *Reynold's Newspaper* (25 Dec 1892), 7.
"Antiquary cannot . . . ," *Notes and Queries* 4 (1857: 2nd series), 40.
"April Fool Extraordinary," *The Boston Weekly Globe* (10 May 1890), 4.
Arment, Chad. *The Historical Bigfoot* (Landisville: Coachwhip, 2006).
Arnold, Frederick. "Burglaries Past and Present," *The Christmas Story-Teller* (London: Sampson Low, 1877), 313–27.
Arnold, Matthew. *God and the Bible: A Review of Objections to "Literature and Dogma"* (London: Macmillan, 1883).
"Arrest and Release of a Reporter," *Belfast Telegraph* (9 Aug 1889), 3.
Ashby-Sterry, J. "The Bystander," *The Graphic* (16 May 1896), 13.
Ashby-Sterry, J. "The Bystander," *The Graphic* (27 Nov 1897), 2.
Ashliman, D. L., and Anne E. Duggan. "Incest, Various Motifs in A (and T)," *Archetypes And Motifs In Folklore And Literature: A Handbook*, (ed.) Garry Jane and Hasan El-Shamy (Sharpe 2005), 432–41.
Ashton, John. *Chap-books of the Eighteenth Century* (London: Chatto and Windus, 1882).
Ashton, John. *Modern Street Ballads* (London: Chatto and Windus, 1888).
"Aspasia O'Whalley's Mission," *The Boston Globe* (16 Dec 1882), 5.
"At Hickling," *Norfolk Chronicle* (26 Sep 1908), 3.
"At Llanydyssil Village . . . ," *English Lakes Visitor* (2 Aug 1890), 5.
"At Taunton Hospital . . . ," *Londonderry Standard* (8 Jan 1847), 3.

Atkinson, David, and Steve Roud. "Introduction," (ed.) David Atkinson and Steve Roud, *Street Literature of the Long Nineteenth Century: Producers, Sellers, Consumers* (Cambridge: Cambridge Scholars Publishing, 2017), 1–59.
"Attempted Robbery in a French Train," *Boston Guardian* (18 Feb 1899), 2.
Axon, William E. A. "Buried Alive: A Tale of Old Cologne," *Notes and Queries* 4 (1881, 6th series), 518–19.
Axon, William E. A. *Black Knight of Ashton* (Manchester: John Heywood, n.d.).
"Baby Carried Away by an Eagle," *East and South Devon Advertiser* (4 Nov 1899), 8.
"Baby Carried of [sic] by an Eagle," *Edinburgh Evening News* (8 Oct 1888), 3.
"Baby Stolen by an Eagle," *Shields Daily News* (25 Oct 1888), 1.
"Baby Stolen by an Eagle," *Hartlepool Northern Daily Mail* (26 Sep 1891), 3.
Bailey, Henry D. B. *Local Tales: Historical Sketches* (Fishkill Landing: Spaight, 1874).
Baker, J. H. "Dyer, Sir James (1510–1582)," *Oxford Dictionary of National Biography* (online 2008).
"Bank Holiday," *Lincolnshire Echo* (8 Aug 1893), 2.
Baring-Gould, S. *An Old English Home and Its Dependencies* (London: Methuen, 1898).
Barnes, Daniel R., and Paul Smith. "The contemporary legend in literature—towards an annotated checklist, part 4: The Bosom Serpent," *Contemporary Legend* 4 (2001), 126–49.
Barrie, J. M. *Better Dead* (London: Sonnenschein & Co, 1888).
Bartels, Sarah "'A Terrific Ogre': The Role of the Devil in Victorian Popular Belief," *Folklore* 128 (2017), 271–91.
Bartholomew, Robert, and Jeffrey Victor. "A social-psychological theory of collective anxiety attacks: the Mad Gasser re-examined," *The Sociological Quarterly* 45 (2007), 229–48.
Bartholomew, Robert E., with Bob Rickard. *Mass Hysteria in Schools: A Worldwide History Since 1566* (Jefferson: McFarland, 2014).
Bartra, Roger. *Modern Myths of the Wild Man* (Ann Arbor: University of Michigan Press, 1997).
Baughman, Ernest W. *Type and Motif Index of the Folktales of England and North America* (The Hague: Mouton, 1966).
Beaven, Brad. *Leisure, citizenship and working-class men in Britain, 1850–1945* (Manchester: Manchester University Press, 2005).
Beckett, Ian. *Victorians at War* (London: Palgrave Macmillan, 2003).
"Beggars," *Lancaster Gazette* (17 Jul 1869), 5.
Bell, Karl. *The Legend of Spring-heeled Jack: Victorian Urban Folklore and Popular Cultures* (NP: Boydell Press, 2012).
Bennett, Gillian, and Paul Smith. *Contemporary Legend: A Folklore Bibliography* (New York: Garland, 1993).
Bennett, Gillian. *Bodies: Sex, Violence, Disease and Death in Contemporary Legend* (Jackson: University of Mississippi Press, 2005).
Bennett, Rachel E. *Capital Punishment and the Criminal Corpse in Scotland, 1740–1834* (London: Palgrave-Macmillan, 2018).
Berkove, Lawrence L. *A Prescription for Adversity: The Moral Art of Ambrose Bierce* (Columbus: Ohio State University, 2002).
"Bernard Wren's Yarns," *Winona Messenger* (2 Jun 1888), 3.
Bernheimer, Richard. *Wild Men in the Middle Ages* (Cambridge: Harvard University Press, 1952).

Berridge, Virginia. *Opium and the People: Opiate Use in Nineteenth-Century England* (London: Allen Lane, 1981).
"Bicycle Trouble," *Leeds Mercury* (5 Jul 1902), 20.
Bielski, Ursula. *More Chicago Haunts: Scenes from Myth and Memory* (Chicago: Lake Claremont Press, 2000).
"Birch for Lady Shoplifters," *Portsmouth Evening News* (22 Jan 1903), 2.
Birch, Edmund. *Fictions of the Press in Nineteenth-Century France* (London: Palgrave, 2018).
Bisagni, Jacopo. "Leprechaun: A New Etymology," *Cambrian Medieval Celtic Studies* 64 (2012), 47–84.
Bishop, Julia, and Steve Roud. *The New Penguin Book of English Folk Songs* (London: Penguin, 2012).
"Bishop's Ghost Story," *Shoreditch Observer* (9 Apr 1910), 3.
Bland-Sutton, John. "The Psychology of Animals Swallowed Alive," *The British Medical Journal* 2 (1925), 104–8.
Blank, Trevor, and Lynne S. McNeill (ed.). *Slender Man Is Coming: Creepypasta and Contemporary Legends on the Internet* (University of Colorado Press: Boulder, 2018).
Blank, Trevor. *Folklore and the Internet: Vernacular Expression in a Digital World* (Boulder: University of Colorado Press, 2009).
Bodio, Stephen J. *Eternity of Eagles: The Human History of the Most Fascinating Bird* (Guildford: Lyons Press, 2012).
Boese, Alex. *The Museum of Hoaxes* (New York: Dutton, 2002).
Bolte, J. "Die Sage von der erweckten Scheintoten," *Zeitschrift des Vereins für Volkskunde* 20 (1910), 353–81.
"Bolton Le Sands: Something about Ghosts," *Lancaster Gazette* (15 Oct 1870), 8.
Bombaugh, Charles Carroll. *The Literature of Kissing: Gleaned from History, Poetry, Fiction, and Anecdote* (Philadelphia: Lippincott, 1876).
Bonaparte, Maria. "The Myth of the Corpse in the Car," *American Imago* 2 (1941), 105–26.
Bonaparte, Maria. *Myths of War* (London: Imago Publishing Company, 1947).
Bondeson, Jan. *Cabinet of Medical Curiosities* (Ithaca: Cornell University Press, 1997).
Bondeson, Jan. *Buried Alive: The Terrifying History of Our Most Primal Fear* (New York: Norton 2001).
Bondeson, Jan. *The Lion Boy and Other Medical Curiosities* (Stroud: Amberley, 2018).
Bonum. "There is locally ... ," *Bye-gones, Relating to Wales and the Border Counties* (1895), 417.
Bottani, Giorgia. "Sbadilon in Islanda: il contesto iniziatico di tre racconti lontani," *Ricerca Folklorica* 46 (2002), 117–223.
"Boy's Suicide Club," *Worcestershire Chronicle* (27 Jun 1903), 5.
Boyle, Thomas. *Black Swine in the Sewers of Hampstead* (London: Viking 1989).
Braccini, Tommaso. "Luciano e il diavolo nella sala da ballo: una nota a *Storie Vere* 2, 46," *Quaderni urbinati di cultura classica* 116 (2018), 128–38.
Bradley, Simon. *The Railways: Nation, Network and People* (London: Profile, 2015).
Brand, John. *The History and Antiquities of the Town and County of the Town of Newcastle* (London: B. White and Son, 1789).
Bray, Mrs. "Cotele; and the Edgcumbes of the Olden Time: II," *Gentleman's Magazine* 40 (1853), 444–50.
Brierley, Benjamin. *Lancashire Wit and Humour* (Oldham: Clegg, 1892).
Brooke, J. W. "Rome's Tactics," *Church Record* (1873), 210.

Brougham, Henry Lord. *The Life and Times of Henry, Lord Brougham* (New York: Harper and Brothers, 1871), 3 vols.
"Broughty Ferry," *Dundee Courier* (6 Feb 1867).
Brown, Lucy. *Victorian News and Newspapers* (Oxford: Clarendon Press, 1985).
Brunvand, Jan Harold. *Encyclopedia of Urban Legends* (Santa Barbara: ABC-Clio, 2012), 2 vols.
Burger, Peter. *Monsterlijke verhalen: misdaadsagen in het nieuws en op webforums als retorische constructies* (Leiden: Doctorate 2014).
Burger, Peter. "Komkommers, zeeslangen, canards en faits divers: Nederlandse kranten (1850–1950) als sagenmedium," *Volkskunde* 118 (2017), 291–318.
"Burglary and Chloroform," *Kilburn Times* (18 Nov 1876), 2.
"Burial of a Noted Character," *Swindon Advertiser* (26 May 1877), 5.
"Buried Alive," *Yorkshire Evening Post* (27 Apr 1893), 3.
"Buried Alive: A Horrible Story," *Cambridge Independent Press* (2 Nov 1888), 6.
"Buried Treasure Near Arbroath," *Arbroath Herald* (12 May 1892), 5.
Burnett, J. George. "The 'Downie Slauchter' Legend," *Aberdeen Journal Notes and Queries* 33 (1908), 161–62.
Burton, John, and Eileen McCabe. *We Don't Do God: Blair's Religious Belief and Its Consquences* (London: Continuum, 2009).
"Burying Alive," *Graham's Illustrated Magazine of Literature, Romance, Art, and Fashion* 9 (1834), 379.
Bushaway, Bob. "'Things Said or Sung a Thousand Times': Customary Society and Oral Culture in Rural England 1700–1900," (ed.) Adam Fox and Daniel Woolf, *The Spoken Word: Oral Culture in Britain, 1500–1850* (Manchester: Manchester University Press, 2003).
"But really . . . ," *Buchan Observer* (30 Nov 1897), 5.
C. L. "Buried Alive: A Story of Old Cologne," *Notes and Queries* 5 (1882, 6th series), 118.
Calder, Robert. *A Hero for the Americas: The Legend of Gonzalo Guerrero* (Regina: University of Regina Press: 2017).
Calmet, Augustin. *Dissertations Upon the Apparitions of Angels, Daemons, and Ghosts* (London: Cooper 1759).
Campbell, S. E. "To the Editor," *The Times* (9 Jun 1928), 10.
Campion-Vincent, Véronique. "The Tell-Tale Eye," *Folklore* 110 (1999), 13–24.
"Can Imagination Kill?," *The Lancet* 1 (1886), 1175.
"Capture of a Wild Man in Missouri," *Elgin Courier* (24 Apr 1857), 2.
"Carlisle Races," *The Carlisle Journal* (8 Jul 1859), 8.
Caron, James E. *Mark Twain: Unsanctified Newspaper Reporter* (Columbia: University of Missouri, 2008).
"Carried Off by an Eagle," *Belper News* (13 May 1904), 6.
Carter, Ian. *Railways and Culture in Britain: The Epitome of Modernity* (Manchester: Manchester University Press, 2001).
"Catharine Maria Bainbridge," *Globe* (23 Dec 1870), 1.
"Causes of the Increase of Self-Murder," *The London Magazine* 24 (1755), 22–23.
"Caution to Railway Travellers," *Northampton Mercury* (27 Dec 1862), 8.
Cawnpore: Outbreak and Massacre (Calcutta: Bellamy, 1857).
"Chained Together to Die," *Dundee Courier* (18 Apr 1891), 4.
Chambers, Robert (ed.). *The Book of Days* (London: Chambers, 1832), 2 vols.

"Charles Dickens and the Pickpocket," *Salisbury and Winchester Journal* (18 Jun 1870), 2.
"Charles Dickens ...," *Tit Bits* (22 Oct 1881), 11.
Chesney, Kellow. *Pickpockets, Beggars and Ratcatchers: Life in the Victorian Underworld* (Old Saybrook: Konecky and Konecky, 1970).
"Chicago Sensation," *Hartlepool Northern Daily Mail* (23 Oct 1897), 8.
"Chit-Chat on Anything and Anybody," *Leeds Times* (30 Nov 1861), 5.
"Chloroform and Robbery," *Huddersfield Chronicle* (4 Nov 1891), 4.
"Chloroform as an Aid to Robbery," *Portsmouth Times* (29 Mar 1851), 7.
"Chloroform in Criminal Cases," *Glasgow Herald* (16 Oct 1865), 4.
"Chloroform in Typhus Fever," *Bradford Observer* (3 Feb 1848), 7.
"Chloroform Robberies," *British Medical Journal* (1871), 64.
"Chloroformed in a Railway Carriage," *Dublin Daily Express* (26 Dec 1881), 7.
"Chloroformed in the Street," *Kentish Chronicle* (14 Oct 1865), 3.
"City Scraps," *London City Press* (15 Apr 1868), 5.
Claretie, Jules. *L'Accusateur* (Paris: Charpentier, 1897).
Clay, John. *Prison Chaplain: A Memoir of the Rev. John Clay, with Selections from his Reports and Correspondence and a Sketch of Prison Discipline in England* (Cambridge: Macmillan, 1861).
Cobb, Irvin S. *A Laugh A Day Keeps the Doctor Away* (Garden City, NY: Garden City Publishing, 1923).
Cohen, Daniel. *The Great Airship Mystery: A UFO of the 1890s* (New York: Dodd, Mead & Company, 1981).
"Coin in an Egg," *Daily Gazette for Middlesborough* (25 Sep 1906), 6.
"Committal for Child Murder," *The Observer* (10 Mar 1861), 8.
"Contemporary Press," *Kendal Mercury* (23 Nov 1850), 1.
"Cora Norwood's Christmas Present," *Wheeling Register* (17 Jan 1880), 3.
Cordell, Ryan. "Reprinting, Circulation, and the Network Author in Antebellum Newspapers," *American Literary History* 27 (2015), 417–45.
Corley, Thomas. *Democratic Despot: A Life of Napoleon III* (Greenwood Press: Westport, 1974).
Correspondent. "The Monster Mother," *Reading Mercury* (8 Jul 1843), 2.
"Country House Gossip," *Leicester Journal* (19 Feb 1886), 5.
Cowan, James. *The Adventures of Kimble Bent* (London: Whitcombe & Tombs, 1911).
Cumming, C. F. Gordon "A Highland Joke," *The North Eastern Ensign* (23 Sep 1884), 2.
"Curiosities of Local History," *South Bucks Free Press* (2 Jun 1882), 2.
"Curious Discovery of a Murder," *The Scots Weekly Magazine* 1 (1833), 43.
"Curious Discovery of a Pair of Golden Breeks in Dundee," *Bradford Observer* (17 Mar 1871), 4.
"Curious Story," *Tyrone Constitution* (10 Oct 1851), 4.
"Curious Story about Louis Napoleon in New York," *Chester Chronicle* (6 Mar 1858), 2.
"Curious Time Measures," *Scientific American* 44–45 (1881), 39–40.
Curling, H. "Christmas Eve: The Story of a Skull," *St Peterburg English Review* 5 (1843), 548–61.
Curtis, L. Perry, Jr. *Jack the Ripper and the London Press* (New Haven: Yale University Press, 2001).
"Cyclist's Sore Throat," *Edinburgh Evening News* (8 Jul 1898), 2.
D. H. "Mr. Urban," *Gentleman's Magazine* 33 (1763), 544–47.
"Daring Robbery in Wales," *Grantham Journal* (15 Aug 1891), 7.

"Daring Street Robbery: Use of Chloroform," *Sheffield Independent* (16 Aug 1851), 8.
Dash, Mike. "The Devil's Hoofmarks," *Fortean Studies* 1 (1994), 71–150.
Dash, Mike. *Thug: The True History of India's Murderous Cult* (London: Granta Books, 2005).
Dash, Mike. *Spring-heeled Jack: Calendar of Sources, 1677-2015* (forthcoming).
Davies, Owen. *The Haunted: A Social History of Ghosts* (London: Palgrave-Macmillan, 2007).
Davis, Edward B. "A Whale of a Tale: Fundamentalist Fish Stories," *Perspectives on Science and Christian Faith* 43 (1991), 224–37.
Davis, Y. Egerton "Man in whale," *Natural History* 56 (1947), 241.
"Day by Day," *Dundee Evening Telegraph* (8 Jun 1942), 2.
De Morgan, Augustus. "A Recovery of Things Lost," *Notes and Queries* 12 (1861, 2nd Series), 506–7.
"De Vergissing Van Een Dief," *Tilburgsche Courant* (1906), 2.
"Dead in a Tree Trunk," *The People* (3 Oct 1909), 13.
"Death by Decapitation," *Northampton Mercury* (4 Jan 1834), 1.
Dégh, Linda. "What Is a Belief Legend?," *Folklore* 107 (1996), 33–46.
Delargy, James H. "The Gaelic Story-Teller with some notes on Gaelic Folk-Tales," *The Proceedings of the British Academy* 31 (1945), 177–221.
Dembowski, Charles. "Incidents in Spain," *Bizarre* 6 (1854–1855), 85–89.
Derleth, Augus.t *The Wisconsin: River of a Thousand Isles* (Madison: University of Wisconsin, 1985).
"Devil Must Be Destroyed," *Dundee Evening Telegraph* (29 Jun 1920), 3.
"Devoured a Living Babe," *Ottawa Daily Citizen* (23 Aug 1890), 6.
"Diamond Found in a Sewer," *Cornish and Devon Post* (31 Mar 1900), 6.
Dickens, Charles. *Sketches by Boz* (Philadelphia: Lea, 1839 [1836]).
Dickens, Charles. *The Life and Adventures of Martin Chuzzlewit* (London: Chapman, 1844).
Dickens, Charles. *The Posthumous Papers Of The Pickwick Club* (London: Gresham, 1837).
"Dickens and the Pickpocket," *Bristol Times and Mirror* (24 Mar 1849), 2.
"Disappeared in a Night," *Pall Mall Gazette* (8 Apr 1913), 3.
"Diseases Due to the Wheel," *Coleraine Chronicle* (26 Jun 1897), 7.
Dixon, Thomas, Jr. *The Clansman* (New York: Doubleday 1905).
Dodd, George. *The history of the Indian revolt* (London: Chambers, 1859).
Dorson, Richard M. *The British Folklorists* (London: Routledge, 1968).
"Doubtful Story of Human Flesh Sold in Russia," *Yorkshire Evening Post* (4 Oct 1919), 7.
Douglas, Dorothy. "Sweets and Suzanne," *Washington Herald* (7 Dec 1914), 7.
"Dover," *Canterbury Journal* (7 Nov 1863), 3.
"Drapers Who Cane Their Customers," *Pearson's Weekly* (1 Sep 1904), 10.
Drew, Odo. "News from Nowhere," *Good Morning* (21 Jan 1944), 3.
"Driving Nails into His Skull," *Lancashire Evening Post* (2 Oct 1890), 3.
"Drugged and Robbed in the Train," *Buckinghamshire Examiner* (19 Mar 1897), 6.
"Drugged by a Flower," *Birmingham Daily Gazette* (13 Aug 1926), 1.
"Drugged Chocolates," *Hartlepool Northern Daily Mail* (14 Nov 1911), 5.
"Drugged Cigar in a Train," *Evesham Standard* (5 Oct 1907), 7.
"Drugged Drink and Outrage," *Sheffield Evening Telegraph* (31 Aug 1897), 2.
"Drugged in a Train," *Lakes Herald* (21 Nov 1913), 6.
"Drugged in the Train," *Sheffield Evening Telegraph* (28 Jan 1899), 4.
"Drugged in Train," *Western Gazette* (23 Jan 1920), 10.

Drysdale, Arthur. "Death Counterfeiting Sleep," *The American Homeopathist* 13 (1887), 412–15.
"Duelling Extraordinary," *Western Daily Press* (14 Mar 1882), 7.
Duff, Andrew Halliday. "Who Murdered Downie?," *Household Words* 14 (1852), 325–29.
Dundes, Alan. "The Ballad of the Walled-Up Wife," *The Walled-Up Wife: A Casebook*, (ed.) Alan Dundes (London: University of Wisconsin Press, 1996), 185–204.
Dundes, Alan, and Carl R. Pagter. *Work Hard and You Shall be Rewarded: Urban Folklore from the Paperwork Empire* (Detroit: Wayne State University Press, 1992 [1975]).
"During the Cholera ...," *The Southern Monthly* 1 (1862), 476–77.
E. H. T. "The Sealed Packet Once More," *Cheltenham Examiner* (23 Dec 1874), 8.
"Eccentric Elopements," *Leeds Times* (2 Sep 1882), 7.
Edgerton, William B. "The Ghost in Search of Help for a Dying Man," *Journal of the Folklore Institute* 5 (1968), 31–41.
"Effects of Aristocratic Example," *Globe* (28 Dec 1837), 4.
Elbourne, Roger *Music and Tradition in Early Industrial Lancashire, 1780–1840* (London: Folklore Society, 1980).
Ellis, Bill. "De Legendis Urbis: Modern Legends in Ancient Rome," *Journal of American Folkore* 96 (1983), 200–208.
Ellis, Bill. "Death by Folklore: Ostension, Contemporary Legend, and Murder," *Western Folklore* 48 (1989), 201–20.
Ellis, Bill. "The Roots of 'Perspectives on Contemporary Legend': The 1960 Rhodes-Livingstone Institute Conference, 'Myth in Modern Africa'" *Contemporary Legend* 10 (2007), 1–37.
"Empty Coffin Mystery," *Derry Journal* (8 Dec 1933), 5.
Encyclopédiana: recueil d'anecdotes anciennes, modernes et contemporaines (Paris: Jules Laisné, 1842?).
"English and Irish Juries," *All the Year Round* 7 (1862), 421–25.
"English Girls in the Harem," *Yorkshire Evening Post* (5 Mar 1892), 2.
Erichsen, John Eric. "Punctured Fractures of the Skull," *The London Lancet* (1868), 69–72.
Erll, Astrid. "Remembering across Time, Space and Cultures: Premediation, Remediation and the 'Indian Mutiny,'" (ed.) Astrid Erll and Ann Rigney, *Mediation, Remediation, and the Dynamics of Cultural Memory* (Berlin: Walter de Gruyter, 2009), 109–38.
Ermacora D., Roberto Labanti, and Andrea Marcon. "Towards a Critical Anthology of Pre-Modern Bosom Serpent Folklore," *Folklore* 127 (2016), 286–304.
Ermacora, Davide. "Pre-Modern Bosom Serpents and Hippocrates" Epidemiae 5: 86: "A Comparative and Contextual Folklore Approach," *Journal of Ethnology and Folkloristics* 2 (2015), 75–115.
Ermacora, Davide. "The Comparative Milk-Suckling Reptile," *Anthropozoologica* 52 (2017), 59–81.
Ermacora, Davide. *Pins and Needles, Nails, Witchcraft and Murder: Three Story-Complexes Between Fantasy and Reality* (forthcoming).
Evans, Arthur B. "Optograms and Fiction: Photo in a Dead Man's Eyes," *Science Fiction Studies* 20 (1993), 341–61.
"Ever since ...," *Motherwell Times* (22 Sep 1894), 3.
Everett, Edward. *Orations and Speeches on Various Occasions* (Boston: Little Brown, 1879), 4 vols.
"Exciting Rumour," *Leighton Buzzard Observer* (13 Sep 1870), 4.

"Execution and Resuscitation of a Murderer," *Waterford Mail* (7 Jul 1841), 3.
"Extraordinary Application of Chloroform," *Bath Chronicle* (16 Dec 1847), 2.
"Extraordinary Attempted Robbery," *Witney Express* (21 Dec 1882), 5.
"Extraordinary Circumstance," *North Devon Journal* (22 Apr 1830), 2.
"Extraordinary Conduct of a Maniac," *North Wales Chronicle* (23 Mar 1847), 4.
"Extraordinary Statement," *Derbyshire Chronicle* (25 Feb 1843), 3.
"Extraordinary Story," *Congleton and Macclesfield Mercury* (29 Jul 1871), 3.
"Face Looked from the Tree," *Cincinnati Enquirer* (24 Apr 1897), 3.
"False Reports of Garotting Cases," *Dover Telegraph* (13 Dec 1862), 6.
"Fashionable Hobbies," *Punch* 16 (1849), 107.
"Fatal Frolic," *Hereford Times* (20 Jul 1833) 4.
"Fatal Joke," *Oxford Chronicle* (17 Apr 1852), 3.
"Father's Dilemma," *Birmingham Daily Gazette* (27 Apr 1907), 7.
Fea, Allan. *Secret Chambers and Hiding-places: The Historic, Romantic & Legendary Stories & Traditions* (London: Methuen, 1901).
Fields, Annie. "A Mysterious Adventure," *Whitstable Times* (26 Dec 1891), 6.
"Finnegan," *Manchester Courier* (10 Oct 1896), 14.
Finucane, R. C. *Ghosts: Appearances of the Dead & Cultural Transformations* (New York: Prometheus 1996).
Flanagan, Kieran. "Conversion: Heroes and their Sociological Redemption," *Conversion in the Age of Pluralism*, (ed.) Giuseppe Giordan (Leiden: Brill, 2009), 33–72.
"Sweeney Todd's Ancestors," https://www.judithflanders.co.uk/sweeney-todds-ancestors/ (28 Mar 2011) [accessed 4 Apr 2019].
Flanders, Judith. *The Invention of Murder: How the Victorians Revelled in Death and Detection and Created Modern Culture* (London: Harper, 2011).
"For several days...," *Bell's Weekly Messenger* (7 Jun 1818), 6.
Forker, Charles R. *Skull beneath the Skin: The Achievement of John Webster* (Carbondale: Southern Illinois University Press, 1986).
Forman, W. Courthope. "The Mistletoe Bough," *Note and Queries* 12 (1924), 198, 273–74.
Forth, Gregory. *Images of the Wildman in Southeast Asia: An Anthropological Perspective* (New York: Routledge, 2008).
Foss, Edward. *The Judges of England: with sketches of their lives, and miscellaneous notices connected with the Courts at Westminster, from the time of the Conquest* (London: NP, 1848–64), 9 vols.
Fox, Adam. *Oral and Literate Culture in England, 1500–1700* (Oxford: Clarendon Press, 2000).
Fox, Adam. *The Press and the People: Cheap Print and Society in Scotland, 1500–1785* (Oxford: Oxford University Press 2020).
Fr. v. R. "Voorspelling en gerucht Lichtgeloovigen opgepast," *Algemeen Handelsblad* (2 Sep 1934), 4.
Frances, Williams-Wynn. *Diaries of a lady of quality from 1797 to 1844* (London: Longman, 1864).
"Frauds on Newspapers," *Bell's Weekly Messenger* (25 Oct 1845), 1.
"Frédéric Kregler," *Le Figaro* (9 Apr 1831), 1.
Free Lance, "The 'Red' in the Tissue of History," *Weekly Irish Times* (16 Mar 1895), 1.
Frog, "Revisiting the Historical-Geographic Method(s)," *Retrospective Methods Network Newsletter* 7 (2013), 18–34.

"From Darkness into Light," *Once a Week* (23 July 1864), 136–40.
"From Our London Correspondent," *West Briton* (19 Dec 1862), 4.
"From Our London Correspondent," *York Herald* (8 Sep 1877), 5.
"From Our London Correspondent," *Manchester Evening News* (14 Jun 1895), 2.
Frost, F. C. "Buried Alive: A Tale of Old Cologne," *Notes and Queries* 5 (1882, 6th series), 196.
Fryer, Peter *Mrs. Grundy: Studies in English Prudery* (London: Dennis Dobson, 1963).
G., "Spring Legs in Broughty Ferry," *Dundee Courier* (2 Feb 1867), 2.
"Galvanic Experiments on the Human Subject," *Cork Examiner* (20 Nov 1843), 4.
"Galvanism," *Norfolk Chronicle* (29 Jan 1803), 4.
Gammon, Vic. "Street Ballad Sellers in the Nineteenth Century," (ed.) David Atkinson and Steve Roud, *Street Literature of the Long Nineteenth Century: Producers, Sellers and Consumers* (Cambridge: Cambridge Scholars Publishing, 2017), 119–53.
"Garotte and Highway Robbers," *Leeds Times* (5 Dec 1863), 7.
Garth, Gibbon. "Can a Mother Forget?," *Blackwood's Magazine* 148 (1890), 97–102.
Gates, Barbara T. *Victorian Suicide: Mad Crimes and Sad Histories* (Princeton: Princeton University Press, 1988).
Georges, Robert A. "The General Concept of Legend: Some Assumptions to be Reexamined and Reassessed," *American Folk Legends: A Symposium* (ed.) Wayland D. Hand (Berkeley: University of California, 1971), 1–19.
"Getting into the Wrong Bed," *Maidstone Telegraph* (12 Sep 1868), 8.
"Ghosts on Wheels," *Dundee Evening Telegraph* (4 Jan 1939), 3.
"Girl and Drugged Chocolate," *Western Morning News* (19 Jan 1935), 7.
"Girl Complains of Being Drugged," *Portsmouth Evening News* (20 Feb 1930), 5.
"Girls' Suicide Club," *Sheffield Evening Telegraph* (27 Aug 1897), 2.
Glaber, Rodulphus. *Historiarum Libri Quinque* (Oxford: Clarendon Press, 1989), 187–89.
Gomme, George. *Folklore as an historical science* (London: Methuen and Co., 1908).
Goodman, Matthew. *The Sun and the Moon: The Remarkable True Account of Hoaxers, Showmen, Dueling Journalists and Lunar Man-Bats in Nineteenth-Century New York* (New York: Basic Books, 2008).
Gorman, W. Gordon. *Converts to Rome: a biographical list of the more notable converts to the Catholic Church in the United Kingdom during the last sixty years* (London: Sands, 1910).
"Gossip of the Week," *Derbyshire Courier* (28 Aug 1888), 7.
"Gossiping Rumours," *Monmouthshire Beacon* (19 Jun 1869), 6.
"Got on the Wrong Trousers," *Sacramento Daily Record-Union* (18 Feb 1884), 1.
Graliński, Filip. *Against the Arrow of Time. Theory and Practice of Mining Massive Corpora of Polish Historical Texts for Linguistic and Historical Research* (Poznań: UaM, 2019).
Gray, Frank. *The Brighton School and the Birth of British Film* (London: Palgrave, 2019).
Green, Anna Katharine. *The Forsaken Inn* (New York: Bonners, 1890).
Green, Anna Katharine. "The Forsaken Inn," *Henley Advertiser* (17 Sep 1898), 7.
Greenberg, M., and R. Littlewood. "Post-adoption incest and phenotypic matching: Experience, personal meanings and biosocial implications," *British Journal of Medical Psychology* 68 (1995), 29–44.
"Greenwich Fair," *Sun* (1 Apr 1834), 3.
"Grim Tragedy," *Auckland Star* (7 Dec 1927), 7.
Grimm, Brüder. *Kinder- und Haus-Märchen* (Berlin: Realschulbuchhandlung, 1812–1815), 2 vols.
Grittner, Frederick K. *White Slavery: Myth, Ideology and American Law* (New York & London: Garland, 1990).

"Gross Outrage in a Railway Carriage," *Morning Post* (14 Jul 1849), 2.
Grundy, Isobel. "Montagu, Edward Wortley (1713–1776)," *Oxford Dictionary of National Biography* (2004), [read online].
"Gulling the British Public," *Edinburgh Evening News* (3 Jan 1885), 4.
H. G. "Death Trance," *The Medical Independent* 1 (1856), 90–99.
H. J. O. "The Genesis of An Anecdote," *Manchester Times* (30 Jan 1891), 4.
H.W. R. "Buried Alive," *The Monthly chronicle of North-country lore and legend* 5 (1891), 427–28.
Hakamies, Pekka, and Anne Heimo. 2019 (ed) *Folkloristics in the Digital Age* (Tallinn: Suomalainen Tiedeakatemia, 2019).
Hall, Carroll D. *Bierce and the Poe hoax* (San Francisco: Book Club of California, 1934).
Hall, Joseph. *Cases of conscience practically resolved containing a decision of the principall cases of conscience of daily concernment and continual use amongst men: very necessary for their information and direction in these evil times* (London: R.H. and J.G., 1654).
Hamilton, Herbert Burce. *On the Portrayal of the Life and Character of Lord Byron in the Novel by B. Disraeli entitled Venetia* (Leipzig: Schmidt, 1884).
Hansen, William. *The Book of Greek and Roman Folktales, Legends and Myths* (Princeton: PUP, 2017).
Hardy, Lucy. "That Terrible Christmas Eve," *North Wales Chronicle* (24 Dec 1892), 7.
Harlow, Alvin Fay. *Paper chase: the amenities of stamp collecting* (New York: Henry Holt, 1940).
Harrison, Fraser. *The Dark Angel: Aspects of Victorian Sexuality* (London: Fontana, 1979).
Hartikka, H. D. "Tales Collected from Indiana University Students," *Hoosier Folklore* (1946), 71–82.
Hartman, Donald K. *Death by Suggestion: An Anthology of 19th and Early 20th Century Tales of Hypnotically Induced Murder, Suicide and Accidental Death* (Buffalo: Themes and Settings, 2018).
Hartmann, Franz. *Buried Alive: An Examination Into the Occult Causes of Apparent Death, Trance, and Catalepsy* (Boston: Occult Publishing Company, 1895).
"Has the Devil Gone out of Fashion," *Todmorden Advertiser* (14 Jul 1899), 8.
Hawkins, Francis Bisset. *Elements of medical statistics* (N.P.: N.P., 1829).
Hayward, James. *Myths and Legends of the First World War* (Stroud: Sutton, 2005).
Hayward, James. *Myths and Legends of the Second World War* (NP: History Press, 2009).
Hearn, Daniel Allen. *Legal Executions in Illinois, Indiana, Iowa, Kentucky and Missouri* (Jefferson: McFarland, 2016).
Henderson, John. "Tales of the Unexpurgated (Cert PG): Seneca's *Audionasties* (*Controversiae* 2.5, 10.4)," (ed.) Monica R. Gale and J. H. D. Scourfield, *Texts and Violence in the Roman World* (Cambridge: Cambridge University Press, 2018), 179–214.
Henderson, Lizanne, and Edward J. Cowan. *Scottish Fairy Belief* (East Linton: Tuckton, 2001).
Henken, Elissa R. *Traditions of the Welsh Saints* (London: Brewer, 1987).
Henken, Elissa R. *National Redeemer: Owain Glyndŵr in Welsh Tradition* (Cardiff: University of Wales Press, 1996).
Herlihy, David. *Bicycle: The History* (New Haven: Yale, 2004).
"Het Goudvischje," *Nieuwsblad van het Noorden* (3 Apr 1892), 2.
Hewitt, Martin. *The Dawn of the Cheap Press in Victorian Britain: The End of the "Taxes on Knowledge," 1849–1869* (London: Bloomsbury Academic, 2014).
Hibbert, Christopher. *The Great Mutiny: India 1857* (London: Penguin, 1980).
Higginbotham, Peter. *A Grim Almanac of the Workhouse* (Stroud: History Press, 2013).

Higginbotham, Peter. *Life in a Victorian Workhouse: From 1834 to 1930* (Andover: Pitkin, 2011).

Higgs, Michelle. *Life in the Victorian & Edwardian Workhouse* (Stroud: Tempus, 2007).

"High Mass, Low Mass and No Mass," *Cheltenham Examiner* (30 Apr 1873), 2.

"Highway Robbery Under Chloroform," *Royal Cornwall Gazette* (19 Jun 1857), 3.

Hindley, Charles. *Curiosities of street literature: comprising "cocks," or "catchpennies," a large and curious assortment of street-drolleries, squibs, histories, comic tales in prose and verse, broadsides on the royal family, political litanies, dialogues, catechisms, acts of Parliament, street political papers, a variety of "ballads on a subject," dying speeches and confessions* (London: Reeves and Turner, 1871).

Hindley, Charles. *The life and times of James Catnach . . . ballad monger* (London: Reeves and Turner, 1878).

"Hint to Druggists," *Worcestershire Chronicle* (7 Mar 1849), 3.

"His Only Duel," *Hampshire Telegraph* (20 Jul 1895), 10.

"Hoax at Chester," *Chester Chronicle* (1 Sep 1815), 3.

Hobbs, Alexander. "Downie's Slaughter," *Aberdeen University Review* 45 (1973), 183–91.

Hobbs, Andrew. *A Fleet Street in Every Town: The Provincial Press in England, 1855–1900* (Cambridge: Open Book, 2018).

Hobbs, Sandy, and David Cornwell. "A behavior analysis model of contemporary legend," *Contemporary Legend* 1 (1991), 93–106.

Hodges, Sydney. "As the question . . . ," *Leeds Mercury* (22 Sep 1888), 3.

Hogg, James. *The Long Pack: A Northumbrian Tale, An Hundred Years Ago* (Newcastle: John Bell, 1817).

Hogg, James. *Winter Evening Tales collected among the cottagers in the south of Scotland* (New York: Kirk, 1820), 2 vols.

[Hogg, James]. *The Long Pack: A Northumbrian Tale, An Hundred Years Ago* (Newcastle-on-Tyne: Ross, 1840).

Hollingshead, John. *Underground London* (London: Groombridge, 1862).

Hopton, Richard. *Pistols at Dawn: A History of Duelling* (London: Piatkus, 2007).

"Horrible Story from the Far West," *Evening Mail* (21 Sep 1866), 7.

"Horrible Story of Supposed Premature Burial," *Leicester Daily Post* (1 Mar 1888), 3.

"Horrible Story," *Evening Mail* (13 May 1844), 7.

Houlding, Henry. "Local Glimpses: Rhymes and Dreams," *Burnley Literary and Scientific Club* 10 (1892), 65–72.

"How I Spent a Very Merry Christmas at an Inn," *Illustrated Times* (24 Dec 1864), 22–23.

Hughes, Geoffrey. *An Encylopedia of Swearing: The Social History of Oaths, Profanity, Foul Language, and Ethnic Slurs in the English-Speaking World* (New York: Sharpe, 2006).

Hulme-Beaman, Emeric. *The Faith that Kills* (London: Hurst & Blackett, 1899).

"Human Flesh Sausages," *Diss Express* (19 Apr 1878), 3.

"Human Sausage Meat," *South Wales Daily Post* (11 Jan 1894), 3.

Hurst, George. *Rural Legends* (London: Provost, 1878).

Hyam, Ronald. *Empire and Sexuality: The British Experience* (Manchester: Manchester University Press, 1990).

"I hear from Cannes," *Kilburn Times* (22 Feb 1895), 6.

"Important Discovery: The Detection of Murder," *Rockford Republican* (23 Oct 1856), 1.

"Important Discovery—The Detection of Murder," *Morning Chronicle* (10 Nov 1856), 7.

"In stealing . . . ," *Nottingham Evening Post* (22 Jul 1904), 5.

"In the pit...," *Western Reserve Chronicle* (17 Jul 1867), 1.
"In the reign of Queen Elizabeth," *Caledonian Mercury* (10 Dec 1763), 1–2.
"In the Talons of an Eagle," *Gloucester Citizen* (10 Dec 1889), 4.
"In the Wrong Bed!," *Leamington Advertiser* (6 Jan 1859), 6.
"In the Wrong Bed," *Indianopolis Sentinel* (6 Dec 1874), 7.
"In view of the fact...," *Uxbridge and W. Drayton Gazette* (6 Oct 1894), 6.
"India," *Globe* (5 Apr 1860), 2.
"Infanticide," *Salisbury Journal* (15 Jan 1853), 3.
Ingemark, Camilla Asplund. "The Octopus in the Sewers: An Ancient Legend Analogue," *Journal of Folklore Research* 45 (2008), 145–70.
Ingoldsby, Thomas. *The Ingoldsby Legends* (London: Bentley, 1866 [1837]).
"Interesting Examination," *Richmond Dispatch* (11 Oct 1856), 1.
"Is Gordon Alive or Dead?," *Portsmouth Evening News* (11 Jun 1885), 4.
"Is the Emperor Napoleon Dead?," *Leeds Times* (19 Apr 1873), 8.
"It is not...," *Hull Daily Mail* (14 Aug 1907), 4.
"It is true that...," *The Referee* (12 Jul 1891), 7.
"It will cost you nothing!," *Preston Herald* (11 Jul 1908), 8.
"Italy," *Morning Post* (12 Jan 1865), 5.
Jackson, Mason. *The pictorial press: Its origin and progress* (London: Hurst and Blackett, 1885).
Jackson, W. A. *The Victorian chemist and druggist* (Princes Risborough: Shire, 1981).
Jaggard, William. "Mistletoe Bough," *Notes and Queries* 187 (1944), 261.
"James Bartley...," *Hull Daily Mail* (13 Jul 1891), 2.
James, M. R. *Collected Ghost Stories* (Oxford: Oxford University Press, 2011).
James, Ronald M. *The Folklore of Cornwall* (Exeter: University of Exeter Press, 2019).
"Jewels &c., Value Right Million Francs, Buried Near Cardiff," *Royal Cornwall Gazette* (31 Aug 1872), 7.
Johnstone, Charles. *Chrysal; or, The adventures of a guinea* (London: Routledge, 1907).
Jones, Aled Gruffydd. *Powers of the Press: Newspapers, Power and the Public in Nineteenth-Century England* (London: Routledge 2016).
Jones, Loyal, and Billy Edd Wheeler. *Laughter in Appalachia: A Festival of Southern Mountain Humor* (Little Rock: August House, 1987).
Jones, William. *Finger-ring Lore: Historical, Legendary, Anecdotal* (London: Chatto and Windus, 1877).
Joshua, Essaka. *The Romantics and the May Day Tradition* (Ashgate: Aldershot, 2007).
Joyce, James. *Ulysses* (London: Secker & Warburg, 1994).
"Judicial Application of Photography," *Norfolk News* (28 Jan 1865), 10.
Justitia, "Chloroform and its Opponents," *London Daily News* (4 Feb 1850), 3.
Keyworth, H. "The Supposed Robbery by Chloroform," *York Herald* (14 Sep 1850), 3.
Khasawneh, Hana F. "The Irish Oral Tradition and Print Culture," *Studies: An Irish Quarterly Review* 103 (2014), 81–91.
Kiernan, V. G. *The Duel in European History: Honour and the Reign of Aristocracy* (Oxford: Oxford University Press, 1988).
Kilburn, Matthew. "Todd, Sweeney," *Oxford Dictionary of National Biography* (2017) [online version].
King, H. Kirwan. "A Curious Incident," *British Medical Journal* (1879), 919.
Kingsley, Charles. *The Water-Babies, A Fairy Tale for a Land Baby* (London: Macmillan, 1863).

Kinsella, Michael. *Legend-Tripping Online: Supernatural Folklore and the Search for Ong's Hat* (Jackson: University Press of Mississippi, 2011).
Kipling, Rudyard. *Life's Handicap: Being Stories of Mine Own People* (New York: Doubleday, 1931 [1891]).
Kirwan, Daniel Joseph. *Palace and Hovel, Or, Phases of London Life* (Hartford: Bellknap, 1871).
"Kissing in a Tunnel," *Dundee Evening Telegraph* (25 Jul 1903), 3.
Klintberg, B. af. "Do the Legends of Today and Yesterday Belong to the Same Genre?" (ed.) L. Rörich, and S.Wienzer-Piepo (eds.) *Storytelling in Contemporary Societies* (Tübingen: GNV, 1990), 113–23.
Kosko, Maria *Le Fils Assassiné (AT 939A): Étude d'un Thème Légendaire* (Helsinki: Academia Scientarum Fennica, 1966).
Krappe, Alexander H. "Our Lady of Rocamadour and the Two Gamblers," *Hispanic Review* 14 (1947), 164–67.
"Lady Castlereagh . . . ," *North Devon Journal* (11 Jul 1850), 7.
"Lady Shop-Lifters," *Dover Express* (28 May 1869), 2.
Lamb, Charles. *The Prose Works of Charles Lamb* (London: Moxon, 1836), 3 vols.
Lambert, Frank. "The Mistletoe Bough," *Notes and Queries* 11 (1922, 12th series), 238.
Lang, Andrew. *Historical Mysteries* (London: Smith, Elder 1904).
Langshank, Laurence. *Things in General* (London: Smith 1824).
Lanska, Douglas J. "Optograms and Criminology: Science, News Reporting and Fanciful Novels," *Progress in Brain Research* 205 (2013), 55–84.
Lanza, Clara. *Scarabæus: The story of an African beetle* (New York: Lovell, c. 1892).
Larsen, Marianne A. *The Making and Shaping of the Victorian Teacher: A Comparative New Cultural History* (Basingstoke: Palgrave-Macmillan, 2011).
"Last of the Suicide Club," *Sunderland Daily Echo* (17 Jun 1904), 4.
Laughton, J. K. "Old Postage Stamps," *Notes and Queries* 2 (1898: 9th series), 425.
Law, Graham. *Serializing Fiction in the Victorian Press* (Basingstoke: Palgrave, 2000).
Lawrence, James. "Downie's Slaughter," *Aberdeen People's Journal* (6 May 1893), 3.
"Le Club des Suicidés," *La Presse* (9 Jan 1873), 4.
Leckey, Edward. *Fictions connected with the Indian outbreak of 1857 exposed* (Bombay: n.p. 1859).
Lee, Alan J. *The Origins of the Popular Press in England: 1855–1914* (London: Crom, 1976).
Legman, G. "Toward a Motif-Index of Erotic Humor," *The Journal of American Folklore* 75 (1962), 227–48.
Lemay, J. A. Leo *The Life of Benjamin Franklin: Journalist, 1706–1730* (Philadelphia: University of Pennsylvania, 2005).
Leslie, Shane. *The Film of Memory* (London: Michael Joseph, 1938).
"Letter from London," *Belfast Morning News* (12 Sep 1863), 2.
Levy, W. Hanks. *Blindness and the Blind, or a Treatise on the Science of Typhlology* (London: Chapman, 1872).
"Libraries of Bones," *Weekly Irish Times* (21 Sep 1895), 1.
"Life in the Glasgow Sewers," *Manchester Courier* (19 Apr 1848), 5.
"Life in the Sewers," *Hampshire Advertiser* (29 Mar 1845), 7.
"Limited Liability," *Bicester Herald* (20 Oct 1855), 14.
Lincos, Sofia. "La nonna della truffa alla nigeriana" www.queryonline.it/2018/10/05/la-nonna-della-truffa-alla-nigeriana/ (5 Oct 2018).

"Literary Notice," *Bedford Record* (17 Nov 1877), 5.
Lloyd, Amy J. "Education, Literacy and the Reading Public," *British Library Newspapers* (Detroit: Gale, 2007) [online].
Lloyd, Sarah. "The Greenland Whale Fishery: The Story in and of a Song," (ed.) David Atkinson and Steve Roud, *Street Literature and the Circulation of Songs* (London: Ballad Partners, 2019), 86–102.
"London," *The Globe* (28 Jun 1841), 2.
"London Gossip," *York Herald* (12 Feb 1880), 8.
"London Gossip," *Birmingham Daily Post* (7 Jun 1889), 5.
"London Letter," *Buchan Observer* (9 Oct 1874), 3.
"London Morning Newspapers," *Chambers's Journal* 12 (1849), 85–90.
"London Sewers," *Lancaster Gazette* (25 Jun 1892), 2.
"London's Queerest Workers," *Edinburgh Evening News* (11 Jul 1896), 3.
Loomis, C. Grant. "The Tall Tales of Dan De Quille," *California Folklore Quarterly* 5 (1946), 26–71.
"Lord Campbell's 'Chloroform Clause,'" *Morning Advertiser* (7 Mar 1851), 2.
"Lost and Found," *Worcestershire Chronicle* (17 May 1879), 3.
"Lottery of Death," *Windsor and Eton Express* (19 Jun 1852), 2.
"Lovers' Kiss," *Edinburgh Evening News* (14 Aug 1873), 4.
"Ludicrous Scene in a Pulpit," *Fife Herald* (27 Aug 1874), 2.
Lurine, Louis. *Les rues de Paris. Paris ancien et moderne; origines, histoire, monuments, costumes, murs, chroniques et traditions* (Paris, Kugelmann, 1844), 2 vols.
Lusinius, Euphormio [John Barclay]. *Satyricon* (Leyden: Hackiana, 1674 [1604-1614]).
"Lynch Law on a Lady-Thief," *Dublin Weekly Register* (17 Jan 1846), 7.
"Lynch Law on a Lady Thief," *Wolverhampton Chronicle* (21 Jan 1846), 2.
M. A. (Oxon). "Notes by the Way," *Light* 10 (1890), 353.
M. C. "Obliterated Postage Labels," *Notes and Queries* 4 (1857, 2nd Series), 421.
Maclean, Neil. *Life at a Northern University* (Aberdeen: Rosemount, 1906 [1874]).
Maidment, Brian. "Illustration," (ed.) Andrew King, Alexis Easley and John Morton. *The Routledge Handbook to Nineteenth Century British Periodicals and Newspapers* (London: Routledge, 2016), 102–23.
Malmene, Professor W. "The Death Dice," *Ross-shire Journal* (12 Nov 1886), 4.
"Man Converted Into Pickled Pork," *Sheffield Evening Telegraph* (12 Mar 1891), 2.
"Man Drugged and Robbed in a Train," *Aberdeen Evening Express* (16 Nov 1891), 4.
"Man in Whale's Stomach: Rescue of a Modern Jonah," *Dundee Evening Telegraph* (15 Jul 1891), 3.
Mankin, Carolyn. "Tales the German Texans Tell," *Singers and Storytellers*, ed. Moady C. Boatright *et alii* (Southern Methodist University Press: Dallas, 1961), 260–65.
"Mansion-House," *The Times* (9 Jan 1838), 4.
Marco, Jorge. "'The Spanish swindle': cartografía literaria trasnacional del timo del entierro," *Relatos infames: breves historias de crimen y castigo*, (ed.) Ignacio Mendiola Gonzalo *et alii* (Beiras: Anthropos, 2017), 71–99.
"Married His Own Daughter," *Sheffield Evening Telegraph* (19 Mar 1894), 2.
Marshall, E. A. "Strange Story," *Notes and Queries* 2 (1862: 3rd series), 118.
Martin, H. "A Lady Restored to Life," *Notes and Queries* 11 (1855), 146.
Martin, Martin. *A Description of the Western Islands of Scotland* (London: Bell, 1703).
"Marvellous Tales," *Kentish Independent* (6 Oct 1860), 4.

Marzolph, Ulrich. *101 Middle Eastern Tales and Their Impact on Western Oral Tradition* (Detroit: Wayne State University Press, 2020).
"Matrimony," *Tickler* 1 (1818), 115–16.
Matthews, Wm. "A Strange Story," *Notes and Queries* 2 (1862: 3rd series), 299.
Mayhew, Henry, *et alii*. *The London Underworld in the Victorian Underworld* (Mineola: Dover, 2005).
Mayhew, Henry. *London Labour and the London Poor* (London: Office, 1851), 4 vols.
McAnally, Henry. "'The Sons of the Rock Come to See Me in Chicago," *Lennox Herald* (7 Jul 1888), 3.
McConnell, Brian. "Browne, Kennedy and the 'Tell-Tale Eye': A Response to Campion-Vincent," *Folklore* 111 (2000), 117–18.
McGovan, James. "The Swell Mobsman's Diamond Ring," *Sheffield Weekly Telegraph* (28 Aug 1886), 3.
"Members of the 'Order of the Black Veil' Arrested," *Dundee Evening Telegraph* (6 May 1908), 3.
Meriton, John. *Small Books for the Common Man: A Descriptive Bibliography* (London: British Library, 2010).
Michell, John, and Robert J. M. Rickard. *Living Wonders* (London: Thames and Hudson, 1982).
Middleton, Jacob. *Spirits of an Industrial Age: Ghost Impersonation, Spring-heeled Jack, and Victorian Society* (NP: Create Space, 2014).
Miller, Hugh. *Tales and Sketches* (London: Ballantyne, 1871).
"Millions of Letters," *Logansport Reporter* (1895), 7.
"Miss Burdett Coutts and the Million of Spoilt Stamps," *Usk Observer* (9 Jan 1859), 4.
"Miss Burdett Coutts does not ...," *Notes and Queries* 5 (1858, 2nd series), 308.
Mitchell, S. Weir. *Characteristics* (New York: The Century, 1892).
Mitchell, Stephen. "A case of witchcraft assault in early nineteenth-century England as ostensive action," *Witchcraft Continued: Popular magic in modern Europe*, (ed.) Willelm de Blecourt and Owen Davies (Manchester: Manchester University Press, 2004), 14–28.
"Money and Valuables Found in a Greenock Sewer," *Greenock Telegraph* (23 Jul 1880), 2.
Monk, Craig. "Optograms, Autobiography and the Image of Jack the Ripper," *Interdisciplinary Literary Studies* 12 (2010), 91–104.
Monk, Maria. *Awful disclosures of Maria Monk, or, The hidden secrets of a nun's life in a convent exposed* (Milner: Manchester, 1836).
"Moonlight," *Leeds Times* (21 Apr 1860), 6.
"More Curious Wagers," *Sheffield Independent* (28 Dec 1892), 8.
"Mortuary Escapade," *Star* (3 Apr 1905), 2.
Morwood, Vernon S. *Wonderful Animals* (London: Hogg, 1883).
Mountcashel, Lord "To the Editor of the Times," *The Times* (22 Jun 1841), 4.
"Mr Arthur Cecil ...," *Yorkshire Post* (21 Oct 1886), 3.
"Mr Gladstone," *Irish Times* (24 May 1888), 3.
"Mr. Hallowes's Sunday Afternoon Theatre Service No. 4," *Barnsley Chronicle* (14 Oct 1876), 3.
"Mr J. L. Toole ...," *Dundee Evening Telegraph* (15 Nov 1898), 2.
"Mr. Wyatt ...," *Reynold's Newspaper* (15 Aug 1897), 8.
"Mrs. Fitzpatrick's Diamond Ring," *Chambers's Journal* 57 (1880), 525–28.
"Mrs. Hunnemune," *Derby Daily Telegraph* (25 Jul 1904), 4.
"Murder by Jest," *Armagh Guardian* (14 Aug 1857), 7.

"Murder Will Out," *Rural Repository* 7 (1830), 21–22.
Mussell, James. "Digitization," (ed.) Andrew King, Alexis Easley, and John Morton, *The Routledge Handbook to Nineteenth Century British Periodicals and Newspapers* (London: Routledge, 2016), 17–28.
"Nearly Buried Alive," *Daily Gazette for Middlesbrough* (24 Jun 1889), 3.
"Nearly Married His Own Daughter," *Cheltenham Chronicle* (19 May 1900), 6.
"New Publications," *London Courier* (19 Nov 1832), 3.
Newman, Paul. *Under the Shadow of Meon Hill: The Lower Quinton & Hagley Wood Murders* (NP: Abraxas, 2011).
Nickell, Joe. "The Doctor's Ghostly Visitor: Tracking 'The Girl In The Snow,'" *Skeptical Briefs* 21 (2012), https://skepticalinquirer.org/newsletter/the_doctors_ghostly_visitor_tracking_the_girl_in_the_snow/ [acc. 1 Jun 2019].
Norris, W. E. "The Lady and the Burglar," *Shipley Times* (9 Mar 1923), 3.
Notes respecting the church of St. Peter, parish of Ballymodan (London: Boys of the Door-Step, 1874).
"Noteworthy and New," *Dorking and Leatherhead Advertiser* (2 Jan 1892), 7.
"Notice," *Burnley Express* (8 Jan 1890), 2.
"Novel Attempt at a Swindle," *Folkestone Express* (20 Feb 1875), 8.
"Occasional Notes," *Pall Mall Gazette* (6 Apr 1870), 3.
"Oddities of B.'s, D.'s and M.'s," *Pearson's Weekly* (19 Aug 1899), 13.
Ogden, John. "The Chimney-Sweep," *Heads of the people, or, Portraits of the English* (ed.) Joseph Meadows (London: Tyas, 1840), 232–40.
"Old Stories," *Chambers's Journal* 19 (1863), 264–67.
"Olympic Theatre," *Evening Chronicle* (17 Mar 1835), 3.
"On Saturday ...," *Bridgwater Mercury* (6 Oct 1886), 7.
"On the Marseilles ...," *The Cincinnati Daily Enquirer* (8 Jan 1881), 12.
"Onder de inbrekers," *Algemeen Handelsblad*, (28 Jun 1885), 5.
"One Guinea for a Penny!," *Liverpool Echo* (24 Nov 1933), 8.
"One hears ...," *Manchester Courier* (20 Aug 1898), 14.
"One of the most radical ...," *Dorking and Leatherhead Advertiser* (16 Apr 1896), 8.
"One Shilling for a Pound," *Luton Times* (7 Feb 1902), 8.
"Op een bal ...," *Provinciale Drentsche en Asscher Courant* (11 Mar 1875), 1.
Opie, Iona, and Peter Opie. *The Lore and Language of School Children* (Oxford: Oxford University Press, 1967).
"Osman Digna," *Newcastle Courant* (2 May 1896), 2.
"Our Essence of News," *Hertford Mercury* (24 Aug 1878), 2.
"Our Ladies' Column," *Kentish Mercury* (8 Jan 1897), 3.
"Outbluffing a Bluff," *The Evening Star* (25 Sep 1909), 3.
"Outrage on British Ladies," *Hampshire Advertiser* (8 Aug 1857), 2.
P. E. A. "A Strange Story," *Notes and Queries* 2 (1862: 3rd series), 67–68.
Palmer, Beth "Prose," (ed.) Andrew King, Alexis Easley, and John Morton. *The Routledge Handbook to Nineteenth Century British Periodicals and Newspapers* (London: Routledge, 2016), 138–50.
"Parallel Stories," *Chambers's Journal* 50 (1873), 569–73.
Pater Filiarum, "A Million Postage Stamps," *Morning Post* (26 Sep 1895), 2.
Patterson, R. Stewart. "Spring-Heeled Jack," *Notes and Queries* 4 (1893), 212.

Paul, Robert A. "Incest Avoidance: Oedipal and Preoedipal, Natural and Cultural," *Journal of the American Psychoanalytic Association* 58 (2010), 10.
Payn, James. *Lost Sir Massingberd* (London: Sampson Low, 1864), 2 vols.
Peake, Richard Brinsley. *Cartouche: The Celebrated French Robber* (London: Hugh Cunningham, 1844), 3 vols.
Pearsall, Ronald. *The Worm in the Bud: The World of Victorian Sexuality* (London: Weidenfeld and Nicolson, 1969).
Pengelly, R. S. "Sweeney Todd," *Notes and Queries* 12 (1922, 10th series), 378.
Peschier, Diana. *Nineteenth-Century Anti-Catholic Discourses: The Case of Charlotte Bronte* (London: Palgrave-Macmillan, 2005).
Pettitt, Thomas. "Legends Contemporary, Current and Modern: An Outsider's View," *Folklore* 106 (1995a), 96–98.
Pettitt, Thomas. "The Hampstead Hogs," *FOAFTALE News* 38 (1995b).
Phegley, Jennifer. "Family Magazines," (ed.) Andrew King, Alexis Easley, and John Morton, *The Routledge Handbook to Nineteenth Century British Periodicals and Newspapers* (London: Routledge, 2016), 276–92.
Photiadès, Constantin. *Count Cagliostro: An Authentic Story of a Mysterious Life* (London: Routledge, 2011).
"Photographing from Dead Eyes," *Popular Science Review* 4 (1865), 394.
Piaschewski, Gisela. *Der Wechselbalg* (Breslau: Maruschke 1935).
Pickford, John. "Buried Alive: A Story of Old Cologne," *Notes and Queries* 5 (1882, 6th series), 117–18.
"Pickpockets and the Late Lord Shaftesbury," *Edinburgh Evening News* (31 Oct 1885), 3.
Picton, J. A. "The Autobiography of Lord Brougham: Mrs. Nightingale's Tomb," *Notes and Queries* 7 (1871, 4th series), 277–78.
"Pictures in the Eye," *Dundee Evening Telegraph* (6 Jan 1882), 4.
Pilkington, Lætitia. *Memoirs of Mrs. Lætitita Pilkington Written by Herself* (London: R. Griffiths, 1754), 3 vols.
Plunkett, John. *Queen Victoria: First Media Monarch* (Oxford: Oxford University Press, 2003).
Poe, Edgar Allan. *The Works of the Late Edgar Allan Poe*, IV vols (New York: Redfield, 1857).
"Poisoning Extraordinary: A Strange Tale if True," *North Wales Chronicle* (23 Nov 1861), 8.
"Popping into the Wrong Bed," *Jamestown Journal* (8 Jan 1869), 7.
Porter, H. C. "The Origin of Sweeny Todd," *Notes and Queries* 9 (1902: 9th series), 345–46.
Pouvreau, Florent. *Du poil et de la bête: iconographie du corps sauvage en Occident à la fin du Moyen Age (XIIIe-XVIe siècle)* (Paris: CTHS, 2015).
"Prayer for a Burglar," *Oxfordshire Weekly News* (28 May 1913), 3.
"Premature Internments," *The Spirit Messenger* 1 (1850) 383.
Presbyter Octogenarius, "To the Editor," *London Evening Standard* (22 Jun 1841), 2.
"Pretty Suffragette's Punishment," *Leeds Mercury* (26 Feb 1913), 3.
Prioreschi, Plinio. *A History of Medicine: Byzantine and Islamic medicine* (Omaha: Horatius Press, 2001).
Pujol, Josep M. *Three Selected Papers on Catalan Folklore* (Tarragona: URV, 2013).
"Queer Hoaxes," *Graham's Illustrated Magazine* 53 (1858), 454–55.
Quin, Charles W. "Photographic Canard," *Notes and Queries* 10 (1866: 3rd series), 18.
R. G. G., "My wife . . . ," *Pearson's Weekly* (4 Jul 1896), 18.
"Raggles, the Burglar: A Queer Story," *Leeds Times* (14 Aug 1880), 6.
"Railway Carriage Robberies," *Morning Chronicle* (2 Apr 1858), 4.

"Railway Robbery by Chloroform," *Jersey Independent* (20 Jan 1859), 2.
"Reformation," *The Leeds Mercury Weekly Supplement* (24 May 1890), 3.
Reid, Donald. *Paris Sewers and Sewermen: Realities and Representations* (Cambridge: Harvard University Press, 1991).
"Remarkable Incident (Very!)," *Buxton Herald* (6 Sep 1860), 6.
"Remarkable Incident," *Saunders's News-Letter* (3 Sep 1860), 3.
"Remarkable Incident," *Bristol Daily Post* (5 Sep 1860), 4.
"Remarkable Story of a Gold Ring," *Whitehaven News* (4 Apr 1872), 7.
"Remedy for 'Bicycle Face,'" *South Wales Daily News* (4 Sep 1897), 3.
Rentilson, John. "Mystery of the 'Lang Pack,'" *Jedburgh Gazette* (19 Jan 1934), 4.
"Resuscitation of the Hammersmith Ghost," *Morning Post* (12 Dec 1833), 2.
"Review," *The Literary Panorama* 2 (1807), 1195–197.
Reynolds, George. *The Mysteries of London* (London: Vickers, 1846), 6 vols.
Richardson, Moses. *The Local Historian's Table Book of remarkable occurrences, historical facts, traditions, legendary and descriptive ballads, connected with the Counties of Newcastle-upon-Tyne, Northumberland, and Durham* (Newcastle: Richardson, 1841–1846).
Richter, Dieter. "Wie Kinder Schlachtens mit einander gespielt haben (AaTh 2401). Von Schonung und Verschonung der Kinder—in und vor einem Märchen der Brüder Grimm," *Fabula* 27 (1986), 1–11.
Rickard, Bob. "EAGLE & BABY 1 - The Svanhild Hartvigsen Story" (https://web.archive.org/web/20180720083713/https://blogs.forteana.org/node/154), 26 Jan 2011 [accessed through the Way Back Machine 1 Jul 2019].
Rickards, J. C. "Obliterated Postage Labels," *Notes and Queries* 4 (1857, 2nd Series), 421.
"Robberies effected . . . ," *The Advocate* (11 Sep 1850), 4.
"Robbery by Chloroform," *North Devon Journal* (3 Feb 1848), 5.
"Robbery by Chloroform," *Manchester Courier* (30 Dec 1864), 3.
"Robbery by Chloroform," *Perthshire Advertiser* (15 Jun 1865), 2.
"Robbery by Chloroform," *Western Times* (21 Oct 1848), 5.
"Robbery by Chloroform in a Railway Train," *Londonderry Standard* (11 Jun 1864), 4.
"Robbery by Means of Chloroform," *Grantham Journal* (25 Jul 1857), 4.
"Robbery under Chloroform," *Gloucester Citizen* (28 Nov 1888), 4.
"Robbery with Chloroform," *Eastern Daily Press* (23 Dec 1879), 4.
Roberts, D. "How Cruel Was the Victorian Poor Law?," *Historical Journal* 6 (1963), 97–107.
Rogers, Samuel. *Italy: A Poem* (London: Cadell, 1830 [1828]).
Rollins, Hyder Edward. *The Pack of Autolycus* (Cambridge: Harvard University Press, 1927).
"Romantic Story from Russia," *Aberdeen Press* (17 Feb 1900), 3.
"Romantic, If True," *Huddersfield Chronicle* (9 Dec 1886), 4.
"Romantic," *Western Times* (9 Nov 1866), 6.
Roper, Jonathan. "Folk Disbelief," *Storied and Supernatural Places*, (ed.) Ülo Valk and Daniel Sävborg (Helsinki: Finnish Literature Society, 2018), 223–36.
Rose-Soley, J. F. "Do Suicides' Clubs Really Exist?," *San Francisco Call* (12 Dec 1897), 22.
"Rossendale Boggart Tales," *Burnley Express and Advertiser* (28 August 1897), 3.
Rossetti, Dante Gabriel. *Dante Gabriel Rossetti: His family-letters* (Boston: Robert Brothers, 1895), 2 vols.
Roud, Steve. *London Lore: The Legends and Traditions of the World's Most Vibrant City* (London: Random House, 2008).

Roud, Steve. "Introduction," (ed.) David Atkinson and Steve Roud, *Street Ballads in Nineteenth-Century Britain, Ireland, and North America: The Interface between Print and Oral Traditions* (Dorchester: Ashgate, 2014), 1–17.
Rowe, Richard. *Episodes in an Obscure Life* (London: Routledge, 1871).
Rowles, George. "The Burglar's Story," *Blackburn Standard* (27 Jan 1900), 11.
"Rumour Concerning the Queen," *Cork Examiner* (3 Aug 1842), 2.
Russell, Herbert. "An Idol of Clay," *Bridgnorth Journal* (3 Jun 1899), 3.
"Ryssel," *Bataafsche Leeuwarder Courant* (9 May 1805), 1.
S. A. S. "A Lady Restored to Life," *Notes and Queries* 12 (1855: 1st) 215.
Sacco, Lynn. *Unspeakable: Father-Daughter Incest in American History* (Baltimore: John Hopkins University Press, 2009).
Sailer, Susan Shaw. "Leaps, Curses and Flight: Suibne Geilt and the Roots of Early Irish Sulture," *Études celtiques* 33 (1997), 191–208.
Sanderson, Ivan. "An Oological Outrage," *Pursuit* 2 (1969), 15.
"Save Us From Our Friends," *Oxford Times* (6 Dec 1862), 3.
"Saw the Devil in Jersey City," *New York Herald* (25 Dec 1893), 9.
Schiffer, Michael. *Draw the Lightning Down: Benjamin Franklin and Electrical Technology in the Age of Enlightenment* (Berkeley: University of California Press, 2006).
"Scrambling for Babies," *Troy Times* (10 Jul 1859).
"Sentences," *Morning Advertiser* (14 Apr 1825), 3.
"Sewer Accident," *Leicester Journal* (3 Dec 1852), 1.
"Sewer Thieves," *Bicester Herald* (18 May 1894), 5.
Shaw, Thomas. *Recent Poems, on Rural and Other Miscellaneous Subjects* (Huddersfield: J. Lancashire, 1824).
Shelley, Mary Wollstonecraft. *Frankenstein: Or, The Modern Prometheus* (London: Routledge, 1888).
Shepard, L. *History of Street Literature* (London: David and Charles, 1973).
"Shoplifting by a Lady of Fortune," *Worcestershire Chronicle* (22 Oct 1845), 6.
Simpson, Jacqueline. "The Queen Rat: A Comment," *FLS News* 22 (1995), 4.
Simpson, Jacqueline. "Urban Legends in *The Pickwick Papers*," *Journal of American Folklore* 96 (1983), 462–70.
Simpson, Jacqueline. *Green Men and White Swans* (Long Preston: Magna Large, 2010).
Simpson, Jacqueline, and Steve Roud. *A Dictionary of English Folklore* (Oxford: Oxford University Press, 2000).
Sinclair, Upton. *The Jungle* (London: Penguin, 1936 [1906]).
Sindall, R. "The London garrotting panics of 1856 and 1862," *Social History* 12 (1987), 351–59.
"Singular Freak of a Pauper at a Union House," *Essex Herald* (2 Mar 1847), 3.
"Singular Occurrence Related by Lord Littleton in a Letter to a Friend," *Oxford University and City Herald* (12 Aug 1809), 4.
"Singular Provision in a Will," *Chicago Daily Tribune* (25 Oct 1893), 4.
"Sir Leo Money and shop Assistant," *Surrey Advertiser* (16 Sep 1933), 2.
"Six Days in a Hollow Tree," *Hendon and Finchley Times* (1 Jan 1886), 7.
Skinner, Charles M. *American myths & legends* (Philadelphia: J.B. Lippincott, 1903), 2 vols.
"Skulls and Bones," *Derbyshire Advertiser* (2 Sep 1921), 12.
Smith, Helen R. *New Light on Sweeney Todd, Thomas Peckett Prest, James Malcolm Rymer and Elizabeth Caroline Grey* (London: Jarndyce, 2002).
Smith, J. B. "Killing the Devil," *Tradition Today* 8 (2019), 58–62.

Smith, Paul. "On the Receiving End: When Legend Becomes Rumour," *Perspectives on Contemporary Legend* (Sheffield: Cectal, 1984), 197–205.
Smith, Paul. "Contemporary Legend: A Legendary Genre?," *The Questing Beast: Perspectives on Contemporary Legend, vol. IV*, (ed.) G. Bennett and Paul Smith (Sheffield: Sheffield Academic Press, 1989), 91–101.
Smith, Paul. "'Read All About It! Elvis Eaten by Drug-Crazed Giant Alligators': Contemporary Legend and the Popular Press," *Contemporary Legend* 2 (1992), 41–70.
Smith, Paul. "Definitional Characteristic of the Contemporary Legend," *FOAFTale News* 44 (1999), 5–8.
Smith, Paul, and Sandy Hobbs, "Contemporary Legend on Film: The Vanishing Lady," *FOAFtale News* 26 (1992), 3–6.
"Snake in the Stomach," *Dundee Evening Telegraph* (17 Aug 1904), 3.
"Snake Stories," *Manchester Courier* (31 Oct 1885), 9.
Snow, John. "The Alleged Employment of Chloroform by Thieves," *London Medical Gazette* (1850), 327.
"'Snowball' or 'Chain' Letters," *The Times* (21 Jul 1906), 17.
"Society Gossip," *York Herald* (13 Mar 1889), 5.
"Some of the Northern papers . . . ," *Canterbury Journal* (22 Sep 1894), 7.
"Some very strange stories . . . ," *Morning Advertiser* (14 Oct 1844), 2.
"Southampton Races," *Hampshire Advertiser* (18 Jul 1840), 2.
"Sovereign Gulls," *London Saturday Journal* 3 (1840), 212–13.
"Sovereigns at a Penny a Dozen," *Orcadian* (6 Jun 1903), 6.
"Sovereigns in the Sewer," *Hull Daily Mail* (27 Mar 1899), 2.
"Spanish Inquisition in London," *Kendal Mercury* (14 Jan 1837), 4.
"Spanish Swindle Again," *Perthshire Advertiser* (29 Nov 1905), 5.
Spirago, Francis, and James Joseph Baker. *Anecdotes and examples illustrating the Catholic catechism* (New York: Benziger, 1904).
"Squeezing the Wrong Hand," *Liverpool Echo* (6 Mar 1884), 3.
Squires, S. Augusta. "Saved By Death," *Derbyshire Times* (31 Aug 1898), 3.
St John, Charles. *Natural History and Sport in Moray* (Edinburgh: Douglas, 1882 [1863]).
Stevenson, Robert Louis. *New Arabian Nights* (New York: Scribner, 1915 [1882]).
Stewart, W. R. H., "The Bicycle and Nasal Disease," *New York Lancet* 2 (1898), 79.
"Stone Bodies in Hollow Tree," *Plain Dealer* (31 Mar 1902), 5.
"Stories about Burglars," *Manchester Courier* (5 Jan 1895), 10.
"Story of a Muff," *Lancaster Gazette* [Ohio] (27 Mar 1851), 1.
"Strange and Stranger Still," *Worcestershire Chronicle* (5 Jun 1880), 3.
"Strange Duels," *Aberdeen Journal* (13 Apr 1927), 5.
"Strange if True," *Portsmouth Evening News* (28 Oct 1879), 3.
"Strange Southern Duel," *Leeds Times* (17 Aug 1895), 4.
"Strange Story," *London and Evening Standard* (2 Apr 1870), 5.
"Strange Wagers," *Northern Whig* (9 Jul 1924), 10.
Stratmann, Linda. *Chloroform: The Quest for Oblivion* (Stroud: Sutton Publishing, 2003).
"Striking Occurrence," *Leicestershire Mercury* (19 Jun 1841), 2.
"Strong's Sonnets," *Blackwood's Edinburgh Magazine* (1835), 587–99.
"Suicide 'De Luxe,'" *Dundee Evening Telegraph* (17 Dec 1896), 3.
"Suicide Club: Theory of Tragedies on an Atlantic Liner," *London Daily News* (17 Apr 1909), 5.
"Suicide Clubs," *Weekly Freeman's Journal* (30 Jul 1898), 12.

Summers, Montague. "The Mistletoe Bough," *Notes and Queries* 182 (1942), 320.
Summerscale, Kate. *The Suspicions of Mr Whicher or The Murder at Road Hill House* (London: Bloomsbury, 2009).
"Summoned by Ghosts," *Western Mail* (4 May 1894), 7.
"Superstition in Russia," *St. James Gazette* (13 Mar 1890), 12.
"Surprising Wagers," *Sheffield Weekly Telegraph* (6 Apr 1912), 8.
"Swallowed by a Whale: A Splendid Yarn," *Lancashire Evening Post* (25 Jan 1892), 3.
Swan, Annie S. "The Prodigal's Christmas," *Taunton Courier* (17 Dec 1916), 3.
Sweet, Matthew. *Inventing the Victorians* (London: Faber & Faber, 2001).
"Szkielet . . . ," *Głos Narodu* (1 Jul 1903), 4.
T. G. *The Flowers of Parnassus* (London: J. and T. Dormer, 1735), 169.
"Taking Arsenic in the Court Room to Win a Case," *The Magazine of American History with Notes and Queries* 1 (1877), 144–46.
"Tarantulas for Two," *Gloucester Citizen* (15 Jul 1892), 3.
Taylor-Blake, Bonnie, and Garson O'Toole. "On the Trail of the Vanishing Lady," *FOAFtale News* 76 (2010), 7–11.
Taylor-Blake, Bonnie, and Garson O'Toole. "On the Trail of the Vanishing Lady," *FOAFtale News* 77 (2011), 6–7.
"10 'Shock' Police Arrested on Suspicion," *The Scotsman* (14 Jul 1936), 9.
Tennant, Kara. "Female Space, Feminine Grace: Ladies and the Mid-Victorian Railway," *Britain and the Narration of Travel in the Nineteenth Century: Texts, Images, Objects*, (ed.) Kate Hill (London: Routledge, 2016), 53–72.
"Terrific Story of the Rue del la Harpe at Paris," *The New London Gleaner* (1827), 313–14.
"Thames Police," *Morning Post* (15 Nov 1830), 4.
"That Buried Treasure," *Leeds Times* (17 Feb 1894), 3.
"That Fatal Diamond: A Thief's Confession," *Leeds Times* (13 Feb 1886), 6.
"The Adventures of a Wedding Ring," *North Devon Journal* (24 Jul 1879), 3.
"The Alledged [sic] Murder at Walworth," *Coventry Herald* (9 Jul 1830), 3.
"The Alleged 'Drugging' on the Tynemouth Train," *Shields Daily Gazette* (18 May 1885), 3.
"The Alleged Outrage and Robbery at the West End," *Globe* (11 Sep 1891), 5.
"The alleged robbery . . . ," *Hampshire Advertiser* (3 Apr 1858), 4.
"The American Chain Letter," *The Times* (19 Nov, 1895), 4.
"The American Clergyman and the Burglar," *Alnwick Mercury* (1 May 1863), 6.
"The American Eagle," *Taunton Courier* (3 Feb 1869), 7.
"The Archbishop Lays the Ghost," *Luton Times* (29 Aug 1913), 3.
"The authorities," *The Times* (Apr 20 1852), 5.
"The Awful Fate of a Mercer County Blasphemer," *Xenia Daily Gazette* (4 Aug 1886), 1.
"The Bicycle Face," *Worcestershire Chronicle* (1 Aug 1896), 2.
"The Bicycle Face," *Dundee Evening Telegraph* (24 May 1897), 4.
"The Bicycle Hand," *Weekly Irish Times* (27 Jun 1896), 1.
"The Birch for Lady Shoplifters," *Edinburgh Evening News* (28 Jan 1903), 2.
"The Birch for Lady Shoplifters," *Edinburgh Evening News* (9 Feb 1903), 2.
"The Bishop and the Ghost," *Luton Times* (26 Jan 1894), 7.
"The Biter Bit: A Laughable Story," *Leicestershire Mercury* (9 Feb 1856), 4.
"The Bloody Hand," *The Table Book* 1 (1827), 258–59.
"The Box Tunnel," *Monmouthshire Beacon* (28 Jan 1843), 4.
"The Box Tunnel—A Railway Story," *Ballymena Observer* (3 Mar 1860), 2.

"The Buried Treasure Swindle," *Dundee Evening Telegraph* (3 May 1879), 2.
"The Buried Treasure Swindle," *Barnsley Chronicle* (3 Mar 1894), 7.
The Charming Young Widow I Meet in The Train (NP: NP, ND).
The Chimney-Sweeper's Boy: A Poem (London: Longman and Co., 1807).
"The Crocodile as a Scavenger," *Gloucester Citizen* (13 Apr 1892), 4.
"The Danbury News . . . ," *The Edwardsville Intelligencer* (22 Jun. 1871), 2.
"The Dead Alive," *Morning Advertiser* (5 Apr 1855), 2.
"The Detroit Man," *Portsmouth Evening News* (29 Jul 1881), 3.
"The Devil and the Balloon," *Cheltenham Chronicle* (21 Oct 1899), 8.
"The Devil Scare in New York," *St. Andrews Citizen* (5 Sep 1896), 6.
"The Eagle and Child Story," *Stonehaven Journal* (12 May 1904), 3.
"The Eagle and the Baby," *The Quiver* 1 (1865), 110–11.
"The Eagle and the Baby," *Knaresborough Post* (12 Oct 1889), 5.
"The Eagle and the Child," *Leicester Daily Mercury* (9 Oct 1890), 3.
"The East Indian Revolt," *The Tribune Almanac* (1858), 47–49.
"The Elephant and Castle," *The Stage* (28 Jun 1917), 14.
"The Empress Eugenie's Jewels," *East and South Devon Advertiser* (18 Nov 1882), 3.
"The following good story from Berlin . . . ," *Daily Telegraph* (4 Oct 1881), 5.
"The following strange story . . . ," *Globe* (8 May 1829), 3.
"The following strange story," *Exeter and Plymouth Gazette Daily Telegrams* (8 Feb 1883), 2.
"The following very unusual . . . ," *Dublin Evening Post* (7 Jan 1779), 2.
"The French Press," *Cornhill Magazine* 28 (1873), 411–30.
"The Garoters," *Cambridge Independent Press* (20 Dec 1862), 4.
"The Garrotte Panic," *John Bull* (13 Dec 1862), 9.
"The Ghost of the Cross-Roads," *South London Press* (23 Dec 1893), 2.
"The Ghost Story," *The Globe* (11 Jan 1838), 4.
"The Golden Hen," *Tit-Bits* (3 Dec 1881), 12.
"The Great Diamond Robbery," *Yorkshire Post* (2 Nov 1886), 6.
"The Great Western Railway," *Wiltshire Times* (13 Apr 1895), 2.
"The Hidden Room," *Worcester Journal* (29 Dec 1894), 3.
"The Horrors of Sanitation," *The Graphic* (23 Aug 1884), 2.
"The Innkeeper's Daughter," *Bradford Daily Telegraph* (29 Jan 1894), 4.
"The Innocent Letter," *Indianapolis Journal* (3 Feb 1895), 13.
"The Kiss in the Tunnel," *Herts Advertiser* (31 Oct 1868), 3.
"The Kiss in the Tunnel," *Gloucester Citizen* (29 Jan 1895), 3.
"The Lady and the Burglar," *The Era* (7 Oct 1905), 25.
"The Lady and the Burglar: A Strange Story," *Sheffield Daily Telegraph* (15 Oct 1872), 2.
"The Land of Cakes No. III," *New monthly magazine and universal register* 28 (1830), 504–11.
"The Late Case of Robbery with Chloroform," *Essex Standard* (1 Feb 1850), 2.
"The Late Extraordinary Story," *Worcestershire Chronicle* (23 Apr 1862), 4.
"The Lost Found," *Advocate and Family Guardian* 33 (1867), 237–38.
"The Lost Found," *Daily Gazette Middlesbrough* (5 Dec 1885), 2.
"The Lost Ring," *Northern Daily Telegraph* (31 Aug 1892), 4.
"The Lost Ring," *Ballymena Observer* (26 Apr 1895), 6.
"The Lottery of Death," *Montrose Review* (31 Aug 1863), 2.
"The Lottery of Death," *Leeds Times* (28 Aug 1886), 6.
"The man who . . . ," *Workington Star* (29 Jan 1909), 6.

"The Ministerial Crisis," *Westmorland Gazette* (1 Mar 1851), 4.
"The Missing Austrian Archduke: A Strange Story," *St. James Gazette* (16 Apr 1895), 8.
"The Mohawks at St James's Hall," *The Era* (22 Sep 1900), 18.
The Mowing-Devil or, Strange News out of Hartford-shire (NP: NP, 1678).
"The Murder," *Newry Examiner* (30 Aug 1865), 4.
"The Murdered Tailor," *Leeds Times* (16 Apr 1870), 7.
"The Murderer in the Jury Box," *Fulton Democrat* (22 Jan 1890), 1.
"The New Hammersmith Ghost," *Pierce Egan's Life in London* (25 Jan 1825).
"The New Sensation," *The Atlanta Constitution* (5 Aug 1873), 3.
"The Newest in Swindling," *Dublin Weekly Nation* (1 Oct 1898), 11.
"The Old Clock: Or 'Here She Goes, There She Goes,'" *Tit-Bits* (21 Jan 1882), 7.
"The Old, Old Story," *Edinburgh Evening News* (30 Jan 1893), 2.
"The paragraph-makers . . . ," *Reading Mercury* (26 Apr 1773), 2.
"The Peddler's Ruse," *Cork Examiner* (14 Apr 1900), 11.
"The Poisoned Draught," *Daily Gazette for Middlesborough* (11 Dec 1888), 4.
"The Railroad Essay," *Bristol Times* (24 Jul 1841), 4.
"The Record of a Suicide Club," *Edinburgh Evening News* (24 Apr 1905), 4.
"The Rev. J. F. T. Hallowes at the Public Hall," *Barnsley Chronicle* (14 Aug 1886), 3.
"The Road Murder," *Western Daily Press* (27 Jul 1860), 3.
"The Romance of a Prayer," *The San Francisco Examiner* (7 Jan 1873), 1.
"The Scorcher's Spine," *Globe* (13 May 1897), 1.
"The Somali War," *Edinburgh Evening News* (30 Apr 1903), 4.
"The South Australian police . . . ," *Beverley and East Riding Recorder* (17 Feb 1894), 2.
"The South Norwalk Sentinel tells . . . ," *Boston Daily Advertiser* (23 May 1871), 1.
"The Southernhay Servants," *Western Times* (5 Feb 1842), 2.
"The Spanish Treasure Swindle," *Evening Star* (18 Nov 1898), 3.
"The Spectre Monk," *North Wales Chronicle* (25 Dec 1886), 6.
"The story of the confusion . . . ," *The Globe* (16 Aug 1905), 4.
"The Story of a Muff," *Fort Wayne Daily Gazette* (8 Mar 1870), 3.
"The Story of a Muff," *Cornish and Devon Post* (31 May 1879), 6.
"The Strangest of Wagers," *Evening Herald* (22 Aug 1895), 1.
The string of pearls, or, The barber of Fleet street: a domestic romance (London: E. Lloyd, 1850).
"The Suicide Club," *Manchester Courier* (23 Mar 1901), 12.
"The Suicide Club," *Northern Whig* (4 Sep 1915), 9.
"The suicide of . . . ," *Evening Herald* (1 Dec 1892), 2.
"The *Sunday Times* . . . ," *Cork Constitution* (14 Nov 1896), 6.
"The Superstitions of the Nineteenth Century," *Morning Chronicle* (10 Mar 1857), 6.
"The Suppression of Mendicity," *Clerkenwell News* (1 Jun 1871), 4.
"The Terrible Explosion at Bremer-Haven," *The Irishman* (24 Dec 1875), 7.
"The Tragic Farce," *Portsmouth Times* (13 Dec 1862), 7.
"The train . . . ," *Leighton Buzzard* (2 Mar 1869), 2.
"The Unhired Servant," *Londonderry Standard* (31 Mar 1859), 4.
"The Value of Solid Silver," *Pall Mall Gazette* (9 Nov 1917), 7.
"The wealth of detail . . . ," *Evening Star* (6 Apr 1898), 2.
"'The Wild Man' Again," *Kentish Gazette* (1 Dec 1868), 6.
"The Wild Man of Alabama," *Tipperary Free Press* (16 Apr 1853), 4.
"The Woman Who Failed," *Dominion* 1 (13 Nov 1907), 4.

The Workhouse Boy (Preston: Harkness Printer, nd).
"Theatre Royal Lyceum," *Tablet* (18 Oct 1862), 14.
"Theatrical Examiner," *The Examiner* (23 Aug 1829), 4.
"They Are Strangers Now," *Greenock Advertiser* (15 Sep 1882).
Thomas, Herbert. "An Anti-Garotte Machine," *Morning Post* (4 Dec 1862), 3.
Thompson, C. J. S. *Poison mysteries in history, romance and crime* (London: Scientific Press, 1923).
Thompson, Liz. "The Queen Rat," *FLS News* 21 (1995a), 5.
Thompson, Liz. "The Queen Rat (2)," *FLS News* 22 (1995b), 4–5.
Thompson, Stith. *Motif-Index of Folk-Literature: A Classification of Narrative Elements in Folk-Tales, Ballads, Myths, Fables, Mediæval Romances, Exempla, Fabliaux, Jest-Books, and Local Legends* (Copenhagen: Rosenkilde and Bagger, 1955–1958), 6 vols.
"Thrilling Discovery," *Norfolk Chronicle* (12 Apr 1862), 6.
Thurber, James. *Writings and Drawings* (New York: Library of America, 1996).
Thurston, Rev. Herbert. *The Myth of the Walled-up Nun* (Belfast: Books Ulster, ND).
Timbs, John. *Romance of London: strange stories, scenes and remarkable persons of the great town* (London: NP, 1865), 3 vols.
Todd, Laurie. "Letters from Laurie Todd: Number Four," *The Knickerbocker* 5 (1835), 503–6.
"Topics of To-day," *Shields Daily Gazette* (18 Jul 1896), 2.
"Town Topics," *Chepstow Weekly Advertiser* (11 Apr 1903), 2.
Town, Harold. "Ghosts and Witches," *Bedfordshire Times* (19 Dec 1930), 13.
Townend, R. "Springheeled Jack," *Yorkshire Evening Post* (11 Oct 1924), 7.
"Traditions of Louth," *Drogheda Argus* (10 Jun 1871), 5.
"Treasure Seekers," *Jersey Independent* (4 Jan 1879), 6.
"Treasure-Seeking in the Sewers," *North Devon Gazette* (4 May 1869), 2.
"Treasures in Sewers," *Lincolnshire Chronicles* (19 Jan 1867), 6.
Tregortha, John. *News from the Invisible World* (Burslem: Tregortha 1808).
Trevelyan, George Otto. *Cawnpore* (London: Macmillan 1866).
"Tricks in a Tunnel," *Sheffield Weekly Telegraph* (12 Jan 1884), 4.
Tripp, Henry. "Buried Alive: A Tale of Old Cologne," *Notes and Queries* 5 (1882, 6th series), 159.
"True Tales of Very Wonderful Dogs," *Leeds Times* (8 Feb 1868), 6.
Trusler, John. *Proverbs in Verse, Or, Moral Instruction Conveyed in Pictures* (London: Souter, 1811), 37–40.
"Truth Stranger than Fiction," *Shoreditch Observer* (11 Aug 1860), 3.
"Truth Stranger than Fiction," *Tower Hamlets Independent* (31 Jul 1897), 5.
"Tuesday 24," *The Gentleman's Magazine* 6 (1736), 486.
Turner, Llewelyn. *The memories of Sir Llewelyn Turner: memories serious and light of the Irish Rebellion of 1798, Welsh judicature and English judges, admirals and sea-fights, municipal work and notable persons in North Wales, strange crimes and great events* (London: Isbiter, 1903).
"20 Dollar gold pieces were offered for 19 Dollar and no one would buy them," *Santa Cruz Sentinel* (8 Apr 1908), 6.
"Two Gloucestershire Ring Stories," *Stroud Journal* (22 May 1886), 2.
"Two men . . . ," *York Post* (26 Jul 1928), 5.
"Two men, named . . . ," *Brighton Gazette* (5 Nov 1840), 4.
"Two very strange stories . . ." *The Days' Doings* (3 Jun 1871), 2.

"Uit Tsarentijd," *Limburgsch Dagblad* (19 Aug 1964), 15.
"Un 'Club de Suicides,'" *Le Journal* (16 Apr 1912), 7.
"Une Cure Merveilleuse," *Images Enfantines* (Paris: Société Française D'Editions d'Art, ND).
Ure, Andrew. "An Account of some Experiments made on the Body of a Criminal immediately after Execution, with Physiological and Practical Observations," *Northampton Mercury* (16 Jan 1819), 4 [originally given at the Glasgow Literary Society 10 Dec 1818].
Uther, H., ed. 2004. *The Types of International Folktales. A Classification and Bibliography Based on the System of Antti Aarne and Stith Thompson* (Helsinki: Suomalainen Tiedeakatemia, Academia Scientiarum Fennica, 2004), 3 vols.
Valk, Ülo. *The Black Gentleman: Manifestations of the Devil in Estonian Folk Religion* (Helsinki: ASF, 2001).
Van Lennep, J. H. "The Throw for Life or Death," *Notes and Queries* 9 (1860, 2nd series), 10–11.
Venbrux, Eric, and Theo Meder. "'The False Teeth in the Cod': A Legend in Context," *Contemporary Legend* 5 (1995), 115–31.
Veritas, "Old Postage Stamps," *Yorkshire Gazette* (3 Mar 1860), 5.
Verne, Jules. *Les Frères Kip* (Paris: Collection Hetzel, 1903).
"Very Strange Story," *Lancaster Gazette* (3 Jan 1857), 2.
Vincent, David. *Literacy and Popular Culture: England 1750–1914* (Cambridge: Cambridge University Press, 1989).
W. C., "To the Editor," *West London Observer* (8 Dec 1933), 12.
Walker, W. J. *Chapters on the early registers of Halifax parish church* (Halifax: Whitley and Booth, 1885).
Walter, *My Secret Life* (np: np, 1888) [online http://www.horntip.com/html/books_&_MSS/1880s/1888_my_secret_life/vol_09/index.htm, accessed 22 Apr 2019].
"War To Garotters," *The Times* (11 Nov 1856), 12.
Ward, Andrew. *Our Bones Are Scattered* (London: Hodder and Stoughton, 2004).
Watts, Joshua. *Remarkable events in the history of man* (London: Robertson, 1825).
"We think it our duty ...," *The Times* (18 Jun 1841), 5.
"Weekly London Letter," *Sussex Express* (17 Apr 1896), 6.
"Weird Find Haunts Men Near Ladysmith," *Sheboygan Press* (19 Mar 1926), 11.
Westwood, Jennifer, and Jacqueline Simpson. *The Lore of the Land* (London: Penguin, 2005).
"Weymouth," *North Devon Journal* (4 May 1848), 3.
"What an Egg Brought," *Emporia Daily Republican* (19 Jan 1891), 3.
"What Hanging is Like," *Manchester Evening News* (14 Oct 1885), 2.
"Who Murdered Downie?," *Falkirk Herald* (28 Mar 1861), 2.
Whymper, Henry. "English and American Postal Defacement Marks," *The Stamp Collector's Magazine* (1 Jun 1863), 77–79.
Widdowson, John. *If You Don't Be Good: Verbal Social Control in Newfoundland* (St John's: Institute of Social and Economic Research, 1977).
Wiener, Joel. *The Americanization of the British Press, 1830s-1914: Speed in the Age of Transatlantic Journalism* (London: Palgrave-Macmillan, 2011).
"Wild Man of the Woods," *Daily Gazette for Middlesborough* (4 Feb 1882), 4.
"Wild Man of the Woods," *Dundee Evening Telegraph* (30 Mar 1923), 7.
"Wit and Anecdote," *Bedford Record* (6 Jul 1889), 7.
"Witchcraft and Exorcism," *Dundee Evening Telegraph* (21 Nov 1892), 3.
"Without a Rag," *Cincinnati Enquirer* (16 Jul 1895), 9.

"Woman Finds $50,000 Diamond ... Inside an Egg!," *Weekly World News* (2 Feb 1988), 35.
"Women's Suicide Club," *St. James Gazette* (26 Jul 1904), 15.
"Women's Suicide Club," *West Somerset Free Press* (7 Nov 1903), 3.
"Wonderful if True," *Durham County Advertiser* (18 Feb 1853), 8.
"Wonderful if True," *Sheffield Daily Telegraph* (22 Aug 1863).
Woodyard, Chris. *The Ghost Wore Black* (Dayton: Kestrel Publications, 2013).
Woodyard, Chris. "The Tomb Challenge of the Russian Princess," *Haunted Ohio Blog* (8 Sep 2015), http://hauntedohiobooks.com/news/the-tomb-challenge-of-the-russian-princess/ (accessed 9 Apr 2019).
"Ye Olde Murder Inn," *Gloucestershire Echo* (18 Mar 1925), 5.
Young, Julian Charles. *Last Leaves from the Journal of Julian Charles Young* (Edinburgh: Edmonston and Douglas, 1875).
Woodyard, Chris. "Midwife to Murderers," *Contemporary Legend* 7 (2017), 40–74.
Woodyard, Chris. "The Reay Mermaids: In the Bay and in the Press," *Shima* 12 (2018), 24–36.
Ziolkowski, *Fairy Tales from before Fairy Tales: The Medieval Latin Past of Wonderful Lies* (University of Michigan Press: Ann Arbor, 2007), 65–92.

About the Author

Photo credit Simon Young

Simon Young, a British historian, lives with his wife and three daughters in Italy. He has published several folklore and history books, including *The Boggart* (2022), and scores of peer-reviewed articles on British folklore and the supernatural.

www.ingramcontent.com/pod-product-compliance
Lightning Source LLC
Chambersburg PA
CBHW030615230426
43661CB00053B/2005